All on Stage

Book 2: group scenes for students

Selected by Mary Greenslade

Samuel French — London
New York - Toronto - Hollywood

CONTENTS

ACKNOWLEDGMENTS

For permission to print or reprint copyright extracts from copyright works in this volume the compiler and publishers are grateful to the following authors, translators, their representatives and publishers. Every effort has been made to trace the copyright holders, but should any inaccurate information be given below please contact the publishers.

Adam Bede © 1990 by Geoffrey Beevers. By permission of the author. Published by Samuel French Ltd.

Animal Farm © 1985 by George Orwell, adapted by Peter Hall, lyrics by Adrian Mitchell. By permission of Peters, Fraser & Dunlop, 503/4 The Chambers, Chelsea Harbour, London SW10 0XF. Published by Methuen London Ltd.

Blood Brothers © 1986 by Willy Russell. By permission of Casarotto Ramsay Ltd, National House, 60-66 Wardour Street, London W1V 3HP, to whom all enquiries regarding professional performance should be made. Published by Samuel French Ltd and Stanley Thornes (Publishers) Ltd.

Bonaventure © 1950 by Charlotte Hastings. By permission of Film Rights Ltd, 483 Southbank House, Black Prince Road, Albert Embankment, London SE1 7SJ. Published by Samuel French Ltd.

Bottom's Dream © 1979 by Samuel French Ltd. Published by Samuel French Ltd.

Cold Comfort Farm © 1993 by the estate of Stella Gibbons and Paul Doust. By permission of Curtis Brown, 162-168 Regent Street, London W1R 5TB. Published by Samuel French Ltd.

Daddy Long-Legs by Jean Webster.

Daughters of Venice © 1992 by Don Taylor. By permission of Casarotto Ramsay Ltd, National House, 60-66 Wardour Street, London W1V 3HP, to whom all enquiries regarding professional performance should be made. Published by Samuel French Ltd.

The Day After the Fair © 1973 by Frank Harvey, based on the short story *On the Western Circuit* by Thomas Hardy. By permission of The International Copyright Bureau Ltd, 22A Aubrey House, Maida Avenue, London W2 1TQ. Published by Samuel French Ltd.

Dear Octopus © 1938 by D. G. Smith, © (Act... permission of Film Rights Ltd, 483 Southba... Embankment, London SE1 7SJ. Published |

Find Me © 1980 by Olwen Wymark. By pern... Ltd, 24 Pottery Lane, Holland Park, Lond regarding professional performance should l Ltd.

The compiler would like to thank Amanda Smith and Peta Kuck for all their help and patience.

PREFACE

With the emphasis more and more on training in oral communication skills in schools, a high standard of performance becomes increasingly important.

Teachers of Drama and English know that preparation time spent on a good script is not only satisfying but reaps its rewards on stage. The process of studying a scene in depth is made more enjoyable when the background of a scene is gradually built up in discussion by the group working as a disciplined team. This involves the vocal and physical aspects of characterization, and the relationship and reactions of characters one to another. 'The approach to every role is an act of research' (Eric Hollis, *The Performer*, the Guildhall Journal, November 1993). It also includes the understanding of style in performance, with an awareness of period, language and the rhythm of speech patterns. This, in turn, means clarity of speech, audibility and projection. Within this framework, emotional levels, timing and climaxes must be realized and communicated with conviction. Gradually, the truth of the scene is understood and appreciated. This leads to a sense of exhilaration in performance, when a polished piece of drama is produced.

Within the two volumes of *All on Stage*, there is material for classroom drama lessons, for concerts, festivals and group performance examinations at all levels. Each excerpt is self-contained, but will need thought in planning, and with imagination, originality and inventiveness, the director and the production team will 'orchestrate' the scene and bring the script to life. It is amazing what a high standard may be accomplished with careful use of space, simple imaginative staging, an eye to grouping and levels and, most important, with an energetic, enthusiastic group of players and backstage crew achieving together and responding to direction.

Although each of these scenes has an introduction to help set it in context, it is always important to study the whole play for a thorough knowledge and appreciation of character, plot and style. There is comedy and tragedy and a cross-section of modern and classical, including lively adaptations from novels, and scenes for small and large casts, some with challenging crowd scenes. May you enjoy performing in them all.

So now: 'Go make you ready ... Bid the players make haste.'

MARY GREENSLADE

CASTS AND PLAYING TIMES

NB. The playing times indicated are approximate.

Adam Bede
   16 speaking parts may be played by M3 F3. Playing time: 18 minutes.
Animal Farm
   M5 F2, 1 boy. Extras. Playing time: 9 minutes.
Blood Brothers
   M2 F5, 1M or F. Playing time: 12 minutes.
Bonaventure
   M2 F4. Playing time: 20 minutes.
Bottom's Dream
   F5. Playing time: 8 minutes.
Cold Comfort Farm
   M10 F9. Playing time: 15 minutes.
Daddy Long-Legs
   M4 F3, 1 boy 3 girls. Extras. Playing time: 14 minutes.
Daughters of Venice
   M8 F6, 1 boy 1 girl. Extras. Playing time: 29 minutes.
The Day After the Fair
   M2 F4. Extras. Playing time: 16 minutes.
Dear Octopus
   M3 F4, 1 boy, 2 girls. Playing time: 13 minutes.
Find Me
   11 speaking parts may be performed by M3 F5. Playing time: 17 minutes.
The Golden Pathway Annual
   M3 F1. Playing time: 10 minutes.
If You're Glad I'll Be Frank
   M6 F4, 1M or F. Playing time: 9 minutes.
Killers
   M4 F2. Playing time: 25 minutes.
Lark Rise
   M5 F4, 1 boy 1 girl. Playing time: 11 minutes.
Other People
   M2 F2. Playing time: 11 minutes.
Pack of Lies
   First scene M1 F3. Playing time: 9 minutes. Second scene F4. Playing time: 8 minutes.

The Passing-Out Parade
   F9. Playing time: 17 minutes.
The Roses of Eyam
   M22 F18 (many of these are non-speaking). Playing time: 29 minutes.
Trafford Tanzi
   M3 F3. Playing time: 12 minutes.
Trelawny of the 'Wells'
   M4 F3. Playing time: 18 minutes.
Visiting Hour
   M5 F9, may be played by M2 F4. Playing time: 30 minutes.
Vivat! Vivat Regina!
   M8 F2. Extras. Playing time: 20 minutes.
Warrior
   M4 F3. Playing time: 15 minutes.
Wuthering Heights
   M2 F3. Playing time: 11 minutes.

Also published by Samuel French Ltd

SCENES FOR TWO
Book I Duologues for Young Players

SCENES FOR TWO
Book II Duologues for Girls and Women

Edited by Mary Greenslade and Anne Harvey

ADAM BEDE
adapted by Geoffrey Beevers from the novel by George Eliot

Originally written for the Orange Tree Theatre, Richmond, this adaptation from George Eliot's masterpiece sustains the dimension and warmth of the characters in their fated drama. The extract begins at the trial of Hetty Sorrel, accused of murdering her own child whilst searching for Squire Arthur Donnithorne, the child's father. We move on to Arthur's return, then to Hetty's cell, to Adam Bede's room and finally to the day of Hetty's execution. Written for six actors, doubling and trebling, it *could* be played by more actors, but still offers excellent ensemble playing with a cast of six. There are many ironies to be gained from doubling in minor roles.

Set: Various simple settings. Period: 1799.

Cast: Sixteen named speaking parts (counting the narrator, George Eliot, as one voice). May be played by M3 F3.
Actor 1: Counsel/Dinah, a Methodist lay preacher. Actor 2: Adam, a carpenter/Servant. Actor 3: Sarah Stone/Woman. Actor 4: John Olding/Captain Arthur Donnithorne/Hangman. Actor 5: Hetty, Farmer Poyser's niece/Driver. Actor 6: Judge/The Reverend Mr Irwine, the parson/Bartle Massey, the schoolmaster/Man.

Playing time: 18 minutes.

SCENE A

The Court

There is the sound of a drumbeat and a bright light on the witness stand

We can dimly see Hetty, and Adam watching her

From the darkness come the voices of the Counsel and the Judge

The drumbeat fades

Counsel Your name?

Sarah Stone Sarah Stone.

Counsel And where do you live?

Sarah Stone I keep a shop in Church Lane here in Stoniton. That Saturday night ...

Counsel February twenty-seventh.

Sarah Stone Yes. (*She points*) She came and asked for a lodging at my house. She looked ill and tired.

Counsel You are sure it was the prisoner?

Sarah Stone Oh yes. Her condition, and something respectable about her clothes, made me as I couldn't find it in my heart to send her away. (*Slight pause*) In the night a child was born.

Reaction in the Court

Counsel Did you send for a doctor?

Sarah Stone There seemed to be no need.

Counsel (*holding up baby clothes*) Do you recognize these baby's clothes?

Sarah Stone Yes—I made them myself. I'd kept them ever since my last child was born. I dressed the child in them.

Counsel And the next day?

Sarah Stone She would get up. She said she felt quite strong enough. But I wasn't quite easy about her, and towards evening next day I made up my mind to speak to our minister about it. I left the prisoner sitting up by the fire in the kitchen with the baby on her lap. When we got back, the candle was burning just as I left it, but the prisoner and the baby were gone.

Reaction in the Court

Judge Stand down.

Silence, apart from the sound of the drumbeat

G. Eliot/Actor 2 And Adam thought "How can she be guilty? Else why should she have taken her baby with her? She might have left it behind ..."

The drumbeat fades

Counsel Your name?

John Olding John Olding. I'm a labourer at Hetton Farm. I first saw the prisoner in a red cloak sitting under a bit of a haystack. She got up when she saw me and seemed as if she'd be walking on the other way. I thought she looked a bit crazy, but it was no business of mine. I had to go to the other side of Hetton Coppice.

Counsel What happened then?

John Olding I hadn't got far before I heard a strange cry. It didn't come from any animal I knew. For a good while I kept looking up at the boughs; and then I thought it came from the ground. I looked about, but could find nothing, and at last the cry stopped. (*Slight pause*) But when I came back the same way pretty nigh on an hour after, I couldn't help laying down my stakes to have another look. Then I saw something odd and round and whitish lying on the ground under a nut-bush by the side of me. And I stooped down to pick it up, and I saw it was a little baby's hand. (*A thrill of horror*) There were a lot of timber-choppings under the bush and the hand came out from among them. But there was a hole left in one place and I could see down it and see the child's head. I took out the child. Its body was cold. I made back home to my wife. She said it was dead and I'd better take it to the parish and tell the constable. And I said "I'll lay my life it's the young woman's child as I met going to the coppice." And the next morning another constable came with me to the spot where I found the child. And when we got there, there was the prisoner a-sitting against the bush where I found the child. She cried out when she saw us, but she never offered to move.

Judge Stand down.

There is only the sound of the drumbeat

G. Eliot/Actor 2 And Adam thought "She's guilty."
Judge Gentlemen of the Jury, what is your verdict?
All Guilty.
Judge Hester Sorrel. You have been found guilty of child-murder. You are to be taken to a place of execution and then to be hanged by the neck till you be———

Hetty shrieks and falls

Adam tries to reach her, but is too late

The drumbeat fades

Scene B

Arthur's return—bright daylight

G. Eliot/Actor 6 When Arthur first learnt of the old Squire's death he felt———
Arthur Poor grandfather.
G. Eliot/Actor 1 It's impossible to say that his grief was deeper than that.
G. Eliot/Actor 3 But it is not in human nature—only in human pretence—for a young man like Arthur, with a fine constitution———
G. Eliot/Actor Thinking well of himself, believing that others think well of him———
G. Eliot/Actor 6 And just coming into a splendid estate through the death of a very old man whom he wasn't fond of, to feel anything very different from ...

G. Eliot/Actor 4 Exultant joy!

Arthur Now my real life is beginning! I'll show them what a fine country gentleman is!

A coach is arranged for him. Arthur has his back to the driver

G. Eliot/Actor 5 Arthur was at ease about Hetty. Mr Irwine had sent him word that Adam Bede was to marry pretty Hetty Sorrel.

Arthur *(to the audience)* The little puss can't have cared for me half as much as I cared for her. I'm a great fool about her still—indeed I haven't cared much to look at any other woman since I parted from her. Strange how long this sort of business lasts ... I'm not in love with Hetty now, oh no—I've earnestly hoped she should marry Adam and *now* it's actually in my power to do a great deal for them. Thank heaven it's turned out so well! I should have plenty of interests to fill my life now and not be in danger of playing the fool again.

G. Eliot/Actor 5 Pleasant the sense of being swept along in swift ease through English scenes, till here was dear old Hayslope at last ...

Driver Whoa!

G. Eliot/Actor 5 He was happy and would make everyone else happy that came within his reach.

Arthur tips the driver

Driver Thank you, sir!

Servants remove the coach and bring on an easy chair and a letter

Arthur greets them all warmly

G. Eliot/Actor 3 To Arthur it was nothing that the servants looked grave and sad.

Servant From Mr Irwine, sir.

Arthur *(with pleasure)* Ah, good ... *(He sits, opens the letter and then reads it)*

Mr Irwine's voice I send this letter to meet you on your arrival, Arthur, because I may be at Stoniton, whither I am called by the most painful duty it has ever been given to me to perform. Any other words I could write at this moment must be weak and unmeaning by the side of those in which I must tell you the simple fact. Hetty Sorrel is in prison, being tried for the crime of child-murder.

Arthur is absolutely still for a time, then quickly leaves

Arthur *(calling back)* Tell them I've gone to Stoniton.

Scene C

Hetty's prison cell

A bed and a window

Hetty sits without hope

Dinah's voice Hetty.

No reaction

   Hetty—it's Dinah.

Hetty reacts slightly

   Dinah enters

Hetty rises and stares at her like an animal, in silence

Dinah Don't you remember Dinah? Did you think I wouldn't come to you in trouble? (*Pause*) I've come to be with you, Hetty ... not to leave you ... to be your sister to the last.

Then they are in each others arms

There is a pause

Hetty's arms slowly drop

   Hetty, do you know who it is?
Hetty Yes.
Dinah Do you remember the time when we were at the Hall Farm and I told you to be sure and think of me as a friend in trouble?
Hetty Yes, but you can do nothing for me—they'll hang me o' Monday. (*Pause*) It's Friday now.
Dinah No, Hetty, I can't save you from that death.
Hetty You won't leave me, Dinah? You'll keep close to me?
Dinah I'll stay with you. But here's someone else besides me.
Hetty (*looking about, frightened*) Who?
Dinah Someone who's been with you through all your hours of sin and trouble, who's known every thought you've had and all the deeds you've tried to hide. And on Monday when I can't follow you He'll be with you then. It makes no difference whether we live or die, we're in the presence of God.

Hetty Dinah, won't nobody do anything for me? Will they hang me for certain? I
wouldn't mind if they'd let me live.

Dinah I know death is dreadful. But if you had a friend to take care of you after
death—someone whose love is greater than mine———

Hetty But I can't know anything about it———

Dinah Because you're shutting your soul against Him by trying to hide the truth. I
love you, Hetty, but if you'd not let me near you, you'd have shut me out from
helping you. Don't shut God's love out. He can't bless you till you open your heart
to Him. (*She kneels*)

Slowly Hetty kneels too

Hetty, we're before God. He's waiting for you to tell the truth.

There is silence

Hetty Dinah, help me... I can't feel anything like you ... my heart is hard.

Dinah Jesus, thou hast known the depths of all sorrow. Thou hast entered that black
darkness and hast uttered the cry of the forsaken. Lord, rescue this lost one. She's
clothed round with thick darkness; she can only feel her heart is hard and she is
helpless. She cries to me; Saviour—it's a blind cry to Thee. I believe in thy infinite
love ... Breathe on her soul, and it shall arise. Yes, Lord, I see Thee coming through
the darkness, coming like the morning, with healing on thy wings. Let the eyes of
the blind be open. Let her see that God encompasses her. Let her tremble at nothing
but the sin that cuts her off from Him. Melt her hard heart. Make her cry with her
whole soul—"Father I have sinned"———

Hetty (*crying out*) Dinah—I will tell—I won't hide it anymore ... (*Pause*) I did do it,
Dinah. I buried it in the wood—the little baby—and it cried ... I heard it cry. I was
so very miserable, Dinah. I tried to drown myself and I couldn't. It was partly
thinking o' you made me come toward Stoniton, I didn't think you'd be cross with
me, but then I began to feel frightened because I was so near home. And then the
little baby was born when I didn't expect it, and the thought came all of a sudden
that I might get rid of it, and go home again. It got stronger and stronger. And I
walked on and on and there came the moon. Oh Dinah, it frightened me when it
first looked at me out o' the clouds—it never looked so before. And I saw the
wood a little way off and I thought I could hide the child there and go home and tell
'em I'd been to try for a place and couldn't get one. I longed so for it, Dinah, I
longed so to be safe at home. I seemed to hate the baby—it was like a heavy
weight hanging round my neck, and yet its crying went through me and I daren't
look at its little hands and face. But I went—(*She stops. She sits on the bed and
shudders*) I came to a place where there was lots of wood-chips and turf and I sat
down on the trunk of a tree. And all of a sudden I saw a hole under the nut-tree, like
a little grave. And it darted into me like lightning — I'd lay the baby there and

cover it with the grass and the wood-chips. And I'd done it in a minute—and oh, it cried so—I couldn't cover it quite up. I thought perhaps somebody 'ud come and take care of it and then it wouldn't die. And I made haste out of the wood but I could hear it crying all the while—and it was as if I was held fast—I couldn't go away. And I sat against the haystack. But after hours and hours the man came and looked at me so, I was frightened and went on. And then there was a barn and I went to sleep—but oh, the baby's crying kept waking me. And then I turned back, I couldn't help it—it was the baby's crying made me go. I saw nothing but that place in the wood where I'd buried the baby ... I see it now. Oh, Dinah, shall I allays see it? (*She shudders again*) I knew the way to the place, and I could hear it crying at every step. I thought it was alive. I don't know whether I was frightened, or glad. I don't know what I felt till I knew the baby was gone. Then I was struck like a stone with fear. I knew I couldn't run away and everybody as saw me 'ud know about the baby. My heart went like a stone. It seemed like as if I should stay there forever. But they came and took ... me ...

There is silence

(*She shudders again and then bursts out*) Dinah, do you think God will take away that crying and the place in the wood, now I've told everything?
Dinah Let's pray. Pray to the God of all mercy.

SCENE D

Adam's room in Stoniton

Perhaps distant Sunday church bells can be heard

G. Eliot/Actor 2 The eve of the execution, at Adam's lodgings.
Bartle Massey A visitor—wants to see you.

Adam turns sharply

Adam Dinah. Bless you for coming to her. Mr Massey brought me word yesterday as you were come.

They stand in silence for a moment

Bartle Massey Sit down, young woman, sit down.
Dinah Thank you, I won't. Hetty entreated me not to stay long away. What I came for, Adam Bede, was to pray you to go and see her. It should be today, rather than in the early morning when time will be short. (*She waits*) Though her poor soul is very dark, she's no longer hard. When I told her you were in Stoniton she said "I should like to say goodbye to Adam and ask him to forgive me."

Adam I can't—I can't say goodbye while there's any hope. I can't bring my mind to it. There'll perhaps come a pardon, Mr Irwine said.

There is a pause

Dinah waits for an answer

I will come, Dinah. Tomorrow morning. I may have more strength to bear it if I know it *must* be. Tell her I forgive her. Tell her I will come at the very last.

Dinah I must hasten back to her. Farewell Adam. Our heavenly Father comfort you and strengthen you to bear all things.

They clasp hands

(*To Bartle Massey*) Farewell friend.

Dinah exits

Bartle Massey Well, if there must be women to make trouble in the world, it's but fair there should be women to be comforters, and she's one, she's one. (*Slight pause*) It's a pity she's a Methodist. But there's no getting a woman without some foolishness or other.

The Lights fade as Adam paces up and down

G. Eliot/Actor 6 It was a long and dreary night.

Adam It's the very day we should ha' been married.

Bartle Massey Ay, my lad, it's heavy, it's heavy. But you must remember, when you thought of marrying her you'd a notion she'd got another sort of nature inside her.

Adam I know. How could I think any other way? And if he'd never come near her and I'd married her and been loving to her, she might never ha' done anything bad. What would it ha' signified—my having a bit o' trouble with her. It 'ud ha' been nothing to this.

Bartle Massey There's no knowing, my lad—there's no knowing. The smart's bad for you now—but there may be good come out of this that we don't see.

Adam (*flaring up*) Good come out of it! I hate that talk o' people as if there was a way o' making amends for everything. Her ruin can't be undone.

Bartle Massey Well, lad—it's likely enough I talk foolishness. I'm an old fellow and it's a good many years since I was in trouble myself. It's easy finding reasons why other folks should be patient.

Adam Mr Massey, I'm very hot and hasty. I owe you something different, but you mustn't take it ill of me.

Bartle Massey Not I, lad, not I.

G. Eliot/Actor 1 So the night wore on in agitation, till the chill dawn.
Adam I must go to the prison now, Mr Massey.

SCENE E

The street

People crossing the stage—a rope is set up

G. Eliot/Actor 3 In the streets the eager people were astir already.
Woman What's happening?
Hangman There's to be no pardon——
Man No reprieve?

The crowd pass on the news

Hangman The cart is to set off at half-past seven——
Woman Come on then——
Man There's to be no pardon ...
Others It won't be long—make haste——

The stage clears into stillness

　　Adam enters on one side, and Hetty on the other, supported by Dinah

Hetty is shocked by the reflection of her suffering in Adam

Dinah Speak to him, Hetty.
Hetty (*like a child*) Adam ... I'm very sorry—I behaved very wrong to you—will you forgive me ... before I die?
Adam Yes, I forgive thee, Hetty. I forgave thee long ago.

Hetty moves towards him

Hetty (*frightened; still holding Dinah's hand*) Will you kiss me again, Adam, for all I've been so wicked?

They kiss—a lifelong parting

　　And tell him—for there's nobody else to tell him—as I went after him and couldn't find him—and I hated him and cursed him once—but Dinah says I should forgive him ... and I try ... for else God won't forgive me.
Hangman It's time.

A crowd gathers again quietly

Adam goes

Hetty is taken towards the rope

Dinah Let's pray, Hetty. Let's pray to God.

Hetty and Dinah whisper prayers. As she gets to the rope, Hetty sees something. She shrieks and clings to Dinah

Everyone looks, some are pointing

Dinah What is it?
G. Eliot/Actor 4 A horseman is cleaving the crowd at full gallop.
G. Eliot/Actor 3 The rider's eyes are glazed by madness——
G. Eliot/Actor 6 He has a paper in his hand——
G. Eliot/Actor 3 Holding it up as if it were a signal——
G. Eliot/Actor 4 It is Arthur Donnithorne carrying in his hand a hard-won release from death.
G. Eliot/Actor 3 A reprieve!
All A reprieve!

Intense excitement

Black-out, then Lights up

G. Eliot/Actor 5 A reprieve—but not a full pardon. Hetty was to be transported overseas.

ANIMAL FARM
by George Orwell, adapted by Peter Hall

Based on George Orwell's novel, the scenes are linked by the narration of a young boy. The play starts with the rebellion of the animals against their drunken farmer and master. Once they are free of him, the pigs take over, with Napoleon gradually becoming their leader so that the farm becomes a Stalinesque Communist Russia. The gentler animals, with their simple natures and faith, are completely swamped. This scene from Act Two is the old faithful horse Boxer's departure.

Set: The farm, outside the barn and the farmhouse.

Cast: M5 F2, 1 boy. Extras.
Napoleon, a pig. Boy, narrator; 8-9. Boxer, huge cart horse. Clover, a stout motherly mare. Squealer, a pig. Minimus, a pig, the first Animalist poet. Benjamin, the old donkey. Man, who leads the horse, who draws the van, non-speaking. Muriel, the white goat. Animals: Hens, Pigs, Sheep, Cows.

Playing time: 9 minutes.

Napoleon I have created a new decoration: The Order of the Green Banner. I have conferred it on myself.

The Lights go down

Boy And the very next morning, the attack came. The animals awoke to find that the men had surrounded the windmill in the night. It was clear they intended to blow it up.

The Lights come up

The animals look nervously at the distant windmill. It is surrounded by men. One is poised over an explosive plunger

Napoleon (*rallying them*) It's impossible! We have built the walls far too thick for that. Courage, comrades!

The plunger is driven home. A huge explosion. All the animals fling themselves flat on the ground. The windmill is in ruins

Boy Without waiting for any orders, the animals charged.
All the Animals Charge!
Boy They chased the men over the fields and off the farm.

The animals stand among the ruins of the windmill

Boxer Our windmill is gone. Even the foundations are destroyed.
Clover It's as though it had never been.
All the Pigs Hooray!
Boxer (*amazed*) Why are you cheering?
Squealer To celebrate our victory!
Boxer What victory?
Squealer What victory, comrade? Have we not driven the enemy off our soil, the sacred soil of Animal Farm?
Boxer But they've destroyed our windmill. And we have worked on it for two years!
Squealer What does it matter? We will build another windmill.
Minimus And another windmill.
Squealer We will build six windmills if we feel like it. You do not appreciate, comrade, the mighty thing that we have done. The enemy was in occupation of this very ground that we stand upon. And now—thanks to the leadership of Comrade Napoleon—we have won every inch of it back again.
Boxer Then we have won back what we already had.
Squealer Yes. That is our victory.

Napoleon appears at the window

Napoleon On this day of joy, you must hear the other good news. There is now no more fear on Animal Farm. The traitor Snowball has been eliminated. One of our comrades, a Bull, who I will not name for reasons of security, is enslaved on the farm where Snowball has been wallowing in luxury. This hero broke into Snowball's sty and gored him to death. Snowball is no more! You need be frightened no longer.
Minimus I shall write a poem about it!
Napoleon Excellent!

The pigs and Napoleon exit

Boxer For the first time, it occurs to me that I am getting old.
Clover A horse's lungs do not last forever.
Boxer They'll keep me going long enough to see the windmill rebuilt.

The Lights change. The animals begin to rebuild the windmill

All the animals   There was a whacking great limestone boulder
But the animals worked as one.
Yes, through animal co-operation
Anything can be done!
Anything can be done!
Anything can be done!

During the above, Boxer collapses on the floor. The animals gather round

Clover Boxer! What is it?
Boxer It's my lung. It doesn't matter. I think you'll be able to finish the windmill now without me. There is a pretty good store of stone.

Squealer enters

Squealer *(full of concern)* Comrade Napoleon has learned with the deepest distress of this misfortune to one of the most loyal workers on the farm. He is already making arrangements to send Boxer to be treated in the village hospital.
Clover Why? I don't like animals leaving the farm.
Benjamin And I don't like to think of a sick comrade in the hands of human beings.
Squealer The veterinary surgeon in the village can treat Boxer's case more satisfactorily. It is the best thing for him.

Boxer begins to struggle to his feet, helped by the other animals. He reaches a kneeling position

Boxer   I will be well, friends,
And I'll retire, friends,
To the shadow of the chestnut tree
With time for thinking
And time for learning
The remainder of my ABC—
Um ... D.

He struggles to his feet. The Lights fade

Boy The next day, a van arrived to take Boxer away.

The Lights come up on a man shutting the rear door of a horse-drawn van. He begins to lead the horse out of the gate

Glover Goodbye, Boxer.

All the Animals (*quietly*) Goodbye, Boxer! Goodbye!

Benjamin comes running in braying at the top of his voice

Benjamin Fools! Fools! Can't you see what is written on the side of that van.

Muriel begins to spell out the words

Muriel Alfred Simmonds, Horse S L... er, Horse S L...
Benjamin Oh shut up! Let me read it. "Alfred Simmonds, Horse Slaughterer and
  Glue Boiler". They are taking Boxer to the knackers!
All the Animals Boxer!

Cries of horror from the animals

Clover Boxer! Boxer! Get out! Get out quickly! They are taking you to your death!
All the Animals Boxer!

Clover pleads with the horse pulling the van

Clover Comrade, don't take your brother to his death.
All the Animals Boxer!

*Boxer's face appears at the small window at the back of the van. He tries to kick his
way out. The man whips the horse and the van moves down the road*

Boy In a few moments, the sound of drumming hoofs grew fainter and died away.
  Three days later, Squealer made an announcement.

Squealer enters

Squealer It has come to my knowledge that a foolish and wicked rumour has been
  circulating. Some of you noticed that the van which took Boxer away was marked
  "Horse Slaughterer", and have actually come to the conclusion that Boxer was
  being sent to the knackers. It is almost unbelievable that any animal could be so
  stupid. Surely, surely you know your beloved leader, Comrade Napoleon, better
  than that? The explanation is really very simple. The van had previously been the
  property of the knacker, and had been bought by the veterinary surgeon who had
  not yet painted the old name out. That was how the mistake arose.
Clover (*weeping*) I am very relieved to hear it.
Muriel So am I.
Squealer Our beloved Comrade Boxer is dead. He died in the village hospital in
  spite of receiving every attention a horse could have.

Napoleon appears drunk at the window of the farmhouse

Napoleon Comrades. It has not after all been possible to bring back our lamented
   Comrade's remains. In a few days time, we pigs intend to hold a memorial banquet
   in Boxer's honour. Whisky will be drunk to his memory.

Squealer I am happy to say that I was present during Boxer's last hours. It was the
   most affecting sight I have ever seen. "Forward Comrades," he whispered. "Forward
   in the name of the rebellion. Long live Animal Farm! Long live Comrade Napoleon!
   Napoleon is always right."

Napoleon I believe those maxims are ones which every animal would do well to
   adopt as his own.

Clover Were those his last words?

Squealer They were.

Napoleon "Napoleon is always right."

All the animals bow their heads

BLOOD BROTHERS
by Willy Russell

An adaptation of the popular musical set in Liverpool, the story tells of twins separated soon after birth. The one, Mickey, brought up in poverty in a fatherless, overcrowded home, where his mother, Mrs Johnston, struggles to raise her family and the other, Eddie, given to the wealthy, childless Mrs Lyons, for whom the mother formerly worked. But the two boys, living so close, are constantly drawn together without realizing they are related and Mrs Lyons becomes increasingly worried — especially as her husband believes Eddie to be his own son.

Set: There are various simples settings in and around Liverpool. There are eight short scenes from Act Two which are played in a fixed acting area. Period: 1980s.

Cast: M2 F5, 1 M or F.
Eddie, rich, well-brought up boy. Mickey, his twin, poor, scruffy. Linda, their friend. The Mother, Mrs Johnston, their real mother, poor. Mrs Lyons, Eddie's adoptive mother. Policewoman. Narrator.

Playing time: 12 minutes.

SCENE A

We see Mickey and Linda appear. They stand, craning until they spot Eddie. They are all aged nearly eight

Mickey (*loud conspiratorial whisper*) Eddie ... Eddie ...

Eddie looks up

You coming out?
Eddie (*equally loud whisper*) I ... my mum says I haven't got to play with you.
Mickey Well my mum says I haven't got to play with you. Don't take any notice of mothers. They're soft. Are you coming? I've got Linda with me. She's a girl. But she's all right. Come on, bunk under the fence and she won't see you.

Eddie looks from his mother to the two kids. Eventually decides to risk it. He creeps away

   As he joins the others Mrs Lyons exits

Mickey Hiya.
Eddie Hiya, Mickey. Hallo, Linda.
Linda Hiya, Eddie. (*Producing an air pistol*) Look. We've got Sammy's air gun. Do you want to have a go?
Eddie Yes, please.
Mickey Come on, Eddie, you can come and have a shot at our target in the park.
Eddie Which target?
Linda Peter Pan.
Mickey We always shoot at that don't we, Linda?
Linda Yeh. You know what, Eddie, the last time we was there we nearly shot his thingy off.
Eddie What, what's a thingy?
Linda You know.

Eddie is still puzzled

   Come here, I'll whisper it to you.

She does so and the three of them break up with the giggles

Eddie Agh.
Mickey Come on gang ... let's go ... (*With an Indian call and arm wave he prepares to lead his men out*)
Eddie (*standing firm*) But, Mickey ... I mean ... are we allowed to do that?
Linda What?
Eddie Suppose we get caught. By a policeman.
Mickey Agh ... take no notice. We've been caught loads of times by a policeman. Haven't we, Linda?
Linda Oh my God, yeh. Hundreds of times. More than that.
Mickey We say dead funny things to them don't we, Linda.
Eddie What sort of funny things?
Linda All sorts don't we, Mickey. My God, yeh.
Mickey You know like when they ask you what your name is, eh eh. Well we say, Linda, don't we, we say things like, like Adolf Hitler.

Eddie, impressed and laughing with them

Linda And tell him that other one Mickey, that we say to them ...

Mickey Yeh. Listen ... listen; you know when a policeman says "What do you think you're doing?"—because they always say that—we say, don't we Linda, we say "waiting for the ninety-two bus".

Eddie (*greatly impressed as they exit*) Do you? Do you really?

Linda Yeh. We're never frightened are we, Mickey?

Eddie Goodness that's fantastic ...

The kids run off

SCENE B

Mrs Lyons (*entering with telephone*) I want you to come home, Richard ... For God's sake leave the office. ... Because I don't know where Edward is. ... But out playing where? ... There's nothing wrong with my nerves ... It's, it's this place; I hate it, I want to move. It doesn't have to be far away ... It's these people, these people Edward has begun mixing with. ... You don't see it, Richard. You don't see how he's drawn to them. ... I don't need to see the doctor. (*Making an effort to control herself*) I'm fine. I'm fine. I just want to move away from this neighbourhood. ... Well I'm frightened. I'm frightened for Edward. Please ... please ... pl ...

He has hung up. She replaces the receiver

Mrs Lyons screams and runs off

SCENE C

The children run on with the air pistol. Mickey takes aim. He fires

Linda Missed!

Eddie loads and fires

Missed!

She loads and fires. There is a clunk as she hits. Mickey loads and fires

Missed!

Eddie loads and fires

Missed!

She loads and fires. There is a clunk as she hits

Mickey (*taking the gun*) We're not playing with the gun no more.
Linda Ah why?
Mickey It gets broke if you use it too much.
Eddie What are we going to do now, Mickey?
Linda Go on tell us, tell us.
Mickey I'll tell ya.
Linda What?
Mickey We're going to throw some stones through those windows there.
Linda I'm going for me tea now.
Mickey Scared.
Linda I'm not. We're having chips. I'm going.

Linda exits

Mickey You're not scared are you, Eddie?
Eddie No.
Mickey Here's your stone. You've got to throw in through that window there, right? After three. One, two, three ...

A Policewoman enters

Policewoman ... Me mother caught a flea. She put it in the teapot to make a pot of tea ... And what do you think you're doing?
Eddie (*very excited*) Adolf Hitler!
Policewoman What's your name, son?
Eddie Waiting for a ninety-two bus ...
Mickey He's not with me ...

The Mothers enter

Scene D

Policewoman (*to Mrs Johnston*) And he was about to commit a serious crime, love, a serious crime. Now do you understand that?

The Mother nods

You don't want to end up in court again, do you? Eh?

She shakes her head

Because that's what's going to happen if I have any more trouble from one of yours. I warned you last time didn't I, Mrs Johnston, over your Sammy, didn't I?

She nods

Well there'll be no more warnings from now on. You keep them in order or it'll be the courts for you, or worse. Won't it?

She nods

Yes, it will.

The Mother and Mickey exit

The Policewoman turns and approaches Mrs Lyons

As I say, it was more of a prank really, Mrs Lyons. I'd just dock his pocket money if I was you. But one thing I would say, and excuse me if I'm interfering, but I'd not let him mix with the likes of them in future. Make sure he keeps with his own kind, Mrs Lyons, not running round with them at the other end. Well, er thanks for the drink. All the best now. Tarar.

The Policewoman leaves

Mrs Lyons Edward. Edward, how would you like to move to another house?
Eddie Why, Mummy?
Mrs Lyons Erm, well, various reasons really; but, erm, well Mummy's not too well and we thought we'd move a bit further out, towards the country somewhere. Do you think you'd like that?

Mrs Lyons exits

Eddie I want to stay here.

SCENE E

Mother enters and stands as if in an office

The Mother (*to the audience*) You see, and I just feel that if I could leave here and, and, you know, sort of start again, in a new house, in a new place where I wasn't known, where the kids weren't known, well we could start again with a clean sheet. Do you know what I mean? You know if we could just like, find a place to start again. See, we've tried, here. We've tried to like turn over to a new page, but like, like the blotches keep showing through. But if we could move. (*Pause*) Well could you put me on the waiting list? Please. Thank you. (*Pause*) Well even if it is a few years, I mean as long as I knew there was a chance well, well it'd be something to hold on to, wouldn't it?

Eddie Hallo, Mrs Johnston. How are you?

She looks at him and suddenly her face breaks into a smile and she laughs

I'm sorry. Is there something wrong?

The Mother No! I just don't usually have kids enquiring about my health. I er, I'm all right. And how are you, Master Lyons?

Eddie Very well, thank you, Mrs Johnston.

She looks at him for a moment

The Mother Yeh. You look it. You look very well. Does your mother look after you?

Eddie Of course.

The Mother Listen, I told you not to come to our house again.

Eddie I'm sorry, but I just wanted to see Mickey.

The Mother No. It's best ... if ...

Eddie I won't be coming here again. Ever. We're moving away, to the country.

The Mother Lucky you.

Eddie But I'd much rather live here.

The Mother Would you? When are you going?

Eddie Tomorrow.

The Mother So we won't see you again, eh?

Eddie shakes his head and quietly begins to cry

What's up?

Eddie (*through the tears*) I don't want to go. I want to stay here, where my friends are, where Mickey is.

The Mother Come here. (*She takes him, cradles him to her, letting him cry*) Now listen, listen ... don't be silly. You'll probably love it in your new house. You'll meet lots of new friends. In no time at all you'll forget Mickey ever existed.

Eddie I won't. I won't, I'll never forget.

The Mother Shush ... shush ... Listen, listen, Eddie; here's you wanting to stay, and here's me, I've been trying to get out for years. We're a right pair, aren't we?

Eddie Why don't you, Mrs Johnston? Why don't you buy a new house near us?

The Mother Just like that?

Eddie Yes, yes!

The Mother looks at him and laughs

The Mother Mickey's round the back. Go on, you can go and see him. But don't blame me if your mother finds out.

Eddie Thank you. Thank you, Mrs Johnston. (*He looks at her for a moment too long*)

The Mother What you looking at?

Eddie I thought you didn't like me. I thought you weren't very nice. But I think you're smashing.

The Mother (*looking at him*) God help the girls when you start dancing.

Eddie Pardon?

The Mother Nothing. Now go on. Beat it. Go and see our Mickey before I change me mind.

Eddie Goodbye, Mrs Johnston.

Mrs Lyons enters in outdoor clothes

Goodbye.

Scene F

Birdsong. The Mother watches them for a moment before she exits

Mrs Lyons Well Edward, do you like it here?

Eddie (*unenthusiastic*) It's very nice.

Mrs Lyons (*bending and pointing*) Look Edward ... look at those cows ... and those trees. Oh Edward, you're going to like it so much out here, aren't you?

Eddie Yes. Are you feeling better now, Mummy?

Mrs Lyons Much better, darling. Oh look, Edward ... look, look at those birds ... look at that lovely black and white one ...

Eddie (*immediately covering his eyes*) Don't Mummy, don't ... don't look ...

Mrs Lyons Edward!

Eddie It's a magpie. Never look at one magpie. It's one for sorrow.

Mrs Lyons Edward that's just a silly superstition.

Eddie It's not, it's not, Mickey told ... me ...

Mrs Lyons Edward, I think we can forget the silly things that Mickey says.

Eddie I'm going inside, I want to read.

Mrs Lyons Edward, children take time to adapt to new surroundings. But you soon won't even remember that you once lived somewhere else. In a few weeks you'll forget him — Mickey.

She smiles at him and nods. They stand together for a moment, surveying the land before them

Eddie What's that, Mummy?

Mrs Lyons (*craning to see*) What?

Eddie There ... look ... below the hill.

Mrs Lyons What? Oh those houses? That's the beginning of a council estate. But we've arranged with the gardener, he's going to plant a row of poplars down at the end of the paddock there. Once they're in we won't even be able to see that estate. Oh, I love it out here. I feel secure here. I feel warm and safe. Once the trees are planted we won't even see that estate.

She beams a smile at him as they turn and head for the house

Scene G

As they exit we see Mickey and The Mother enter, each carrying a suitcase. The Mother is vigorously taking in the fresh air and leading the way as Mickey struggles with the case, behind her. He is now twelve

Mickey (*stopping and pointing*) Is that our new house there, Mam?

The Mother (*looking*) Where?

Mickey There ... look, you can just see it behind that row of trees.

The Mother (*laughing*) Mickey ... give over will you. The Corporation don't build houses like that. That's a private house, son. (*She points in the other direction*) No ... look, down the hill ... that's where ours is. Look. Oh ... son, isn't it nice out here eh? Eh?

Mickey It's like the country isn't it, Mam?

The Mother Eh, we'll be all right here, son. Away from the muck and the dirt. And the bloody trouble. You can breathe out here, Mickey. Hey, I could dance. Couldn't you?

Mickey (*alarmed*) What?

The Mother (*grabbing him*) Come on ... (*She lilts a tune and waltzes him around the road as he protests vigorously*)

Mickey Mother ... Mother put me down will you. (*Breaking away, leaving his mother to dance alone, looking around and checking that nobody saw him then watching his mother as she dances. Slowly a huge smile breaking across his face*)

The Mother And what are you laughing at? I used to be a good dancer you know. A very good dancer in fact.

Mickey I'm not laughing. I'm smiling. I haven't seen you happy like this for ages.

The Mother Well I'm happy now. You never know, Mickey, play your cards right, we might have tea from the chippie. (*She picks up her case*)

Mickey (*picking up his case*) Ooh, can we, Mam, can we?

The Mother Come on, come on. Hey, Jesus, where's the others? Where's our Sammy and the others?

Mickey They went into that field, Mam.
The Mother Which field?
Mickey (*pointing*) That field.
The Mother (*craning, horror stricken, shouting*) Sammy, Sammy get off that cow
    before I bleedin' kill you. Oh Jeez, what's our Donna Marie put her sodding foot
    in? Sammy, get hold of her ... wipe it off ... oh ... come on, Mickey ... come on ...

They exit

SCENE H

Mrs Lyons enters. She is terrified

Narrator   There's no use clutching at your rosary
                          The Devil's in the garden and he can see
                          Deep inside; he can touch your bones.
                          No he won't, no he's never going to let you alone.
                          You can run you can hide but he'll always find you
                          Wherever you are he's just behind you.
                          When he rings at the chimes then he knows you're in
                          No you won't, no you'll never get away from him,
                          No you won't, no you'll never get away from him.

Repeats last line. Ends with a scream from Mrs Lyons

BONAVENTURE
by Charlotte Hastings

A thrilling drama set in a convent in the Fens, some miles from Norwich. Two prison officials escorting a prisoner, the artistic Sarat Carn, to the gallows, are forced to take refuge in the convent of a French nursing order when the Great Dyke floods. Sister Mary Bonaventure, certain Sarat is wrongly convicted of her brother's murder, is determined to prove her innocent.

Set: Sister Mary's room in the Convent of Our Lady of Rheims. Period: 1947.

Cast: M2 F4.
Sister Mary Bonaventure, tall, beautiful, intelligent; late 30s. Sister Josephine, short, buxom, Scotswoman, rosy, wrinkled. Dr Jeffreys, handsome, poised, charming; 35. Sarat Carn, fierce magnetism, tall. Melling, prison warder, spruce, upright; 40. Miss Pierce, prison wardress, pleasant looking; 32.

Playing time: 20 minutes.

Sister Mary's room

Sarat is standing downstage of the tapestry frame looking through the pages of a book. Pierce is seated on the window seat looking through a book, and Melling is similarly occupied, standing in front of the stove. More books are piled on the desk. Daylight comes through the windows, the lights have not been lit and a bright fire burns in the stove

Pierce (*rising*) Is this any use? (*She indicates something in her book*)

Sarat puts her book down on the stool by the tapestry frame and moves to Pierce

Sarat (*taking the book from Pierce*) Let me see. (*She looks at the page Pierce has indicated*) No, I'm afraid not. Too late. (*She returns the book to Pierce, moves to the tapestry and studies it*) Why *did* this particular figure have to be torn away? Whatever he is, he must have the right boots.

Pierce (*adding her book to the pile on the desk*) Sandals might be correct if he were a priest.

Sarat He has no tonsure.

Mary enters L. She carries a book and some sewing

Mary I think we've found your book. (*She hands the book to Sarat*) Page fifty-six, where the marker is.

Sarat (*reading the title*) Fifteenth-century Embroidery. Sister, what a find. (*She sits on the stool near the frame, opens the book at the marked page and compares the illustrations with the tapestry*) Courtier, groom, processional dress—falconer— yes, why didn't I think of it? (*She looks up at Mary with a smile*) Thank you, Sister.

The telephone rings. Mary puts her sewing on the back of the chair by the desk and lifts the telephone receiver

Mary (*into the telephone*) Sister Bonaventure. ... Yes, he's here. ... Yes, certainly. (*She replaces the receiver. To Melling*) Newlands wants you downstairs, Officer.

Melling Shall I take these books back to the library for you?

Mary I should be grateful.

Melling collects the books together and exits L

Pierce picks up the paper from the window seat, moves to the chair by the stove, sits and starts to read. Sarat rises, moves to the desk, sits at it, and starts to sketch, copying the illustration from the book. Mary moves to the bookcase and picks up her workbasket

(*To Sarat*) Sister Agnes is getting most enthusiastic about starting the embroidery.

Sarat I should like to see it complete. (*Her pencil pauses for a second*) I've not finished my part yet. (*She resumes sketching*)

Mary (*moving to Sarat*) You will. (*She stands watching Sarat*) How quick and sure your strokes are. It must be wonderful to be creative.

Sarat Sometimes it's hell. Things just won't work out. And sometimes everything goes perfectly, and you feel you're God.

Mary picks up her sewing from the chair by the desk and sits. She puts her workbasket on the desk and starts to sew

Mary The newspaper reports said you sketched every day throughout the trial.

Sarat (*without looking up*) I must have drawn everything in sight. The Judge, Counsel—even the ushers. The trouble was they all kept getting the same face.

Mary Whose?

Sarat Jason's.

Mary Was he so much in your mind?

Sarat I couldn't help thinking how he'd have enjoyed the situation. He could draw too, you know, in a facile showy way. He couldn't be bothered to learn properly. (*She pauses*) Poor devil. He made such a mess of his life. Things might have been so different.

Mary (*intent on her sewing*) He made your life intensely unhappy. Yet you have this—this depth of pity for him.

Sarat People can't help the way they're made, can they? Jason's make-up was completely physical. When he became helpless, he had absolutely nothing left. You should understand, Sister. It must be terrible to have no spiritual resources.

Mary (*quietly*) Yes. Was he so very bad?

Sarat Probably only the normal male appetite to start with. But he had an odd perverted streak of mental cruelty which drove him too far. Poor Jason. We had some grim interludes.

Mary Such as the Royal case in Florida?

Sarat puts down her pencil

Sarat Who on earth told you that? No-one knew ...

Mary Martha overheard you talking. The words stuck in her mind.

Sarat Martha?

Mary Would it distress you to tell me?

Sarat No. (*She starts to sketch again*) About eight years ago I was working on a commission in Florida. Jason followed me—as usual. He got mixed up with a girl, called Bee Royal—a solitary intense fool—God help her. When he let her down, as he always let everyone down, she gassed herself.

Mary Was there trouble afterwards?

Sarat (*laughing shortly*) Jason didn't even appear at the inquest. She wrote him a pathetic raving letter, but she also sent one to the coroner, saying she made no charges against anyone, but the person concerned would be haunted by his conscience for the rest of his life. (*She erases part of her sketch with a quick movement*) She didn't know Jason. (*She resumes sketching*) I wouldn't have known much about it myself, but she sent me a letter, too.

Mary Why you?

Sarat She seemed to think we were of one blood, and therefore one character. Actually, I only met her twice. For a man of his temperament, Jason knew how to be discreet. (*She rises, picks up her sketch, moves to the stool by the tapestry and sits*) Let's talk about something else, shall we? What are you making? (*She props the sketch against the frame and commences to paint the tapestry*)

Mary A christening robe for the Grimes' baby. Poor Mrs Grimes is so bewildered at having a boy that she hasn't the slightest idea what to call him. Any suggestions?

Sarat Personally, I prefer plain names. John or Charles would be nice. What's your choice?

Mary (*after a short pause; quietly*) I rather like David.

Sarat puts down her brush. For a moment she sits very still, then turns on her stool towards Mary

Sarat You've been asked to approach me, haven't you?
Mary Yes.
Sarat (*directly*) And how do you feel about it?
Mary I'm divided between my desire to help you, and my equally strong opinion that it's your own personal business.
Sarat I wish I'd had you to talk to in the beginning. (*She takes up her brush and resumes painting*)
Mary (*putting her sewing on the desk*) Talk to me now, Sarat. Why won't you see him or write to him?
Sarat Haven't I done enough? His career is spoilt—probably the rest of his life affected—just because he knew me.
Mary I'm sure he doesn't see it in that way. If you met—once more ...
Sarat No. I couldn't bear it.
Mary But if he wishes ...
Sarat I can't help that. (*She sweeps her brush across the canvas. Desperately*) Don't you understand—can't you realize—if I saw him again—spoke to him—I should go up like straw?
Mary (*gently*) I'm so sorry. I was wrong to speak of it. (*She resumes sewing*)
Sarat (*looking at the canvas*) Damn. I've smudged it. That's what comes of talking while you work. Pass me that rag, will you, Sister?

Mary rises, picks up the rag from her desk, moves to R of Sarat, gives it to her, then stands watching

Mary (*suddenly*) Sarat ...
Sarat It's best like this, Sister. Please don't try and persuade me otherwise.

Mary moves to the chair L of the desk, sits, picks up her sewing and resumes work

Mary If you must torment yourself, need you do it to him also?

Sarat, with her brush and the rag in her hands, rises and moves above the desk

Sarat (*abruptly*) He'll forget. Men do. (*She dips her brush in the jar of water to clean it*)
Mary (*looking up quietly*) Yes. They do. (*Half to herself*) But—women go on remembering.

Sarat mechanically wipes her brush. Her head is bent and she is lost in her own memories. She does not comprehend Mary's words

Sarat (*slowly*) I hope he won't—forget everything. I suppose everyone imagines her own love affair to be the most wonderful thing that ever happened. (*Quietly*) I know mine was. (*She stands very still above the desk*) We were so—so mentally complete. Our minds struck sparks. (*She pauses*) I've lived it over and over again since. Particularly the little idiotic things. (*Quietly*) You know. (*She pauses, then cleans her brush again*)

Mary (*to herself*) I—know.

Sarat Once, in Paris, we paid three visits to the top of the Eiffel Tower. Once so that he could watch me see the view, once so that I could watch him, and the third time so that we could both see it together.

Mary I can't think of three better reasons.

Sarat Then someone said: "But you could have done all that in one visit." And we just looked at each other. We simply hadn't thought of it. That's how crazy we were, and how close. (*She sits on the stool and resumes painting*) I'm glad I told you. It's made it fresh in my mind again.

Mary sits looking straight in front of her, her thoughts far away for the moment

Melling enters L *and crosses to Pierce*

Pierce puts down the newspaper and rises. Melling and Pierce speak together inaudibly. Sarat glances at them, then resumes painting

(*To Melling*) Now, Officer, we can't have you making overtures to Miss Pierce while you're on duty.

Melling moves quietly to R *of Sarat, Pierce to* L *of her*

Melling (*quietly*) Is there much more to do?

Sarat (*without looking up; concentrating on a tricky curve*) Not very much.

Suddenly, instinctively, Mary rises. There is a pause. Sarat stops working, looks at Pierce, then at Melling

(*Evenly*) Why do you ask?

Melling Now, Miss Carn ...

Sarat (*in the same tone*) Why do you ask?

Melling I thought you'd like to finish if you could. You've been very co-operative so far and ...

Sarat For God's sake come to the point.

Melling Newlands has made some sort of connection with the telephone wires. We contacted a nearby house and finally Norwich. (*Quietly*) I've spoken to the Governor. They're sending out a police launch. (*He glances at his wrist-watch*) I should say maybe another three hours.

There is a pause, then Sarat drops her brush on the stool and rises abruptly. Melling and Pierce steady her quickly, both hands on her elbows. Mary puts her sewing on the desk

Take it easy, Miss Carn.

Sarat Thank you, Officer. Don't worry. Could you and Miss Pierce—give me a few minutes with Sister—quite alone?

Melling We'll go out of hearing. I'm afraid we can't go out of sight.

He moves to the door L, opens it and glances at Pierce, who exits. He follows her off, leaving the door open

Sarat crosses to the window and stands looking out

Sarat (*steadily*) It had to come, of course. We knew that.

Mary (*moving below the stove*) Sarat—would you let me be with you ...?

Sarat (*turning and moving above the desk*) You can do that without leaving here.

Mary Yes. If you wish it.

Sarat I've been lucky to get this peaceful interval. I've had vastly different surroundings, I've completed a piece of work which I think is good. I've known you—and believe me, that means a great deal.

Mary Thank you.

Sarat I'm not sentimental, and I don't particularly believe in the power of thought. But I'll ask Pierce to let you know—and then—if you want to pray or anything ... (*She suddenly grips the edge of the desk with both hands, and looks down, fighting for control. To herself*) Oh, God! (*She sits in the chair above the desk*)

Mary moves quickly to Sarat, puts her arms around her, and holds her close

(*She leans her head against Mary. Exhaustedly*) There's something the Chaplain reads, isn't there? I would only see him once—but he did tell me—and the words were like a roll of drums. "I am the Resurrection and the Life ..."

Mary "I am the Resurrection and the Life, saith the Lord. He that believeth on Me, though he were dead, yet shall——" (*She pauses*)

Sarat Go on.

Mary "—yet shall he live. And he that liveth and believeth on Me, shall never die." (*Quietly*) It *is* like a roll of drums.

There is a pause. Sarat moves away from Mary and leans on the desk

Sarat I've never been religious.

Mary You mean you've never troubled about the accepted forms.

Sarat And I don't want them now. If this has to happen, why can't they just be businesslike—and get it over?

Mary It is thought we need intercession. (*She suddenly raises her hands and covers her face*)

Sarat Why, Sister—dear Sister Mary—what is it?

Mary I would give anything to help you at this moment. (*She turns despairingly to Sarat*) How can I when I'm as full of doubts as you are?

Sarat You could make a pretence. You could offer prayers and platitudes. (*Simply*) Instead, you give me this complete honesty.

Mary (*in a very low voice*) Oh, Sarat.

Sarat (*moving to Mary*) Do you know what I've been afraid of all along? Of losing the only thing left to me. My personal self-respect. My pride. Is that wrong?

Mary No.

Sarat (*sitting at the desk and facing Mary*) To go to pieces at the last moment—disintegrate. The others are scared of that, too. Melling, Pierce, even the Governor. They don't mention it, but each knows it's in the other's mind.

Mary Sarat, you have so much courage. Don't be afraid any more.

Sarat That's what I'm trying to tell you—since I've known and talked to you, I don't think I shall be. (*She reaches out and holds Mary's hand*) Only—stay with me until we leave—please stay with me till we leave.

Mary (*holding Sarat's hand tightly*) I will.

Sarat (*after a pause; rising abruptly*) I must get on.

Mary You hands are shaking. You can't possibly work. (*She moves L and calls*) Officer.

Melling and Pierce enter L

Miss Carn would like to finish her painting. With your permission, I'm going to ask Dr Jeffreys to give her a sedative.

Melling Would you like me to go and find him?

Mary If you would be so kind. I expect he's in his room.

Melling exits L

Sarat leans against the chair by the desk. Pierce crosses and, not unkindly, puts a hand on Sarat's arm

Sarat (*gently removing Pierce's hand*) What you and I need, Pierce, is a large brandy and soda.

She crosses to the door up LC and exits. Pierce follows her off. Josephine enters hurriedly L

Josephine (*breathlessly*) I had to come. Is it right what they say?

Mary If you mean—is she going back—yes.

Josephine (*moving* C) When?
Mary They think in perhaps three hours. (*She sits at her desk*)

Melling and Jeffreys enter L. *Jeffreys carries his bag*

Melling (*as he enters*) Sorry to fetch you down like this, Doctor.
Jeffreys (*crossing to the desk*) It's all right. (*He puts his bag on the end of the desk*)
I'm only surprised she hasn't broken down before. (*He opens his bag, takes out his stethoscope and moves to the door up* LC)

Melling and Jeffreys exit up LC

Josephine Has she—broken down?
Mary No. She has more courage than we have. And in her own way—more faith.

Jeffreys enters up LC. *His stethoscope hangs around his neck*

Jeffreys (*moving to the desk*) What we ought to do is put her right out for twenty-four hours, (*he searches in his bag*) but she insists on finishing that confounded painting. (*He pauses and takes an empty bottle from his bag*) Damn, I'm out of phenobarbitone. Got any in your cupboard, Sister? (*He puts the empty bottle on the desk*)
Mary (*rising*) Yes, Doctor. (*She moves to the bookcase and opens the cupboard*)
Jeffreys (*moving to the door up* LC) Bring it in to me, will you, please?

He exits up LC

Josephine moves to the desk and picks up the empty bottle. Mary takes two small bottles from the cupboard

Josephine An empty bottle is a dreary sight at any time—specially in a doctor's bag. (*She replaces the bottle on the desk*)
Mary Here, give him this full one. We can spare it.

She gives one bottle to Josephine, then moves to the door up LC *and exits*

Josephine opens Jeffrey's bag to put the bottle in it, and shakes her head over the contents

Josephine (*sorting out the items in the bag and tidying it*) Dear goodness—the clutter the man carries about with him. It's a guid thing I don't carry the tools of my trade. A fine sight I'd look with a couple of saucepans and my iron-bottomed frying pan. (*She puts a piece of folded gauze on the desk*)

Mary enters up LC

Mary (*smiling*) You just can't resist tidying people up, can you? (*She picks up the piece of gauze*) Now this gauze has got paint on it. (*She opens it out and a newspaper cutting falls out of it*)
Josephine Oh, mercy!

Mary picks up the cutting, glances at it, then pauses and reads it

Mary What on earth ...?
Josephine What's the matter?
Mary (*slowly*) It's a cutting from my file. (*She looks at the cutting again, then slips it hurriedly under the blotter*) Quickly—put everything back.

Josephine hastily repacks the bag

Wait—give me a newspaper—on the window seat—hurry. (*She picks up the scissors*)

Josephine moves to the window seat, picks up the newspaper and passes it to Mary, who hurriedly cuts out a strip of paper about the length of the cutting and rolls it in the gauze. She then puts the gauze in the bag and shuts it. She pauses a moment, glances at the door up LC, *then takes the cutting from under her blotter and studies it*

Josephine What's it doing in his bag?
Mary I don't—know. (*She pauses*) Wait a minute—he asked me for that gauze yesterday. The cuttings were on my desk when he folded it.
Josephine Ay. He caught that one up and put it in the bag by accident.
Mary I suppose so. (*She looks at the cutting thoughtfully*) And yet—I had all the cuttings in a spring clip. (*She looks up*) I remember—I was at the cupboard—Martha came in and I looked up. He was standing here with the file in his hand, fiddling with the clip. He could have—taken it off.
Josephine Not by chance. He'd need to do more than fiddle.
Mary Then he meant to take it.
Josephine Perhaps it's not one of yours.
Mary Yes. Look—there's the mark of the clip. (*She quickly opens the desk drawer, takes out the bulldog clip and fits it on to the cutting*) It fits the dents exactly. (*She looks towards the door up* LC) Sister Josephine, just what does this mean?
Josephine He didn't want you to study that one too closely. Which one is it?
Mary (*looking at the cutting*) It's the report of his cross-examination. (*She looks up. Slowly*) All my cuttings were burnt—or so I thought. There was nothing I could do but resign myself. And now, by some utterly unlooked-for incident, this is returned to me.

Josephine Do you think you should harry yourself all over again? It might be
coincidence.

Mary Perhaps I've been working in the wrong direction. Perhaps this is an indication
of the right one.

Josephine But why should he bother to take one when the whole lot went in the
stove together?

Mary He didn't know that would happen. It was Nurse Phillips who told the Reverend
Mother about the cuttings.

Josephine (*suddenly*) Who said she did?

Mary Why, no-one. But she must have done.

Josephine When did she ever see them? They weren't on the desk last night. You
put them in the drawer before Phillips came in.

Mary Yes. Who else knew besides you and me?

Josephine (*nodding towards the door up* LC) He did.

Mary But surely—he's done everything to help Sarat. And you've forgotten, haven't
you? When it all happened, he was in Norwich.

Josephine Yes. No getting over that.

Mary I want to think. (*She sits at her desk*) Let me read this through, thoroughly. I
may be wrong, but I feel as though ...

She breaks off as the door up LC *opens and Jeffreys enters*

Mary slides the cutting under the blotter

Jeffreys (*moving to the desk*) I've given her a grain and a half, Sister. (*He puts his
stethoscope in his bag*) Let her have a warm drink in about an hour. (*He closes his
bag, picks it up and moves to the door* L) Whichever way you look at it, this is a
wretched business.

He exits L

Mary and Josephine look at each other, then Mary pulls out the cutting and studies it

Mary But what reason would he have for telling the Reverend Mother about the
cuttings? (*She looks up*) Could it have been Willy?

Josephine Willy? (*She turns to the window*) Och, the puir laddie couldn't read a
newspaper well enough to know what it meant. All he worries about in here is
whether the sweeties are sticky enough to give him two or three in one.

Mary (*suddenly*) Sister Josephine!

Josephine turns, startled at the tone of Mary's voice

Josephine What is it, Sister?

Mary looks at the cutting for a second, then puts it down on the desk

Mary I must—have been—very stupid.

She looks across at the door L

BOTTOM'S DREAM
by Alan Poole

Who dreamt the Midsummer Night's Dream? What were the reactions of the Artisans' relatives to their play-acting activities? Quince and his friends have started rehearsals for their play 'The Most Lamentable Comedy and most Cruel Death of Pyramus and Thisby' in preparation for the wedding celebrations of Theseus, Duke of Athens. The comedy takes a different turn when their wives become suspicious about their activities.

Set: An arena.
The play was originally written to be performed on two levels — either a stage and the auditiorium, or two acting levels. Scenery requirements are simple but a free-standing door is essential . Fixed above it should be a roller (or some other device) that can be turned quickly to indicate from which of the five houses — Starveling's, Flute's, Snout's, Snug's or Bottom's — the ladies emerge.

Cast: F5.
Mrs Agnes Starveling, the tailor's wife. Mrs Flute, the bellow-mender's mother. Mrs Snout, loving wife of the tinker. Mrs Alice Snug, the joiner's wife. Mrs Ursula Bottom, the weaver's wife, strong, determined.

Playing time: 8 minutes.

The Lights come up on the house which becomes Starveling's, Flute's, Snout's, Snug's and Bottom's, in quick succession as the women leave

Mrs Starveling Well if she hadn't called a meeting I would have done. It's time a stop was put to this.

Mrs Starveling goes off, grumbling

Mrs Flute (*wheezing and puffing*) I'm really too tired to go, but I'd better for Francis's sake. Oh dear, I hope he's not getting into bad company.

Mrs Snout (*smiling serenely*) Can't think what this is all about. Still it'll be nice to have a chat with the ladies and then back home to my Tom.

Mrs Snug Poor stuttering creature. I don't know how he'd get on without me. If those men are leading him astray they'll get plenty of words from me.

Mrs Bottom Nick Bottom needn't think he can ride roughshod over me! He's got a rude awakening just round the corner.

The Lights go down on the house and up on the arena

Mrs Starveling and Mrs Snug arrive at the meeting place together

Mrs Starveling Well, Alice, there's something very funny going on, if you ask me.

Mrs Snug I've got my suspicions.

Mrs Starveling Does Ursula Bottom know anything?

Mrs Snug What she doesn't she'll make up.

Mrs Starveling You can be sure of that.

Mrs Snug I'd never blame her husband, anyway, whatever he did.

Mrs Starveling Nor I. Must be a dog's life.

Mrs Snug Trouble is, he's leading our men astray.

Mrs Starveling Him and that Peter Quince.

Mrs Flute arrives all of a flutter

Mrs Flute Oh dear, thank goodness I'm not the last. I made sure I'd be late. It's me legs, you see.

Mrs Snug Here, sit down, Mrs Flute. Take the weight off your poor feet.

Mrs Flute They swells something terrible in the summer. I can't hardly get along.

Mrs Snug You poor thing. And now this worry. It's too bad.

Mrs Flute (*much agitated*) Oh Mrs Snug, what is it? I've been hearing such things.

Mrs Starveling That's what we're here to find out.

Mrs Snout enters wreathed in smiles

Mrs Snout Now, you lovely ladies. How nice to see you again!

Mrs Starveling Can't think what you have got to be so cheerful about.

Mrs Snout And why not, indeed?

Mrs Starveling You're in the same boat as the rest of us, you know. Your husband's running loose at nights.

Mrs Snout I don't know what you mean. He may go out with his friends once or twice but that is all.

Mrs Starveling But is that all? You wait till you hear what Mrs Bottom has to say. Look, here she comes.

Mrs Bottom enters

Mrs Bottom Now ladies. Are we all here?

Mrs Snug You're the last, Ursula.

Mrs Bottom Well let's get straight down to business. You all know why we've met?

Mrs Starveling (*grimly*) We do. We want to know what our men folk are up to.

Mrs Flute (*whimpering*) Oh dear; my poor little Francis.

Mrs Snout I don't know what you're worrying about. You can't want to deny our men a few simple pleasures.

Mrs Bottom But what pleasures? That's what we'd like to know.

Mrs Snout My Tom says they are just getting up a play.

Mrs Snug If you'll swallow that, you'll swallow anything. Snug in a play! I ask you!

Mrs Bottom The plain facts are that after living normal lives for years, Bottom, Snug, Snout, Starveling and ...

Mrs Flute (*wailing*) Oh, not my Francis, too!

Mrs Bottom (*glaring at her*) The plain facts are that our men have taken to going out secretly at nights, neglecting their wives and families.

Mrs Snout My Tom doesn't neglect me.

Mrs Starveling More's the pity.

Mrs Bottom We all have the evidence of our own eyes and ears. There's Bottom mumbling over his pottage every supper time, and last night he reared up in bed and called out "Thisby, Thisby, my love", all in his sleep.

Mrs Snug I knew it! They're after the women.

Mrs Starveling Nick Bottom always had a roving eye. Not that anyone would blame him, as Alice was saying just now.

Mrs Bottom And what may you mean by that, Agnes Starveling?

Mrs Starveling Well, he hasn't got much to keep him at home, has he?

Mrs Bottom How dare you! There's a warm house and a good table. I'd be ashamed to own a man as skinny as yours.

Mrs Starveling And a tart tongue for afters, too.

Mrs Snout Now, ladies, now. Don't let's fall out.

Mrs Snug They're at a very funny age you know. And there are some girls around this town'll run after anything in breeches.

Mrs Flute My Francis is only a boy. I hope he never thinks of things like that.

Mrs Bottom Don't you believe it. Ask him what he was doing up Goose Lane the other night.

Mrs Flute Goose Lane? Oh dear!

Mrs Bottom Yes, with that Jenny Golightly from the forge.

Mrs Flute (*tearfully*) And he gave me his word!

Mrs Bottom Men are all alike. None of 'em can be trusted. I want to know who this Thisby is.

Mrs Snug There's no-one of that name in these parts.

Mrs Bottom Just let me catch her, that's all. She'll soon feel the length of my nails.

Mrs Starveling Well, you've certainly got problems, Ursula. I'm only thankful my man isn't like that.

Mrs Bottom I shouldn't think he'd have the energy on what you feed him.

Mrs Starveling (*with assumed dignity*) Just because we don't all eat like pigs at the trough it doesn't mean we're undernourished.

Mrs Bottom So that's the way of the wind. Pigs indeed! You forget, Agnes Starveling, I've been in your kitchen, and I doubt if your Robin could fancy anything out of there.

Mrs Starveling You vixen! Anyone could eat off the floor in my house, and you know it.

Mrs Bottom Ay, could!

Mrs Snout Ladies, ladies!

Mrs Snug Well, none of us can afford to be complacent. We just don't know what they're up to.

Mrs Flute Oh dear!

Mrs Snug Now take Snug ...

Mrs Bottom No, you take him!

Mrs Snug Very funny. All right, I did take—poor, witless creature when it comes to talking. He could hardly get out "I do" when Parson married us—we looked like being there till Martinmas.

Mrs Starveling I remember it well. We were all breathing on the words for him.

Mrs Snug But when it comes to cutting a mortice his hand's as steady and true as his heart.

Mrs Bottom (*acidly*) You've got off the point, Mrs Snug. Is he steady and true now?

Mrs Snug I don't know. I don't know. He's always played with the children of nights, made them toys out of little scraps of wood, and funny—he can always talk to them; the words come easy like fresh shavings from a plane.

Mrs Bottom The point, the point.

Mrs Snug Well, only yesterday our Mary came running in with tears streaming down her cheeks—her dad had frightened her, she said. Jumped out from behind his bench and roared at her like a lion, she said.

Mrs Starveling Poor little mite.

Mrs Snug Well, I gave him a piece of my mind at supper-time, I can tell you, and what do you think he said!

Mrs Starveling Go on!

Mrs Snug "I've got to practise to escape a hanging," he said.

Mrs Flute Oh terrible, terrible! What can be going on? It's the fairies, I know it is. Why can't they leave us alone? Our men, they've been pixilated.

Mrs Bottom I know what's bewitching them and it's not the fairies! Ladies, if we are going to keep our men the battle is on. We've everything to lose. Be vigilant, watch and follow! We shall meet again secretly, wherever our husbands meet, and then their devices shall be known. And now to our homes! Courage!

They all go off, talking

COLD COMFORT FARM
by Stella Gibbons, adapted by Paul Doust

An adaptation of the classic novel set in the 1930s. The ironic humour requires a very special style of playing, as these are larger-than-life characters. Under the influence of Flora Poste, who is visiting her strange relatives at the Farm in Howling, Sussex, all is changed. But Grandmother Ada Doom is a strong challenge to Flora, and the conflict reaches its climax in this amusing scene: The Counting, where the Starkadder family assemble before Grandmother Ada Doom of Cold Comfort Farm.

Set: A farm kitchen. Period: 1930s.

Cast: M10 F9.
Flora Poste, practical heroine. Aunt Ada, her very eccentric aunt. The number of Starkadders may be expanded or contracted as necessary: Urk, Amos, Mark (his half-brother), Phoebe (with their three children), Michah (Urk's father) and his wife, Susan, Luke (Amos's half-brother), Polly (Luke's daughter), Naphthalie, her husband, and three babies. Distant relatives: Sheba, Meg and Peg (twins), Rennet (a daft Starkadder). Elfine, Seth, Reuben Starkadder. Mr Neck, a Hollywood producer.

Playing time: 15 minutes.

The kitchen, set up for The Counting

The sukebind has grown enormously and is now in flower. The plant, in blooming, has released its perfume and the sweet, sickly smell hangs heavily in the air. (Perhaps incense can be burnt in the kitchen beforehand.) Ada sits in an enormous high-backed chair. Urk lies on the floor, face down and motionless. Rennet, in gum-boots, is huddled in a corner. Amos kneels, mumbling prayers, with a magazine in his hands. Judith is also present, as is the extended Starkadder family. These include: Mark (Amos's half brother) and Phoebe Starkadder, and their three children—Dandelion, Jane and Jacob. The children range from nine years old to fourteen. Dandelion huddles behind Ada's chair, Jane is at Ada's feet, and Jacob sits on Ada's knee. The following relatives cower about the kitchen, all within Ada's sight: Michah Starkadder and his wife, Susan. (Michah is Amos's cousin and Urk's father.) Luke (Amos's half brother). Sairy-Lucy's Polly (Luke's daughter), her husband, Naphthalie, and their three babies (dolls) in three appalling prams. Naphthalie's half sister, twice removed, Sheba. Meg, an unmarried female whom nobody can remember having been born of the Starkadders, but who quite certainly was. Meg's twin, Peg. Various other Starkadders are also present

The collected Starkadders play a vital role in this scene, contributing a variety of moans, murmurs, gasps and wails. Their principal reactions are included, but many more may be introduced; they should underscore the action almost constantly. Any periods of absolute silence are indicated

There is a deadly hush in the room; nobody says a word apart from Amos and Ada. Ada sings discordantly as she rocks Jacob to and fro. A single oil lamp hangs from one branch of the sukebind and illuminates Ada's face horribly. The fire gives a more than usually hellish glow, with lurid shadows

Ada (*looking up to the audience*) Ay! Gather in around me —gather in! You're all mine! Mine! Ivery one o' you! And none o' you mun leave! (*She claws a hand into the air and draws it to her heart*)

A great groan from the Starkadders. The Lights fade further. Ada stands Jacob up

Jacob! Fetch me my copy of the *Milk Producers' Weekly Bulletin and Cowkeepers' Guide*!

The Starkadders mumble: "Milk Producers' Bulletin", "Cowkeepers' Guide", etc. Judith moves forward to Amos and snatches the bulletin from his hands

Amos 'Tes gone! Lord! 'Tes a sign! A sign!
Ada Amos!

Amos clasps his hands and returns to his quivering

Judith 'Ere ...

Judith gives the magazine to Jacob, who moves fearfully toward Ada and, trembling, holds it out toward her. Ada takes the magazine. She rolls it into a tight tube, and the Starkadders twist and groan as she does this. She gives a final twist to the magazine; the Starkadders convulse. Jacob bursts into tears

Ada Silence!

She clubs Jacob with the magazine and he falls to the floor, unconscious. There is a gasp from the Starkadders. Ada looks around. Silence. Phoebe now dashes forward and tries to pick up her son. Ada points at her with the rolled-up magazine

Phoebe ...

Phoebe lays her son, the sacrificial lamb, down again. She withdraws, weeping. Ada points at her with the magazine.

Phoebe!

Phoebe stands up straight

Starkadders Phoebe.

Ada now scans the room, picking out the Starkadders with the magazine and calling their names. They each stand up and move forward when called

Ada Mark!
Starkadders Mark.
Ada Luke!
Starkadders Luke.
Ada Judith!
Starkadders Judith.
Ada Amos!
Starkadders Amos.
Ada Susan!
Starkadders Susan.
Ada Michah!
Starkadders Michah.
Ada Sairy-Lucy's Polly!
Starkadders Sairy-Lucy's Polly.
Ada Sairy-Lucy's Polly's husband, Naphthalie!
Starkadders Sairy-Lucy's Polly's husband, Naphthalie.
Ada Sairy-Lucy's Polly's husband Naphthalie's half sister twice removed, Sheba!
Starkadders Sairy-Lucy's Polly's husband Naphthalie's half sister twice removed, Sheba.
Ada Meg!
Starkadders Meg.
Ada Peg!
Starkadders Peg.
Ada Dandelion!

Silence

Dandelion!

Dandelion, behind her at the chair, taps Ada on the shoulder

Argh!

Ada bludgeons Dandelion with the magazine, and she falls to the ground with a moan. She lies unconscious on top of Jacob

Elfine!

Silence

Elfine!

Silence

Seth!

Silence

Seth! Seth, Seth, Seth!

Silence. Ada throws herself back in the chair

Argh! Woodshed, woodshed! Narsty! Narsty! Woodshed, woodshed! Narsty, Narsty! Argh! (*She collapses, unconscious, in her chair*)

A great commotion goes up from the Starkadders. Some of them edge bravely forward, peering at Ada. Suddenly the door is thrown open and a great gust of wind sweeps through the kitchen. The Starkadders moan and retreat. Silence

Flora, Elfine, Seth, Reuben and Neck enter. Flora carries a tyre pump and moves to Amos

Flora (*whispering*) Cousin Amos—the pump for the tricycle.

Amos takes the pump gingerly

Well, well ... (*To the audience*) The gang's all here!
Judith You must greet your Aunt Ada.
Ada I saw something narsty in the——
Flora Yes, so I've heard.
Judith Mother, 'tes Flora Poste. Robert Poste's Child.

Ada 'Twas a burnin' noonday ... all them years ago. And me no bigger than a titty-wren ...

Flora (*to the audience*) Not much of a conversationalist, is she?

Ada (*rising slowly from her chair and shuffling forward*) Seth? Where is my Seth? Where is my darling boy?

Seth 'Ere, Gran'mother. 'Ere I am.

Ada Ah!

Seth And I will niver leave 'ee—niver ...

Judith moves toward Seth with a moan

Amos (*leaping at Judith*) Woman!

Ada enfolds Seth in her arms. Seth contributes to the picture in a statuesque manner. Neck moves to Flora

Neck What a dude ...

Flora Quiet, Mr Neck!

Ada That's my boy ... my mommet ... my pippet ... Why, how grand he is tonight! But what's this? What's all this? Where 'ave you been? What 'ave you been doing, boy? Tell your granny!

Flora He's been to Richard Hawk-Monitor's twenty-first birthday party. And so have I, and so has Elfine, and so has my friend, Mr Neck. What's more, Aunt Ada, Elfine and Richard are engaged to be married—and will be, too. Just as soon as things can be arranged.

There is a terrible cry from Urk. He rises up from the floor

Neck What the ... ?!

Urk steps crazedly forward. Rennet rushes to him with a pleading, strangulated moan. Urk throws Rennet aside, and she collapses with a shriek. Urk reaches out as if to throttle Flora

Ada I shall go mad! I shall go mad!

Urk suddenly collapses in tears

Urk My liddle water-vole!

Amos Lord!

Judith Seth! (*She rushes toward Seth*)

Seth throws her aside. There is a pained shriek from Judith and a chorus of despair from the Starkadders. Seth gives a wild cry and strikes a pose. Silence. Neck comes forward, making a screen shape with his hands and looking at Seth through it

Neck That's it, sweetheart! That's got it! Now—hold it!
Flora (*to the audience*) And Seth, soaked as he is in movie slang, holds it with perfection.
Neck Wow! Baby—would you like to be in the talkies?

There is a gasp from the Starkadders

Seth Me?
Neck Who else!
Flora Mr Neck is a film producer, Cousin Seth. He has a studio in Hollywood.
Seth Oh! Do 'ee know Lotta Funchal?
Neck Old Lotty? Sure I do! I got her under contract right now!
Seth Oh!
Ada I saw something narsty!
Neck You can meet her, if you want. Hey! She can be your first leading lady! Would you like that?
Seth Lotta Funchal! Oh! More 'an anythin' in the woarld!
Neck Well, ain't that dandy? He wants to be a movie star and I want to make him one!
Ada I saw something narsty!
Flora Cousin Seth, go to your room and pack at once. You're going on a long, long journey.
Amos Journey!
Judith No!
Neck Can it!
Ada I saw something narsty!
Neck You know, honey, someone oughta write you some new dialogue. Seth?

Seth looks from Judith to Ada and exits

Neck Attaboy!

Neck exits

Ada and Judith wail. Amos steps forward

Amos If a sinner can leave then so mun I!
Ada What?
Amos I mun go, I say! I mun go! For the Lord calls me to it and I mun obey!

There is a gasp from the assemblage

Ah, 'tes terrible a thing, but I mun do it! I 'ave been a-wrestlin' and a-prayin' and a-broodin' over it for months —and now I know the truth at last! I mun go abroad on one o' they nice ol' tricycles! A nice old tricycle—with a platform on the back! Ay, like the Apostles of old I 'ave 'eard my call, and I mun follow it!

Ada No!

Urk Elfine! Elfine!

Amos He flung his arms wide, and stood with the firelight playing its scarlet fantasia upon his exalted face!

Lord! Lord!

I hear the glad voices of the angels calling me!

Out over the ploughed fields! Where the liddle seedlin's are clappin' their hands in prayer!

The tricycle do be ready tonight!

I've no time to lose!

Ada No, no! I cannot bear it! There have always been Starkadders at Cold Comfort Farm!

You must not go!

Argh!

You must not!

None of you might leave!

I shall go mad! I shall go mad! I saw something narsty in the woodshed!

Urk Me and the water-voles! We've failed!

We're beaten!

We planned a nest for her up by Nettle Flitch Weir—me and the water-voles—and would have taken her there when the eggplant was in bloom! And now she has given herself to him—Richard Hawk-Monitor! When she was but an hour old, I did mark her feeding bottle wi' water-vole's blood. She was mine, see? Mine! And I've lost her ... Oh, why did I ever think she was mine?

Ada Arghhh! There have always been Starkadders at Cold Comfort Farm! But that means nothing to you! Nothing!

Amos Ay—*nothing*!

There is a gasp from the Starkadders

'Tes goodbye to you, Mother!

Ada Argh!

Amos 'Tes goodbye to you *all*!

Silence

Flora (*to the audience*) Ada's eyes, like slots of pain in her grey face, turn fiercely upon Amos; they blaze with hate!

Reuben comes forward with Amos's hat, coat, and warming pan

Amos (*snatching the hat, coat, and pan*) Ay—with the help o' the angels and the Lord's word——
Flora (*to the audience*) No mention of me, of course.
Amos —I have broken your chains—forever!
Ada A-m-o-s!
Flora (*to the audience*) A screech from her heart roots that buries itself in his plexus. But he does not turn. He goes to the door, throws it wide——

There is a great gust of wind through the kitchen as Amos opens the door. The Starkadders shriek. Mark and Michah rush to restrain Amos, but he throws them off. Susan rushes to her husband

   Amos exits

Ada Amos ...

   Mark, Michah and Susan charge out after him

Reuben shuts the door

Flora (*to the audience*)—and is gone.
Ada Argh! (*She swoons*)

Judith and Rennet rush to catch her

Judith Mother!
Ada Alone! Alone ...!
Urk Ay! But I'll not be alone!

There is a gasp from the Starkadders

   I will not!
Flora (*to the audience*) He is laughing noiselessly, insanely!

Urk laughs—noiselessly, insanely

Urk Come 'ere Rennet! Ay! I 'ave lost Elfine but I shall not be alone! I 'ave lost my mommet—but I shall take 'ee instead!

Seth enters, wearing a coat and carrying a suitcase. Neck enters behind him

Ada Seth!
Neck Well, well ... How's the girl?
Ada I saw something narsty!
Neck Did *it* see *you*? Seth?
Urk Ay, dirt as you are, I'll take 'ee, and we'll sink in the mud together!
Ada You must not take her, Urk! I forbid it!
Rennet Oh? And what's it to do wi' you?

There is a gasp from the Starkadders

   Ay, gasp if you must, but I 'ave found my voice—and I mean to use it!
Judith Seth! Seth! You must not go! 'Twould break my 'eart! Besides, there's the
   spring onions to bring in.
Neck Gee, ma'am, I know it's raw, I know it's tough—but that's life, girl!
Rennet Right then, Urk; I'll 'ave 'ee, my angel—and to 'ell wi' Mark Dolour!

There is a great gasp from the crowd. Urk gives a wild laugh

Judith No, no!
Neck Look, baby—why not come along with us? I'll get you a job. As my secretary!
   How about that?
Judith Why must you take him? Why? Why?
Neck OK ...

Neck pulls Seth in front of Judith

   Now you see this hunk, honey?

Judith sobs

   You know what this hunk has got?

Judith moans

   He's got passion!

Judith wails

   And do you know what passion is?
Judith I know nothing! I am a dead woman! A broken chaff! A used gourd!

Neck grabs Judith and kisses her passionately

Neck That's passion!

Judith is stunned. She stares at Neck, transfixed

And that's what sells pictures. And your boy here has got passion by the sackful—and the looks. *That's* why I need him! *That's* why I can't give him up! See?

Judith, unable to speak, simply stares at Neck

OK, OK—He'll send you five grand out of his first picture. How's that?

Pause

Judith exits

Urk Come then, my beauty—my handful o' dirt!

He throws Rennet over his shoulder. There is a spontaneous round of applause from the crowd

Rennet And who's coming with us?
Ada No-one, no-one!

But as Urk makes toward the door with Rennet he is followed by a train of squealing Starkadders; this includes everybody in the room apart from Ada, Reuben, Elfine, Seth, Neck and Flora (Phoebe snatches up Jacob and Dandelion on her way)

Argh! Come back! Come back! You must not leave me!
Flora (*to the audience*) Ada Doom stands bolt upright, her eyes closed tight against the world. She is rigid. Her lips move, softly. I listen, and can just make out what she is saying. It is none too festive.
Seth (*moving to Flora*) I jus' wan' t' say—thank 'ee. Thank 'ee—and goodbye.
Neck Come on, baby. I tell you sweetheart, you're going places—and you ain't never coming back!

Seth and Neck exit, leaving the door open

It appears that only Flora and Ada are left in the room; in actual fact Reuben is standing in a shadowy corner and Elfine is asleep in a chair, but we can see neither of them very clearly. Flora crosses to the door and closes it. Silence and stillness

Judith now enters from upstairs wearing her coat and carrying a suitcase and her photograph album

Judith Where did he go?

Flora Who?

Judith My man! My man! My *beautiful* man!

Flora Oh, really, Cousin Judith—we've been through all this. (*She takes the album*) Cousin Seth has gone to be a film star.

Judith Nay—not Seth! (*She takes the album back*) I am not talking about Seth! Seth is my son—nothing but a capsy boy-child. Nay—I am talking of the American gentleman!

Flora Mr Neck?

Judith He has asked me to go away with him. I am his passion!

Flora Well, I'm not sure that's quite what he——

Judith He has asked me! He is very kind. There is a dark force in him. It beats like a black gong! I wonder you cannot 'ear it.

Flora We can't all strike it lucky.

Ada groans a little

Judith Goodbye, Mother! (*She throws the album on to the fire*)

A red glow leaps across the room. Ada trembles. Judith steals toward the door. As her hand touches the latch, Ada lets out a great screech

Ada J-u-d-i-t-h!

Judith stops and looks back at Ada. The fire and the red glow subside. Pause

Judith exits, closing the door quietly behind her

Ada gibbers

Flora (*to the audience* So Judith has gone as well—and I didn't have to lift a finger! (*She glances at Ada*) Oh, I say! What a picture! Yet still no sign of the old-fashioned camera, the tripod and the flashlamp. How very puzzling. Mind you, it is not yet "The End"—and "The End" is where a "Let's-Pretend-To-Be-A-Photograph"-type effect truly belongs—isn't it?

Reuben (*coming forward*) Do 'ee think Father'll return?

Flora Not a chance, my lamb. The farm is all yours now. All of it. Not that this kitchen looks too pretty at the moment. If only I had some snowdrops. Snowdrops would dispel this dismal atmosphere in a trice.

Reuben Snowdrops?

Flora Yes. Quite the most beautiful of flowers, don't you think? Still—Elfine ... Elfine ... wake up my lovely —it's time for bed.

Elfine takes Flora's hand and lifts herself drowsily

Elfine, Flora and Reuben exit

Ada is now alone. She stands, rigid, in the middle of the kitchen. The Lights fade, extremely slowly, until Ada is lit only by a tight pool of light

Ada Amos ... Urk ... Seth ... Judith ... All—gone. Gone ... And who was it that sent them away? Who was it that made 'em go? That brat! That wennet! Robert— Poste's—Child!

Lights out on Ada

DADDY LONG-LEGS
by Jean Webster

The play, first produced in London in 1916, is set in a New England orphanage at the beginning of the century. This scene from the first act takes place on Trustees' Day and Mrs Lippett is anxious to create a good impression. She bullies the orphans, especially Judy, the senior girl, who has become the child drudge during her eighteen years in the home.

Set: The dining-room of the John Grier Home for orphans. Period: early twentieth century.

Cast: M4 F3, 1 boy 3 girls. Extras.
Mrs Lippett, hard-faced, domineering; 40. Judy, spirited; 18. Gladiola, Loretta, Mamie and Sadie Kate, young orphans. Freddie Perkins, orphan; 9. Miss Pritchard, charming old-fashioned gentlewoman, sympathetic; mid 50s. Jervis Pendleton, a Trustee's friend. Cyrus Wykoff, short, chubby, bald-headed, pompous, dignified, wears spectacles. Abner Parsons and Mr Codman, trustees. Other Trustees.

Playing time: 14 minutes.

It is a bare, dreary room with a table, chairs and a cupboard

Judy enters from the pantry. She carries a tray of sandwiches. She is vividly alive girl of 18, dressed in the same blue gingham that the young orphans wear, but made in a more becoming manner. There is an air of all-conquering youth. Neither Mrs Lippett's harshness nor the sordid air of the asylum has succeeded in cowing her. She puts the tray down on the table and then goes and gets a black box from the cupboard. She brings the box to the table, opens it and takes out caps and aprons. During the scene she is humming "Comin' Through the Rye" gaily to herself

Mrs Lippett enters upstage. She has an unpleasant voice that grows shrill when she loses her temper. She is wearing a polka-dotted silk dress, very tight and rather fussily made with a profusion of cheap lace trimmings. It is turned up from the bottom and pinned so that she will not soil it

Mrs Lippett I'm glad to see that somebody's carefree.

Judy stops her song

Is everything ready?

Judy (*at work, smoothing out the aprons*) Yes, Mrs Lippett.

Mrs Lippett Seems as though everything's gone wrong today. And just when we've got a rich Trustee up from the city. (*Turning to the window*) He's out in the play-yard now, talking to Freddie Perkins, with a hole in his pants that big.

Judy laughs

Well, what are you laughing at? It's no laughing matter. Can't you keep that child mended?

Judy I mend Freddie Perkins's trousers every day of my life. There's no trousers left any more. Nothing but patches.

Mrs Lippett (*looking over at the sandwiches, turning in disgust*) Did you make these sandwiches?

Judy Yes, Mrs Lippett. I know they're pretty thick. But the bread was so fresh I couldn't cut it. I'm awfully sorry.

Mrs Lippett (*mollified*) Well, maybe they'll taste all right. Look sharp now. I don't want any more hitches.

Mrs Lippett exits. Gladiola pokes her head into the room

Gladiola Judy, has she gone?

Judy Yes, and it's time for you to go! Come, fly into these.

Led by Gladiola, the orphans enter. They are dressed exactly alike in stiffly starched blue gingham pinafores with a row of white china buttons down the back and a suggestion of red flannel petticoat showing beneath. Each child has her hair strained back tightly and braided into two pigtails

Gladiola and Loretta sit on the bench and begin playing a game of "Peas-porridge hot" during the following. Judy gives Mamie and Sadie Kate a cap and apron each. They are regulation waitress aprons, about three inches longer than the children's dresses, which fasten behind. The caps are muslin bows fastened to an elastic. Mamie and Sadie Kate put on the aprons, Judy buttoning Mamie's and Mamie buttoning Sadie Kate's. Then they put on the caps

Gladiola ⎫
Loretta ⎰ Peas-porridge hot, peas-porridge cold,
Peas-porridge in the pot, nine days old.
Some like it hot, some like it cold,
Some like it in the pot, nine days old!

The children all join in, talking noisily but not loudly. Judy finishes Mamie's apron and gives a precautionary "Hush" to the children. Then she gives the tray of sandwiches to Mamie and the tray of cups to Sadie Kate

Judy Now please be careful, children, and don't make any mistakes.
Sadie Kate No, Judy.
Two others We won't.

The orphans go out

Gladiola Judy! Tell us a story.
Loretta Cinderella!

Judy, with a tired sigh, sits on the bench. Gladiola kneels on the bench beside her and Loretta kneels on the floor. Judy caresses them in a manner that shows her loneliness and longing for love

Gladiola No! Not Cinderella! Tell us Noah's Ark. (*She rises*) I'll be the lion. (*She growls and throws her arms around Judy, pretending to devour her*)
Judy Not now, dear. Some other time.
Both Yes now!
Judy Poor Judy's so tired. This is the first time I've sat down since five o'clock this morning.
Loretta Tell it *while you are sitting* down.
Judy I must learn my lesson for school tomorrow.
Gladiola What? 'Rithmatic?
Judy No, not 'rithmatic. French.
Loretta What's French?
Judy *Tu es un enfant très bon et je t'aime beaucoup.*

The children laugh

Freddie Perkins enters upstage. He is dressed in dark blue knickerbockers and a jumper made of the same striped blue gingham that the girls are wearing, but his knickerbockers have a large three-cornered rent in the back. His hair is shaved close to his head

Freddie When are we going to have supper?
Judy (*good-naturedly, scolding*) Freddie Perkins, turn around.

Freddie turns

Freddie What's the matter?

The children laugh. Freddie turns back to them

What are you laughing at? Cut it out! Cut it out!

He tries to hit Loretta who jumps away

Judy You bad, bad boy, to tear your clothes. (*She discovers a rent in the shoulder of his shirt*) You disgraceful little ragamuffin!
Freddie (*sitting next to Judy*) I don't care, I'm hungry!
Gladiola So'm I.
Loretta Me, too.
Judy You can't have supper till the Trustees go.
Gladiola I hate Trustees.
Loretta So do I.
Freddie What's today? Beans? (*Pause*) Or corn-meal mush?
Loretta This is Wednesday.
Gladiola It's corn-meal mush.

The children all join in the orphan's yell while Judy frantically tries to make each child be quiet. The last line tapes off into a dying wail

Orphans   Mush! Mush! Corn-meal mush!
                        Slush! Slush! Same old Slush!
                        How I hate it,
                        Corn — meal — mush! (*Heads down*)
Judy Hush, you naughty children.

Freddie sits on the floor

Gladiola Judy, tell us a story.
Judy No, no, no!
Gladiola ⎫ (*together; imitating her*) Yes, yes, yes!
Loretta ⎭
Judy (*pleading*) Children! I'm so tired!
Freddie (*rising*) Draw us a picture!
Judy I've no paper!

The children run around looking for paper. Loretta goes around behind the table and discovers the box cover. Gladiola brings the cover to Judy

Gladiola Draw it on this.

Judy looks dubious. Everyone sits as before

Judy But I haven't any pencil!

Freddie (*turning away disgustedly*) Oh, gee!

Judy I can't draw with my finger, you know.

Freddie (*discovering a piece of chalk in his pocket*) Here's a piece of chalk.

Judy Very well — Mercy! It's all over sugar.

Freddie Did I give you sugar! (*He grabs the chalk in an attempt to lick the sugar off*)

Judy (*grabbing it back*) You bad, bad boy!

Freddie moves away

Well, what shall I draw?

Gladiola Elephant!

Loretta Circus!

Freddie Cowboy chasing Indians! (*He gives an imitation of a wild Indian*)

Judy Oh, something easy. I'll draw a bad little boy who's torn his clothes.

The children begin to laugh at Freddie and cry "Shame, shame"

Freddie (*domineeringly*) Cut it out! Cut it out!

Judy Freddie!

Freddie turns away shamefacedly

What'll I draw?

Gladiola Oh! Draw a Trustee!

Loretta Yes, draw a Trustee!

Freddie Yes, one of those guys that goes around like this. (*Imitating Wykoff*) "This won't do, Mrs Lippett! This won't do! And this floor must be scrubbed ... I tell you it won't do, Mrs Lippett ..."(*He stands puffing himself out à la Wykoff*)

The children watch him in ecstasy, laughing and applauding

Gladiola Yes — and make him fat. With a gold watch-chain!

Freddie And with a pair of searchlights!

Judy (*drawing*) There's his body. And there's his head. There's his coat and there's his waistcoat, and there's the buttons on his waistcoat.

Gladiola Where's his whiskers?

Judy Wait a minute, I can't draw his whiskers on his waistcoat, and there's his tie and there's his collar and there's his whiskers and there's his eyes.

While Judy draws the eye-glasses Freddie begins to laugh. Judy turns to him

What are you laughing at?

Freddie Oh, those searchlights!
Judy And there's his searchlights. And those are his arms and those are his legs.
Loretta And where's his gold-watch chain?
Judy And that's his watch-chain!

She holds the picture in front and they all laugh

Gladiola (*taking the picture from Judy*) It looks exactly like a June bug.

Judy takes back the picture

Judy (*writing at the bottom*) "This looks like a June bug, but is meant to be a portrait of any Trustee."

The children laugh. Freddie takes the picture and marches around with it, followed by Gladiola and Loretta

Chorus Looks like a June bug! Looks like a June bug!

Sadie Kate and Mamie return with a half-emptied plate of sandwiches which they place on the table

Sadie Kate Gee! You ought to see them eat!

Judy goes to Sadie Kate and Mamie. The others stop singing and hungrily look at the sandwiches. Freddie puts the picture on the table and goes to Judy, followed by Loretta and Gladiola

Freddie Can I have a piece of bread?
Gladiola Me, too!
Loretta I'm hungry.
Judy (*after a moment's hesitation*) Yes, you may all have one piece.

They help themselves joyously. Freddie gets first piece and biggest, to the disgust of the others. He goes triumphantly to the bench and sits. They keep up a chatter

Freddie Say!

The children all stop the noise to listen

(*Boasting*) I played a joke on those Trustees!
Judy Freddie Perkins! (*Suspiciously*) What have you done?
Freddie I ain't goin' to tell.

The Trustees are heard talking angrily off L

Gladiola (*moving to the door*) Cheese it! They're coming!
Judy (*surprised*) Scamper out, children!

Freddie at first sound has bolted off DR. *Gladiola, Loretta and Mamie exit* DR. *Sadie Kate exits* UR. *Mrs Lippett enters* UL, *followed by a group of Trustees and visitors, Miss Pritchard, Wykoff, Jervis, Codman and Parsons. Miss Pritchard looks worried, Wykoff is indignant, Jervis amused. They have all been talking outside and it has grown in volume until they are well on and in place*

Mrs Lippett (*with the sugar-bowl*) Judy Abbott, what is the meaning of this?
Judy (*bewildered*) The sugar-bowl?
Mrs Lippett It's full of salt!

Judy turns and looks after Freddie

Wykoff We put salt in our tea.

Judy bursts into a quick laugh. Jervis moves downstage, his back to Judy and amused by the scene

Mrs Lippett When you have finished laughing, perhaps you will tell us how it came there?
Judy I don't know.
Mrs Lippett Of *course* you don't know. *You* never know *anything.*
Miss Pritchard It was a mistake.
Wykoff Bad management. Bad management!
Judy (*apologetically*) I didn't know about it, of course — I'm very sorry it happened!

Mrs Lippett sees the empty plate and crumbs on the table

Mrs Lippett What's this?

They all turn and look

So you've been stealing the refreshments that were left?
Judy The children were hungry — it's after their regular supper-time — and I gave them each a piece of bread and butter.

Parsons discovers the broken cup

Wykoff Mrs Lippett, does this young woman run this institution?

Parsons (*coming downstage with the broken china*) Here! Here! What's this?

Judy stares in amazement

Mrs Lippett (*turning upon her sharply*) How did that get broken?

Judy is silent

Well — don't stand there staring!
Wykoff Another little joke?
Mrs Lippett Answer me, Judy Abbott. Did you break that cup?
Judy (*with dignity*) No, Mrs Lippett, certainly not!

Parsons puts the broken cup on the tray

Mrs Lippett Who put it there?
Judy I don't know.
Mrs Lippett Seems as though you are old enough to take a little responsibility.
Judy (*miserably*) I try to, Mrs Lippett — but I can't be in two places at once. And today while the nurse was taking care of the sick babies ——
Wykoff Doesn't pay to educate 'em out of their class.
Mrs Lippett These children are the most *deceitful* creatures I have ever known. It's enough to make one lose one's faith in human nature.
Judy (*facing Mrs Lippett, quietly*) If you would *trust* the children, they would not deceive you.
Mrs Lippett So now, you are going to be *impertinent*, are you?

Wykoff discovers the picture on the table

Miss Pritchard (*pleasantly, trying to end the discussion*) Dishes will get broken — suppose we join the others.

Wykoff is examining the picture which he has casually picked up

Wykoff (*facing front explosively, showing the picture*) Good heavens, madam! What does this mean? Do I look like a June bug? (*He exhibits it to Mrs Lippett*) And may I ask who is the artist?

Judy stands staring at the others with something of the air of a hunted animal

Mrs Lippett (*with ominous quietness*) Is that one of your drawings?

Wykoff shows it to the Trustees

Judy Yes, Mrs Lippett.

Mrs Lippett Have you got anything to say?

Judy (*miserably*) I can't draw. I just do it to amuse the children.

Wykoff To amuse the children! Madam, is this the kind of respect that you teach?

Codman puts the picture on the table

Mrs Lippett How do you dare make fun of a Trustee of the John Grier Home?

Judy (*frightened*) I—I didn't mean to make fun of anybody.

Mrs Lippett Oh! I suppose you think that it is a fitting way to show gratitude for all that's been done for you? This Home has given you every mouthful you ever ate, and as a result, you ridicule your benefactors. I'll tell you this, Miss Judy Abbott — you'll be finishing school next month and then you'll be put to work. The *kind* of place you'll get will depend on your record here.

Wykoff And when you have to shift for yourself, young woman — then maybe you won't think life so funny.

Other Trustees nod approval

Judy (*wearily*) I don't think it's so very funny now.

Mrs Lippett Oh, there's no use trying to make anything decent of her, I shall send you to a boarding-house keeper who wants a little slavey to wash the dishes.

Judy I shall be very happy to go. Any place, anywhere will be better than this.

Mrs Lippett (*beside herself*) You ungrateful little — imp! What do you mean?

Judy (*commencing in low, intense tone, gradually rising to a fever of rebellion*) I mean — I don't feel any *gratitude* because I have nothing to be grateful for. There is no *charity* about it. I have *earned* my living in the John Grier Home. I have worked from the time I was a tiny child. For three years straight I polished brass door knobs until you discovered that I was clever enough to do other things. And you haven't kept me all this extra time just for my own good. When I was eleven years old that lady wanted to adopt me. But you made her take another child instead, because I was useful. I might have had a home, too — like other children — and you *stole* it away from me. And you call me ungrateful because I'm glad to go? I don't care how hard it will be. I can make my own way in the world. Just give me the chance. Anywhere — out of the shadow of this place — you'd see. I've lived eighteen years in this *prison*. I *hate* the John Grier Home!

As she hurls this last defiance, she turns and runs out DR

Jervis has turned his back on the scene and stands DL *with folded arms and head bowed in deep thought, for Judy has won his admiration by her plucky stand. After a pause, the Trustees recover from their astonishment*

Mrs Lippett You see! You see!

Wykoff The quicker you pack her off the better.

Miss Pritchard The child didn't know what she was saying!

Codman Insubordination!

Parsons Bad example.

Wykoff Demoralize the whole institution!

Parsons She must be punished!

They start to go, shaking their heads and talking excitedly at once

Mrs Lippett And punished severely. Oh, if you knew what I have to put up with ——

Wykoff, Parsons, Codman and Mrs Lippett go off C, *the excitement and tumult gradually dying down*

Miss Pritchard follows them to C, *trying to pacify them, then she comes downstage*

Miss Pritchard I'm sorry this had to happen before you, but really, really we have no right to be angry.

Jervis Angry? Oh, no, no! I was only hesitating because — well — I must be sure I'm doing the best thing for the girl. But by jove! (*He turns to Miss Pritchard*) It was great to see that little thing rise up and demand her right to live. (*He looks off* DR *and then slaps his hand as if having arrived at a decision*) She shall have it!

Miss Pritchard What?

Jervis (*turning to Miss Pritchard*) I'll send her to college!

Miss Pritchard (*joyfully*) That *is* generous!

Jervis (*gruffly*) Nonsense! I'm interested. I'd like to see if the girl really can pull it off!

Miss Pritchard She will be so *grateful.*

Jervis No, no. None of that. She's never to know who does it.

Miss Pritchard She will want to thank you.

Jervis Well, she can't. I won't have it. Good Lord! She's had to give thanks for every mouthful she ever ate! I wonder she didn't choke. This college business comes as a free gift from Heaven.

Miss Pritchard Don't you want to watch her progress?

Jervis From a distance. They can send me her reports.

Miss Pritchard A college doesn't send reports.

Jervis (*thinking out loud*) Well, let me see. We're to make a writer of the girl? Hm — there's no better practice in composition than good, old-fashioned letter writing. She may write me a letter on the first of every month, telling about her studies and her daily life — just such a letter as she would write to her parents — if — she had any.

Miss Pritchard She will have to know your name.

Jervis Tell her Smith. John Smith. She will address her letters to Mr John Smith ——

care of my secretary, just as the boys do their reports. But she's never to expect any answer. I can't have Judy a nuisance.

Miss Pritchard I will explain the best I can.

Jervis And don't explain to anyone else. We must keep it a secret for the girl's sake. Let her forget this Home. Blot the word "orphan" out of her mind.

Sadie Kate enters from UR *and puts a spoon on the table*

Miss Pritchard Sadie Kate, run quick and call Judy Abbott.

Sadie exits DR

Sadie Kate (*calling as she goes*) Judy — Judy.

Jervis And now I must run. I don't want the child to see me. Get her some pretty frocks — and all that sort of nonsense. Goodbye.

Miss Pritchard Goodbye! Thank you! Thank you! (*She follows him upstage and watches him off*)

Jervis exits. Judy dejectedly enters DR *and goes towards Miss Pritchard*

Miss Pritchard turns and sees her and goes to her

Judy (*with a dead voice*) Well — what are they going to do with me?

Miss Pritchard (*very kindly*) Nothing dreadful.

Judy I didn't mean to break out that way — but when you think bitter thoughts for years and years, some day — suddenly — they just won't stay inside you any longer. (*She turns away*)

Miss Pritchard Judy — (*by Judy*) — I have good news for you.

Judy faces front

Something wonderful is going to happen to you.

Judy (*slowly facing Miss Pritchard*) Wonderful?

Miss Pritchard Judy — a gentleman — one of our Trustees — is going to send you to college.

Judy To college? Me?

Miss Pritchard nods affirmatively

Miss Pritchard With pretty new frocks and everything.

Judy You mean — I'm going just like any other girl — who has a real father and mother?

Miss Pritchard Yes, dear.

Judy (*slowly grasping the situation, as though choking over her joy, crossing* L) *Oh, oh,* oh! It sounds just like the fairy stories I make up to tell the children.

Miss Pritchard It's true, dear.

Judy (*turning to Miss Pritchard, breathlessly*) Who is he?

Miss Pritchard No-one you know.

Judy He wasn't here? Today? Not one of those men?

Miss Pritchard Yes.

Judy I didn't look at them. What's he like? What's his name?

Miss Pritchard You are not to know his name — his real name. You may call him Mr Smith.

Judy Smith?

Miss Pritchard Mr John Smith. He will be your guardian.

Judy My guardian! I'll belong to him? And I won't belong to the orphanage any more? I'll just belong to him?

Miss Pritchard Yes, dear!

Judy (*turning, crying*) Oh, I'm so happy! I'm so happy! (*She turns to Miss Pritchard*) Where is he? I want to tell him. I want to see him.

Miss Pritchard You cannot see him, dear.

Judy But I want to know what he's like. I'll never bother him — never — if I may see him just once. So I can think about him. Oh, please, please, just this once? Please, please!

Sobbing, she places her head on Miss Pritchard's shoulders who lays her arms around Judy tenderly and mothers her. An approaching car's headlights can be seen through the upper window

Miss Pritchard Hush, dear. I promised to keep it a secret.

Judy sobs again

But, he's there — outside now!

Car horn

Waiting for his car.

Judy turns quickly, but Miss Pritchard holds her at arm's length

No, no, dear — it's too dark to see his face, but there, reflected on the wall, you can see his shadow!

She releases Judy who crosses looking off through the window L

Judy Oh, if I could only see his face. At last I have the shadow of a father. Oh, my daddy — my daddy —— (*Laughing*) Look — what funny long legs the shadow has. I never saw such long legs. I know — (*Turning to Miss Pritchard*) I'll call him my dear old Daddy Long-Legs. (*She turns to the window again*)

DAUGHTERS OF VENICE
by Don Taylor

In Venice in 1720, the Sisters of the Convent of the Pietà care for the young girl orphans of the city. The girls' musical talents are fostered and they have a world-famous orchestra under the guidance of Vivaldi. On the night of the Carnival, the girls are to perform in the Grand Salon, but their teachers are more concerned than the pupils, who are excited by the romance and their clandestine meetings during this festive time. In the second scene a now rich, widowed Contessa comes to claim the daughter she abandoned at the Convent grille thirteen years earlier when she was destitute.

Set: The parlour of the convent and the public part of the room, the divide being a mesh iron grille; an ante room; the Madre's room. Period: 1720.

Cast: M8 F6, 1 boy 1 girl. Extras.
The Madre di Coro, stern-mannered, motherly, nun; 50. Sister Teresa. Milord, good-looking, good-hearted Englishman, stupid beneath his fashionable charm; mid 20s. Bodger, his servant, energetic, keen, always helpful, not too bright which he covers by low cunning; 20. Pazzo, short, unshaven, crafty Italian. Girl, seller of ribbons and laces. Puppet Boy. Tumbler. Punch and Judy Man. Anna-Maria, mature convent musician, fresh; 18-20. Grimaldo, tall, dark, fearsome Italian down on his luck. Maestro Vandini, director of the orchestra and choir; early 40s. Maestra Luciana, suspicious, irritable; 38. Perduta, small, bustling, energetic; 13. Vivaldi, energetic, powerful temper, asthmatic; 40. The Contessa, beautiful, pale, nervous; late 30s. Sister Annunciata. Crowd of ragged children. Girls of the orchestra.

Playing time: 29 minutes.

Scene A

The reception room or parlour of the Convent of the Pietà

A large open room, split down the middle by a wall which contains two openings like huge windows, only instead of glass they contain a wide mesh iron grille, the holes being four or five inches square. Hands can be touched through them, and lips too, I daresay. On the side within the convent a large curtain cuts off any further vision. There are chairs set both sides of the grille for people to converse together, so that, although privacy is not possible, a certain kind of intimacy is

In the public part of the room, there are all kinds of people, a ragged boy who plays the sopranino recorder for two tumblers who perform as he plays, a boy with three puppets, and standing on one side of the room, a Punch and Judy booth. There is also a ragged girl who sells ribbon and lace from a tray, and three or four ragged boys sitting round the walls, apparently doing nothing, who are probably pickpockets. While the room is empty of the public, they all sit round the room bored, but as soon as anyone enters, the whole group bursts into activity

There is a momentary pause, and then Milord enters, led by Pazzo, with Bodger following

Immediately, the recorder player begins to play, the tumblers tumble, the girl comes forward with her tray, and the boy begins to make his puppets dance. The opening speeches are played more or less together

Girl Buy some ribbons and laces, signori, for your mistresses, they will love you for ever with these in their hair!

Puppet Boy Watch the puppets dance, signori, and for a groat they will perform a play!

Punch and Judy Man Come and see the famous Mr Punch beating his wife, signori, no better entertainment in all Venice!

Puppet Boy The story of the Prince, the Princess and the Gondolier!

Tumbler Don't forget the tumblers, sir, remember the acrobats!

Milord Good God, where are we? Bartholomew Fair?

Pazzo No, signore, this is the Parlour of the Convent of the Pietà——

Bodger I've seen duller market days in Leicester.

Pazzo —the nuns' Reception Room, where they meet their friends and lovers.

Bodger Their lovers? I thought they took vows of chastity?

Pazzo But what are vows, signore? Soldiers take vows of loyalty, and change sides if they are losing, dukes takes vows of fealty to kings, and murder them in their palaces, and bankers take vows of honesty. It is the world, signore. We didn't make it, but we must live in it.

Milord But what are all these people doing here?

Pazzo Selling, sir, what else? Lots of people come here, some of them rich. In such places there will always be people with things to sell.

Milord Just us at the moment.

Pazzo That is because it's early, signore. After midday people will be queuing up to take their turn at the grille, and these people will be making money. Or stealing it.

Milord Stealing?

Pazzo Keep your eye on those ragged boys, signore, with nothing to sell. They will have your watch and your wallet if you give them half a chance.

The ragged boys move suddenly in a bunch, and brush past Pazzo and Milord

Keep your hands in your pockets, signore! Like this.
Milord Oh yes, I see ...
Bodger Oh look, the Punch and Judy's beginning! I love Punch and Judy.
Punch and Judy Man "I am the famous Punchinello. And this is Judy my wife!"

Punch hits Judy

Bodger That's the way, Mr Punch, you give her what for!

A crowd of ragged and half-starved children of both sexes runs in noisily, and gathers by one of the grilles, shouting

Sister Teresa emerges from behind the curtain with a basket of bread rolls, which she proceeds to give them through the grille

They eat greedily, and wait, hoping for more

Milord What's happening now?
Pazzo These are the starving children. They come in two or three times a day. The nuns give them bread.
Milord What do they do if the nuns don't give them bread?
Pazzo They starve, signore.
Sister Teresa That's all, there isn't any more ...

The noisy crowd of children immediately begins to leave, in search of another hand-out

Milord is immediately attacked again by the various hucksters, who gather round him with their wares

Puppet Boy The play, signore, let me show you the play ...
Milord Oh, well ... I don't know ...
Puppet Boy (*performing*) This is the story of the famous Prince of Venice, the Princess, and the Gondolier ...

The recorder player is beginning to play, the girl is trying to sell ribbons, and Punch and Judy is progressing. Pazzo gets the attention of Sister Teresa as she is going

Pazzo The English Milord is here, to see Maestr'Anna-Maria.

Sister Teresa Oh ... yes ... I'll get her.

Sister Teresa goes behind the curtain

Punch and Judy Man "Oh Mr Punch, how can you treat me so bad?" "It's easy. I just take my stick and do this!"
Bodger That's the way, Mr Punch! He'll kill her in a minute!

Pazzo turns to the hucksters and yells ferociously

Pazzo Go away, scum, filth, leave the English Milord alone! If you sit quietly at the wall, he will give you a shower of money! Won't you, Milord!
Milord Well, I'd rather give it to them for entertaining me——

The hucksters try to begin again, but Pazzo intimidates them

——but yes, of course I will!

Sister Teresa appears from behind the curtain with Anna-Maria and Sister Annunciata. Anna sits on the stool behind the grille. The two nuns stand behind her

Sister Teresa Signore, Maestr'Anna-Maria is here.
Pazzo Silence, filth, while the English Milord speaks!

The hucksters all scurry to the walls and sit in silence

Bodger Oh, don't stop the Punch and Judy show! Oh ... well ... yes.

Milord sits facing Anna-Maria. He is awestruck, almost speechless at seeing her so close

Milord I ... er ...
Anna-Maria You asked to see me, Milord?
Milord I ... You played beautifully. At the Cardinal's.
Anna-Maria Thank you, Milord.
Milord And ... sang beautifully too ... But now I see you close up, without your violin ...
Anna-Maria You see a body, signore. But the soul is absent.
Milord Oh ... well. I wasn't going to say that. The body is ... wonderful ... on its own.
Anna-Maria I believe you know ... I must leave the Pietà.
Milord I've met the woman who looks after you all ... I mean, the chief nun ...
Anna-Maria La Madre di Coro.
Milord Yes, I suppose that's the one ... I want ... to take you back to England.

Anna-Maria Signore?

Milord I mean, no, I want to marry you. Here. Well, no, I mean in England. I have a very big house, in Leicestershire, and two town houses in London, and a villa in Middlesex ... lots of land, cows, sheep. Farms. Forests ... rivers ... all sorts. You will be very happy in England. And very rich.

Anna-Maria I know nothing about England. What do you do there?

Milord Do? Ah, well ... We ride. We eat ... a lot. Balls of course, we have balls. Go to London for the season. Play cricket.

Anna-Maria What is ... cricket ...?

Milord Ah well ... how long have we got? ... Well, no, it's a game English gentlemen play with their servants, on the grass. I mean, there's two wickets, one at each end, and a bat and ball ... and the two captains toss up at the beginning, and ... Perhaps you don't have cricket in Italy.

Anna-Maria I don't think so.

Milord No, well, Venice. You wouldn't.

Anna-Maria Do you have music?

Milord (*relieved*) Music, oh, good heavens, yes! The opera in London. Italian opera!

Anna-Maria Which composers?

Milord Oh, well, let me see. Handel! He's Italian. Lots of others. Can't remember their names. We go to see the singers really, and to chat to our friends.

Anna-Maria And your house?

Milord What about my house?

Anna-Maria Music in your house?

Milord Oh yes. Every now and again. I play the fiddle myself.

Anna-Maria (*smiling enthusiastically*) You play the violin?

Milord Oh yes, the Chaplain plays the harpsichord, and there's one of the servants plays the gamba, and the chap from the cowshed plays the serpent. Sometimes, when we have a dance, I play myself, though my mother doesn't approve. Jigs and hornpipes, and good old *Sir Roger de Coverley*!

Anna-Maria Who is he?

Milord No, no. It's not a person. It's a tune.

Anna-Maria I don't think I know this music.

Milord No, well, it's English. Very English. Not the sort of thing you play. I'm going to buy lots of that. Lots and lots of it, concertos and cantatas, while I'm here ... You're so beautiful I can't stop looking at you.

Anna-Maria If I went to England, would I be able to play?

Milord Of course! Bring your violin. We'll play together!

Anna-Maria No, I mean concerts. With an orchestra. Do you have a Court Orchestra?

Milord What, in Leicestershire?

Anna-Maria In your house.

Milord Well. Not as far as I know. I've never seen one. It is a big house. I might have missed it.

Anna-Maria Could I play with your orchestra? Is that the custom in England?

Milord Well, er ... you mean in public?

Anna-Maria For concerts.

Milord For friends you mean. Like the Duke of Chandos at Cannons. But, not in public, for money, no. One's wife can't play in public. I mean. That isn't done.

Anna-Maria No ... here it is the same. It is very kind of you to ask me. I am an orphan, like we all are here, and I have no friends but the nuns and my violin.

Milord You have me now.

Anna-Maria Thank you, signore ... Will you ... please allow me to think. Just a few days.

Milord Of course! Take your time! I shall be here for months yet! When can I see you again? Preferably not with this grille between us.

Anna-Maria I will be playing at the Grand Duke of Tuscany's ball tonight. Will you be there?

Milord It will take the Grand Duke and all his armies to stop me!

Anna-Maria Thank you, signore.

Milord No indeed. Thank you.

Gracefully she withdraws behind the curtain with the two nuns

Milord is dazed, shattered, gobsmacked

Oh Bodger! She is an angel! I'm lost!

Bodger Sir, haven't you forgotten something?

Milord What?

Bodger You're married.

Milord We're going to have to do something about that, Bodger! We really are. She's wonderful! I love her to distraction! I *must* marry her!

Bodger Well the least you can do, sir, is ask your wife.

Grimaldo enters, grimly

Grimaldo Pazzo!

Pazzo Signore?

Grimaldo Outside, there is a Frenchman who wants to meet a large number of ballet dancers. Do we know any ballet dancers?

Pazzo No, signore. But I do know where we can find some good-looking sailors.

Grimaldo He wants ballet dancers, not sailors!

Pazzo If he's a Frenchman, signore, he won't know the difference.

Pazzo hurries out with Grimaldo

All the hucksters begin again

Bodger Oh good, the Punch and Judy's beginning again.

Milord (*slightly nervously*) Bodger, I think we ought to get out while the going's good.

Bodger He said you were going to give them some money, sir. I don't think they'll be very pleased if you don't.

Milord Quite right ... (*He feels in his pocket*) Bodger!

Bodger What?

Milord My purse. It's been lifted!

Bodger Don't let on, whatever you do.

Milord How much have you got in your pocket?

Bodger Five pence. All in pennies.

Milord English or Italian?

Bodger English.

Milord It'll have to do. Give it to me. (*He holds up the money in his closed fist*) Here we are. For you. Catch!

He throws the money in the air. They all dive for it

Run!

Bodger and Milord go off, and the Lights fade on the scrum

The scene changes to an ante room in the Grand Duke of Tuscany's palace. Off stage a formal minuet is being played and danced

All the girls come on stage, in their white habits, wearing their cloaks, and carrying their instruments. They talk together as they remove their cloaks and put them on chairs. Perduta hands out folders of music

Maestro Vandini comes in with Maestra Luciana

Luciana Where is the Madre? She said she would be here before the concert began!

Vandini Well, it doesn't matter. We can play without her.

Lucinana But where is she, why is she not here when she is supposed to be?

Vandini The Governors called her to a special meeting this afternoon. She said she would take a fast gondola as soon as she could.

Luciana The Governors? Why?

Vandini I have no idea ...

Vandini talks to some of the girls, while Luciana singles out Lucietta, for some last-minute instruction. Anna-Maria, Silvia and Candida are near the front of the stage

Silvia Will he be here tonight?

Anna-Maria Yes, I think so.

Candida What's he like? Did you like him?
Anna-Maria I think so. He's a pleasant man.
Silvia Well, what does liking have to do with it? Is he better than the nunnery?
Anna-Maria Yes. Better than that.
Silvia So. Brava. I'll throw rose petals at your wedding.
Anna-Maria Yes, I suppose so ...
Sister Teresa Maestro Vandini, the dancing is over ...
Vandini Ah ... My children ... my children!
Sister Teresa And the Madre is here.

The Madre enters, still wearing her warm outdoor cloak

Madre Be quiet, all of you!

They fall silent instantly

We can hear your chatter in the Grand Salon! Compose yourselves to play. Is everything ready?
Vandini Yes, Madre. You have all your music in the correct order?
Perduta Yes, Maestro, they have. I checked every folder.
Vandini Good. Maestra Anna-Maria, you are leading the orchestra tonight?
Anna-Maria Yes, Maestro.
Vandini And Lucietta leading the continuo?
Lucietta Yes, Maestro.
Vandini So we are truthfully superfluous. We can sit back and listen, as if we merely loved music, without the burden of making it!
Sister Teresa They're ready now, Maestro.
Madre All right, Maestr'Anna, lead them in. Remember, don't begin till the Grand Duke's master of ceremonies gives you the signal. It'll be at least five minutes.
Anna-Maria Yes, Madre ...
Madre Off you go then.
Vandini Good luck, my children, daughters of the Muse!

The girls file into the Grand Salon. There is some applause, but little change in the general level of talk from the duke's guests

The three elders look at each other, and the two teachers prepare to follow

Madre Maestra Luciana, Maestro Vandini! Wait here a moment please.

The two teachers stop and return enquiringly

Vandini Madre?
Luciana What is it, Madre?

There is a pause. The Madre is embarrassed

Madre Dear Luciana ... I have some bad news for you.

Luciana freezes before she speaks

Luciana What?

Madre The Governors called me to a special meeting. They are making great changes. To save money, they say, but it seems to me to be purely destructive ...

Luciana What? What is it?

Madre They will not renew your contract to teach organ and harpsichord. From Easter.

A pause. No-one speaks

Luciana But ... what ...?

Madre I did all I could. I argued against them.

Luciana But who will teach my pupils? There will be no-one. I have been here since I was a little girl. Forty years.

Madre They say Lucietta can teach as well: and that only one organist is needed.

Luciana It isn't true! It isn't. She is a beginner!

Vandini Oh, Maestra, my dear ... this is a disaster for all of us.

Luciana Where shall I go? What shall I do? I've been here all my life!

Quite suddenly Vivaldi enters, in a rush. He is a little over forty, a man of consuming vast energy, and powerful temper. In fact he suffers from asthma, and always carries a stick with him to lean on when he gets out of breath, which he occasionally does, though not often when he is really worked up. He has a ruddy complexion, and wisps of his red hair are visible under his wig. He is in a fury

Vivaldi Vandini, there you are!

Vandini Maestro Vivaldi! How long have you been in Venice?

Vivaldi About two hours. And the first thing I hear is that at the Grand Duke of Tuscany's assembly, all the music is to be my concertos!

Vandini Yes Don Antonio, a great honour.

Vivaldi You can have my share of the honour, Vandini, how much money did you get out of him?

Vandini Money?

Vivaldi For me, for my music!

Vandini Reverend Don Antonio, the concertos are the property of the Pietà ...

Vivaldi Of course they are, but when you play them at the special request of the Grand Duke, I expect a substantial present. Ten or fifteen ducats at least!

Madre Don Antonio, no-one asked him.

Vivaldi Then you should have done! You have no right to use my music as though it were your own property! It is mine, Madre, I wrote it for the Pietà, not for public concerts in every salon in Venice! I shall march up to the Grand Duke when the applause is echoing round his great chamber, and in the most courteous manner possible, I shall indicate that some gift would be appropriate! The heir to the Medici can afford to pay a poor Venetian musician, whatever else he can do. My best wishes to you, old friend, and to you, Madre, and to you, Maestra Luciana. Will they play well tonight?

Madre I'm sure they will, Don Antonio.

Vandini What happened to you, Don Antonio? We heard you were in Prague?

Vivaldi I was. But there is not enough money to be made from opera there. They paid me fifty ducats for a whole opera, and spent a thousand on the castrato's helmet! I got out with my skin just about intact, but it was time to leave. I shall stage a season of new operas here in the Summer, at the Teatro San'Angelo.

Vandini Ah, it will be good to have you back after so long ...

Vivaldi Anyway, you know why I am here. I am to be Maestro di Coro again. The Governors wrote to Prague and asked me.

Vandini What?

Madre It's true. They told me tonight. I would have told you later.

Vivaldi Why all the glum faces? Did you not know? Well, nobody told me, of course, they expect me to know these things by instinct! Don't worry, old friend, you aren't to be booted out into the square. You are to teach cello still. And you can play for me in the Summer, write some of the recitatives too, to save my time.

Vandini Ah, thank you, Maestro.

Vivaldi But I do need money, every penny I can get. So the Duke must pay for his pleasures.

The music begins in the Salon. The Spring Concerto, from "The Four Seasons"

Ah. How did I guess! If I had ten ducats every time this music was played, I could retire and live in a castle. But. Everyone enjoys my music, and I get what I can beg!

Madre is comforting Luciana. Vivaldi doesn't notice

Madre Don't cry, my child. We shall do something. We shall manage something.

Luciana Where else can a woman teach the organ?

Madre We shall think of something.

Vivaldi Well. I seem to have cast a gloomy shadow. Shall I go back to Prague, and tell the Governors to go to Hell? No, unfortunately I can't. I need the money, and at the moment it can only be made here.

The solo music begins

Ah. The birds are singing well tonight. Who is playing?

Vandini Maestr'Anna-Maria.

Vivaldi Ah yes. The child is a master. We can teach her nothing. I suppose she must be leaving soon?

Madre After the Carnival.

Vivaldi Have you arranged something. Is she to be married?

Madre I hope so.

Vivaldi The best thing. Get her to the church, and pregnant. Before she does us all out of work. Thank God she's only a girl, eh Vandini? Or where would the next meal come from?

They go into the Grand Salon together, laughing and talking

Madre Will you come in, Luciana?

Luciana No. I can't. I'll listen from here.

The Madre goes in to the Grand Salon

Luciana slowly sits on a chair, amid all the cast-off cloaks and instrument cases, as the music sweeps in from the next room. She lowers her head and cries, sobbing uncontrollably like an injured child

Black-out

SCENE B

The Madre's room in the Pietà

The Madre is on stage with Sister Annunciata. Neither speaks

Sister Teresa enters

Sister Teresa The Contessa is here, Madre.

Madre Tell her ... to wait just a moment.

Sister Teresa To wait, Madre?

Madre Just a moment.

Sister Teresa goes

Sister Annunciata What are you going to do?

Madre There is a mother who has lost her child. A child who has lost her mother. What should I do?

Sister Annunciata But, Madre——

Madre What are we talking about, Sister Annunciata? Strokes made by a pen on a page, which may or may not be accurate.

Sister Annunciata There's no reason to think they are not, Madre.

Madre Nor any reason to think they are. There are three hundred years of entries in those ledgers. Do you imagine there are no mistakes in all that time? That poor woman needs her child. And all the children here need parents. What would we achieve for either by telling them the child died? Nothing but pain. Perduta will have to leave us eventually, and will never have another chance like this. This is a miracle, Sister, and we must not reject miracles when they are offered.

Sister Annunciata It isn't true, Madre.

Madre What is truth, Sister Annunciata ...? Pen strokes in a book? Or the chance of happiness?

Sister Annunciata And a substantial gift, no doubt.

Madre is angered

Madre (*quietly*) You speak above your place, Sister. The whole of Venice may be corrupt. You may be corrupt. But I am not! I remind you as a nun you are under obedience to your superiors, and in this matter, I am your superior. I command you to keep silent!

Sister Annunciata Yes, Madre.

Madre Tell Sister Teresa to send the Contessa in. And wait yourself in the ante room.

Sister Annunciata Yes, Madre.

The Contessa enters, shown in by Sister Teresa, who immediately leaves. She looks pale and nervous

Contessa Madre ...

Madre My lady.

Contessa You have some news for me.

Madre Yes.

Contessa (*her face lighting up*) You've found my child. You have! I can tell from the look on your face! You've found her!

Madre I believe we have ... Our little Perduta. Our lost one.

Contessa Perduta ... She is found now. I have found her. Who gave her that name?

Madre One of my predecessors, my lady.

Contessa I shall keep it. She could not have been better named. It is a kind of miracle, Madre, isn't it. After all these years.

Madre Yes my lady, it is.

Contessa When can I see her?

Madre I have to tell you, my lady ...

Contessa What?

Madre There can never be ... absolute certainty. They say a father can never be quite sure of his paternity: and a mother whose child has been lost is in the same position. All we can say ... is that the evidence is there.

Contessa But the day I left her ... the note, the locket and shawl ...?

Madre Yes my lady, we have found them ... I say only what I must say when these occasions arise—and they are rare enough, rarer than we would wish. There is no certainty in any of the things of this world. The only absolute truth is with God, and in Heaven, not in Venice.

Contessa That is true, Madre, of spiritual things. But we have the locket, the shawl! There can't be any possibility of error!

Madre No, my lady. Very likely not.

Contessa Is she here? Can I see her now?

Madre Yes, she is.

Contessa Does she know?

Madre Yes. I told her myself.

Contessa What did she say?

Madre Almost nothing. She was dazed. They all make up stories about their parents all the time. But they never think they will come true, and when they do, it changes everything. But she is one of our very liveliest girls. I've no doubt she will be herself again by now.

Contessa Let me see her. Please.

Madre I'll bring her in.

Madre goes out

During the short pause while she is off stage, the Contessa walks quietly across the room, in an agony of expectation and fear

Madre enters with Perduta, who looks much paler and more subdued than usual. She carries a small bundle

There she is, my lady.

Perduta (*curtsying*) Good-morning, my lady.

Contessa Good-morning.

Madre I shall attend you in the ante room.

Madre goes

The woman and the girl look at each other, not knowing what to say, feeding on each other's physical reality after so many years of imagination

Perduta I am called Perduta here. I have no other name. The Madre has told me you are my mother.

Contessa Yes. I believe I am.

Perduta She gave me these things for you. (*She hands the Contessa the bundle, the shawl and the locket*)

Contessa Oh, yes. Yes. (*She is near tears*) There is no question ... There was a note too?

Perduta The Madre gave me no note, my lady.

Contessa No ... well. Destroyed years ago, I daresay ... You were wrapped in this tiny shawl. The locket was round your neck. May I put it there again?

Perduta Yes, my lady.

The Contessa replaces it with great emotion and tact, taking care not to touch the child

Contessa You must wear it there for ever.

There is a pause, the Contessa full of an emotion Perduta cannot share. She watches with a kind of fearful curiosity, aware that her whole life is changed, but not yet sure how to react

Perduta Did you really leave me at the grille?

Contessa Yes. I can never ask forgiveness enough ... But if I hadn't done so ... you would probably have died.

Perduta Why didn't you want to keep me: when you were so rich?

Contessa I wasn't rich then. And I did want to keep you. But I couldn't.

Pause

Perduta Am I to go with you now?

Contessa Yes, soon. I hope so.

Perduta Are you *very* rich?

Contessa I am rich, yes. You are my only child. Your life will be very different. You will have everything you want. You will never have to work.

Perduta I have always dreamed of my mother finding me. And in my dreams it was always someone like you. Rich and beautiful.

Contessa I'm very glad. Your dream has come true.

Perduta But it was just a dream. I never thought it would happen.

Pause

Contessa What's the matter?

Perduta I ... I am the chief copyist. I make all the parts for the orchestra to play, and the soloists too, Maestra Silvia and all the others.

Contessa That must be very hard work.

Perduta But I don't just copy. I have studied counterpoint and harmony. The others all tease me because I can't play any instrument except the keyboard, but I know more about music than any of them. I have to be able to adapt the music to suit our players if it was written for other instruments. I have to write bits too sometimes, to make everything fit.

Contessa That's all finished now. You need never do anything like that again.

Perduta No, but ... what *shall* I do then?

Contessa You need do nothing at all. You will be my daughter.

Perduta But ... you see ... I love it here ... You're very kind, but ... I don't really want to go.

The Contessa sits, shattered

Contessa Oh ...

Perduta (*confused*) Oh ... I mean ... that sounds very unkind ... I know you are my mother, and I'm sure I shall come to love you, and it must be wonderful to be rich ... but I do love it so, being with all the musicians, and especially Maestra Silvia ... Will there be music in your house?

Contessa There will be whatever you wish there to be. There is music in almost every street in Venice, and in Rome it is very grand, with the opera, and the great concerts in the palaces, and the oratorios and masses in the churches. We might employ one or two musicians to play for you, if that would be what you want.

Perduta Really! ... I would have my own orchestra?

Contessa Not orchestra exactly. But some servants who would play, whenever you want them to.

Perduta That would be wonderful!

Contessa We must get to know each other, Perduta. We are strangers yet. It will take a little time, for both of us. My name is Livia.

Perduta I think I shall just call you Mother.

Contessa I would like that.

Perduta Will I have to go ... I mean ... will I come with you before the end of the Carnival?

Contessa Would you like to stay till then?

Perduta Yes please! I love Carnival best of all the year!

Contessa Then why not? We shall see a good deal of each other from now on.

Perduta (*not quite certain*) Yes ...

Contessa Madre?

The Madre enters, and Sisters Teresa and Annunciata stand in the door

The Contessa speaks quietly to the Madre

I don't have the slightest doubt, Madre, now I've seen her. She's adorable, and I *know* she's mine. She is very uncertain at the moment, and I must get her used to the idea of changing her life slowly, and with great care. She wants to stay till the end of the Carnival, and I see no harm in that. I shall take her immediately after.

Madre There are some formalities to be completed with the Governors, but there is plenty of time. Are you happy now, Perduta, to have found your mother?

Perduta (*slightly unconvinced*) Yes Madre. Wonderfully happy.

Madre Take her back to her quarters now, Sister Teresa.

The Contessa crosses to Perduta, holds her lightly by the shoulders, and kisses her forehead. Perduta barely responds

Contessa Goodbye, my child: for the moment.

Perduta Goodbye, Mother.

Sister Teresa takes Perduta out

Contessa I can never thank you enough. To have lived the life I have lived, and then to be rewarded like this ...

Madre Your pleasure is my reward, my lady.

Contessa Indeed, but it will take a more practical form. I intend to settle a very large sum on the Ospedale ...

Madre That will be most generous.

Contessa And I shall not forget your part in this business ...

Sister Annunciata is looking at the Madre almost with a grin

Madre No, my lady. I need nothing. What has passed between us is more important than money.

Contessa Is that what you mean by the truth of Heaven, Madre, rather than the truth of Venice?

Madre In my prayers, I most fervently hope it is. (*She bows her head*)

The Contessa leaves through the door opened for her by Sister Annunciata

When she has gone, Sister Annunciata looks at the Madre, almost with contempt, and follows the Contessa out

The Madre stands quite still

THE DAY AFTER THE FAIR
(based on a short story by Thomas Hardy) by Frank Harvey

Set in the nineteenth century, this is the culmination of an unusual romance with Anna, the servant girl, marrying the London barrister, Charles, whom she met at the fair some months earlier and with whom Charles thinks he has been corresponding ever since. The writing of Anna's letters has gradually been taken over by her mistress, Edith, who is organizing the wedding reception in her home, with the help of her husband, Arthur Harnham. Edith's and Arthur's relationship is not a happy one, hence Edith's involvement in the correspondence. She ultimately finds she has fallen in love with Charles herself. This scene is the moment of truth on the morning of the wedding.

Set: The front room of the Brewer's House, in a west country cathedral city. Period: nineteenth century.

Cast: M2 F4. Extras.
Edith Harnham, gentle, attractive, with a certain nervous vitality suggesting concealed tension. Arthur Harnham, her husband, red-faced, solidly built; middle 50s. Letty Harnham, Arthur's sister, forceful, attractive; late 50s. Anna, servant girl; 18. Charles Bradford, the bridegroom, a barrister from London. Sarah, housemaid. Wedding Guests.

Playing time: 16 minutes.

The front room of the Brewer's House

The study door opens and Arthur appears in time to detain Charles

Arthur Ah, Bradford? I'm Harnham.
Charles How do you do, sir.
Arthur Everything went off all right, I hope?
Charles Oh, splendidly, sir.
Arthur Good. Then I think, before the revels start, my lad, we'd better just have a word together, you and I, eh?
Charles Certainly, sir.

Arthur grips Charles by the arm in a friendly manner and leads him back into the room

Arthur Don't be afraid. I'm not proposing to make a long speech or anything of that sort. I know you've a train to catch, but they're expecting a *few* words from me, of course. And you'll have to reply.

Charles I think I can manage that, sir.

Arthur But the thing is, in the ordinary way, these affairs are entirely local and everybody knows everybody else. But this is different. Down here, you're what we call a foreigner—a bit of a dark horse. So I thought it might be a good idea if I could tell 'em a bit about you.

Charles Such as?

Arthur Well, now—You're a Londoner, aren't you?

Charles I was born in London, yes.

Arthur Then what *are* you? What do you do for a living?

Charles I'm a barrister, but—er—I thought ...

Arthur Eh? What?

Charles A barrister, sir.

Arthur (*incredulous*) A barrister?

Charles Of Lincoln's Inn.

Arthur Lincoln's Inn? A barrister? (*His whole attitude changes*) My dear fellow, I'd no idea you were a professional man. No idea at all. Nobody told me that. Good heavens. But how extraordinary!

Charles (*sharply*) In what way, sir?

At this moment, the remainder of the wedding-party passes down the hall from the front door towards the breakfast-room. All sidle past shyly and awkwardly, two men in ill-cut suits of some heavy material wearing white carnations, three women wearing sprays of flowers pinned to their voluminous but shapeless gowns

Arthur You're the same young man that Anna met at the fair, aren't you?

Charles I imagine so. We did first meet at the fair.

Arthur That's right, Mansell. It's in the breakfast-room. You know the way. You just carry on without me—I'll be with you in a moment. Yes—well—when I say extraordinary, all I mean is it's extraordinary that Anna should have—er—been fortunate enough to encounter someone in such good standing as you on a fairground. That's all I mean.

Charles It was quite fortuitous, I agree, but for my part, sir, a very *happy* encounter.

Arthur Oh, but of course. And one that has led on to an equally happy conclusion. Well, you've certainly given me plenty to talk about, but don't worry, my dear fellow. I shall keep it short and sweet. And you, I realize, must be well accustomed to getting up on your feet.

Charles Naturally, I shall welcome an opportunity to thank everyone for all their kindness, and in particular, of course, Mrs Harnham.

Arthur Yes—well, it's quite fair to say that if it hadn't been for Mrs Harnham it's most unlikely that you'd be here today.

Charles I don't doubt that at all, sir.

Arthur There's no blame attaching to Anna, of course—none whatsoever. But the aunt must have been a stupid woman.

Charles I don't quite ... ?

Arthur I blame the aunt entirely.

Charles What for, sir?

Arthur Why, for not seeing that Anna went to school and learnt to read and write. Ah, here we are.

Sarah enters, carrying a silver tray on which are several glasses of champagne

Sarah (*suppressing a giggle*) Mrs Bradford says she's waiting to cut the cake, sir.

Arthur We're just coming. (*To Charles*) A glass of champagne, my dear fellow?

Charles (*who has been thinking hard*) I beg your pardon?

Arthur A glass of champagne?

Charles Oh. (*Taking a glass*) Oh, thank you.

Arthur (*also taking a glass*) But let me tell you you're not the only one with something to celebrate, is he, Sarah?

Sarah Oh, no, sir.

Arthur This has been a memorable week for Harnham's, too. We are now not only the oldest and the best, but also the biggest, the biggest brewery in the whole of the South-West of England. There! What do you think of that?

Charles I'm interested in what you were saying about the aunt, sir.

Edith enters

Edith Oh, do come along, Arthur. Their glasses are all filled. Everybody's waiting. They want to cut the cake.

Arthur (*finishing his glass and taking another*) We're coming, we're coming. Let's get it over, my dear fellow. Come along. Yes, the biggest in the whole of the South-West of England—that's something, isn't it? And, mark my words in five years ... I repeat ... five years we will be the biggest in the whole of England.

Taking their glasses with them, Arthur and Charles go off towards the breakfast-room

Sarah *You* haven't had a glass of champagne yet, ma'am.

Edith (*moving to the windows*) No, thank you, Sarah. I don't want anything just at the moment.

Sarah Mr Mansell's brought a great bag of rice in his pocket, ma'am, so I told him, I said, if *one single speck* of that stuff gets into my hall, I'll scratch your eyes out, I said.

Edith (*from the window*) There's that poor man waiting outside with the fly. If you like, Sarah, you may take *him* a glass of champagne.

Sarah Ooh! It won't make him squiffy, ma'am, will it?

Edith I should hardly think so.

Sarah All the same, I expect he'll say he'd rather have a glass of beer any day, although champagne'll make a nice change for him, won't it, ma'am?

As Sarah moves up into the hall with her tray of glasses, there is a burst of laughter from the wedding-party in the breakfast-room. Sarah puts the tray on the hall table, picks up a single glass and goes off with it to the front door. Letty enters

Letty Arthur's now in full spate, Edith. Do you want to hear him?

Edith All I want is for them to go. The thing's done. It's over. If only they'd go.

Letty (*gently*) They'll be off presently, Edith.

Edith They should never have come back here. They could so easily have gone straight to the station.

Letty It wouldn't have been quite the same, would it?

Edith It was Arthur, of course. He insisted.

Letty I think he was curious to see the young man. And I must confess so was I. He's—he's very handsome, Edith.

Edith Well, I've done my best for Anna. Now, there's no more I *can* do.

Letty And how pretty she looks, too, in the new clothes you had made for her. Of course, I think it's a pity they weren't married in church, but I suppose it's just as well in the circumstances.

There is a burst of clapping from the wedding-party in the breakfast-room

Sarah, carrying her tray, comes down into the room a step or so

Sarah I give him the champagne, ma'am, and he drunk it down. And do you know what he said? He said, "Very nice, but I'd sooner have a glass of beer any day." I knew that's what he'd say, ma'am. Didn't I say he would?

Sarah goes off with her tray, giggling, towards the breakfast-room

Letty Does that girl sound to you as if she's been helping herself rather too freely, Edith?

Edith So far as I'm concerned, she can fall down in a stupor, if she likes. (*Moving towards the hall*) I shall come down to wish Anna goodbye.

Letty Oh, but won't that look rather ...

Edith You go and join the others, Letty.

Letty Very well, Edith, but ...

Edith goes off up the stairs

Letty watches her go anxiously. There is a sustained burst of applause from the wedding-party, followed by a buzz of general chatter, laughter, and the clink of glasses. Letty still stands bewildered

Charles suddenly enters

Charles Oh, Miss Harnham ... ?

Letty Can I help you, Mr Bradford?

Charles I was wondering where Mrs Harnham was. She seems to have quite disappeared.

Letty She's gone up to her room, but she'll be down presently, Mr Bradford. Is there anything I can do?

Charles I think not, thank you. It's just that Anna and I—well—we've a little surprise for her.

Letty Oh?

Anna enters

Anna Yes, Charles? What is it?

Charles Ah, Anna. My dear, I want you to do something for me.

Anna Anything, Charles—anything in the world.

Charles If Miss Harnham will excuse us both for a moment?

Letty Of course. I should be helping with the guests, in any case.

Letty goes out to rejoin the wedding-party

Anna Well? What am I to do?

Charles First, let me show you something. (*From him pocket he produces a jeweller's box which he opens, showing Anna the contents—a pendant of paste and semi-precious stones*) Look—isn't that pretty?

Anna Oh, Charles! It's lovely. But—oh, my dear, you shouldn't—you've already given me so much.

Charles It's not meant for you, Anna, no.

Anna No? Then who is it for?

Charles It's a present for Mrs Harnham. For all her kindness, a present from us both.

Anna For Mrs Harnham? Yes, yes! Oh, I'm so glad you remembered her, Charles. She'll be so pleased. Now I know what you want me to do. You want me to give it to her.

Charles Not that exactly, Anna.

Anna Oh?

Charles What I'd like you to do is write a little note ...

Anna (*fearfully*) Write a little note?

Charles Yes—to go with it.

Anna But if we're going to give it to her ourselves, there's no need. We can *say* ...

Charles (*firmly*) I would like you to write a few lines, Anna. It shows a proper concern and it'll please Mrs Harnham, too. Besides, you can do it so charmingly. (*He moves to the desk and sets the chair for her*) Come and sit here, Anna. It'll only take you a moment, and then we shall have to start thinking about our train.

Like a person going to the scaffold, Anna walks to the desk and sits

That's it. There, now—just a few words of thanks for all her past kindnesses. And try to work in one of those little turns of phrase which I used to find so delightful.

Miserably, Anna takes up the pen. There is a burst of laughter from the wedding-party in the breakfast-room. Charles moves to look out of the window. Anna begins to write, but her eyes fill with tears. At length, she lets her head fall on her arms and breaks into loud, uninhibited sobs. Charles moves to her quickly

Why, Anna—my dear—what on earth's the matter?

Anna (*through her sobs*) I can't do it. I can't.

Charles Oh, nonsense! (*Moving to her*) Of course you can.

Anna (*through her sobs*) I can't. I can't.

Charles Here, let me see what you've done.

Charles takes up Anna's abortive note, an action which triggers off a further outburst of sobbing, and looks at it

Anna (*through her sobs*) Oh, Charles! I—I didn't write those letters, Charles. She did. (*She twists herself round in the chair and grasps Charles about the waist, hiding her face against him*) I'm learning, though. I *am* learning, my dear. You'll forgive me, won't you? You'll forgive me for not telling you before?

Pause

Charles (*gently*) You mustn't cry on your wedding-day, Anna. It's unlucky, they say.

Anna rises and puts her arms round his neck

Anna Oh, Charles, I feel so bad about it. Oh, my dear!

Charles gently removes her arms

Charles You have some things to bring down from upstairs, haven't you?

Anna Yes.

Charles Then dry your eyes, my dear, and go and get ready, for we must be off shortly.

Anna I knew. I knew I was right. I knew it wasn't those old letters.

Tearful still, Anna goes off towards the rear of the house

Charles turns back to the desk and picks up the sheet of paper

Edith starts down the stairs

Charles drops the paper on the desk as she comes into the room

Edith Oh. Anna's not with you, Mr Bradford?

Charles She's just gone to gather her belongings together. It's nearly time for us to go.

Edith Yes, I suppose it must be.

Charles Mrs Harnham—I find it hard to thank you for all you've done, not only for Anna, but for me also.

Edith Please don't try, I—I've done little enough.

Charles (*producing the pendant in its box*) Both Anna and I would be most happy if you'd accept this very inadequate ...

Edith (*taking the box*) Mr Bradford, this is quite unnecessary. (*Opening the box*) Oh, how lovely!

Charles It's not genuine, I'm afraid, but it looks pretty, I think.

Edith It's most beautiful. I shall always treasure it.

Charles Anna began a little note to go with it. (*He picks it up from the desk*) Unhappily, she didn't get very far.

Edith takes one corner of the note, so that they are both holding it. She glances at it, then their eyes remain fixed on each other. Charles then lets go of the note, leaving it in Edith's hand

So ... (*Pause*) The letters were yours?

Edith Yes.

Charles No part of them was Anna's?

Edith They were written *for* Anna.

Charles But you wrote them without her—alone?

Edith Some of them. Yes—many. But only on her behalf. I was trying to help her.

Charles Then the thoughts and feelings expressed were yours—not Anna's?

Edith I put down what I would have written had I been in her position.

Charles I see—yes. I think I understand. You had such concern for her.

Edith (*clutching at a straw*) Yes, I had. I *was* concerned for her.

Charles And—quite naturally—you'd no concern for me.

Edith Oh, but I had!

Charles (*shaking his head*) No concern. So—you deceived me.

Edith But it wasn't—I didn't mean ...

Charles (*interrupting firmly*) You deceived me, Mrs Harnham.

Edith (*almost a whisper*) Yes.

Charles Cleverly. Successfully.

Edith Cleverly? Oh no, no. It wasn't clever, it wasn't that.

Charles To have chained me to a little—peasant——

Edith No! (*She groans*)

Charles —a pretty, little peasant.

Edith Don't!

Charles That was very clever, Mrs Harnham.

Edith It wasn't. It was wrong of me. I'd no intention of hurting you—not *you* ...

Charles Then why did you do it? (*Pause*) Why?

Edith I began—I think I began in simple kindness. Kindness to her—to Anna. What else could I have done, and then when I knew the girl was in trouble? But I admit I—I went on—for other reasons.

Charles Other reasons?

Edith Yes.

Charles What other reasons?

Edith Writing freely to someone—brought me a sort of—happiness, I think.

Charles Why?

Edith Because—no. No, I mustn't say.

Charles But you must say, Mrs Harnham. Why?

Edith Because—to open my heart to someone—and to find a response—was something I'd never known.

Charles (*after a pause*) Do you mean your letters to me were not all make-believe, that you were not just pretending? Is that what you're saying?

Edith Yes.

Charles You were expressing your true feelings—your true feelings towards me?

Edith Yes.

Charles You meant every word you wrote?

Edith Every word.

Charles And you still do?

Edith With all my heart.

Charles I see. (*Pause*) Well, then—it would appear that you and I are lovers, Mrs Harnham. Lovers by correspondence. In fact, more than lovers now.

Edith Now?

Charles Legally, I've married Anna—God help us both—but in soul and spirit I've married the writer of those letters and no other woman in the world.

Edith But I couldn't—you must know that we could never—ever ...

Charles (*interrupting*) Why try to dodge the whole truth? You've admitted half of it. I've married you. So let me now make one claim. For the first time—and the last.

Charles moves to within arm's length of Edith and puts out his hand slowly towards her face. Edith is terrified. He suddenly pulls her towards him and kisses her, fiercely. As he does so, there is a burst of loud laughter from the breakfast-room. Edith breaks away from the embrace, bewildered by its ferocity and uncertain of Charles's real feelings

Edith Then—you forgive me?
Charles Forgive you, Mrs Harnham?
Edith Can you?
Charles No. I can never forgive you.
Edith But—perhaps—in time—with Anna, you may find ...
Charles Never. And with Anna there to remind me, it's unlikely I shall ever forget.

Anna appears in the hallway. She carries her belongings in a small, basket-like trunk held together by a leather strap

Ah—here's my little Mrs Bradford. Are you ready, my dear?
Anna Yes, Charles.
Charles Then we must make a start.

Edith remains silent. Charles takes Anna's luggage from her. Anna runs to Edith and flings her arms about her. The two women hold each other tightly for a moment

Anna exits

Goodbye, Mrs Harnham.

Charles follows Anna off, joining her in the hall

Sarah (*off*) They're going! They're going—everybody! Mr and Mrs Bradford are just going. Come and see them off! Come on, everybody! They're leaving for the station now!

The wedding-party, their former inhibitions now softened by alcohol, troop through the hall laughing and chattering

Edith remains motionless as, to cries of "Good Luck!" and "Every happiness!" and much shouting and laughing, the newly married pair prepare to set forth. Suddenly, as the fly is heard to pull away to a ragged cheer, the new steam roundabout emits three short blasts on its whistle and the organ bursts into gay, marital music

As the wedding-party begins to retrace its steps towards the breakfast-room and the drinks, Arthur comes bustling into the room. He proceeds at once to close the upper sashes of the open windows, thus reducing the sound of the music to a reasonable level

Arthur It's high time they put a stop to this. Come next Michaelmas our new by-laws come into force so they'll have to hold it somewhere out in the country. (*He is moving towards the hallway when a thought strikes him and he turns back to Edith*) I dare say the others will be here for quite a while yet, you know. They're expecting to see something of *you*, Edith, so come along and join in the fun.

Arthur goes off towards the breakfast-room

Edith remains as though turned to stone. The music from the steam-organ swells a little

DEAR OCTOPUS
by Dodie Smith

It is 1938, and all the family has gathered for the weekend to celebrate
Charles and Dora Randolph's Golden Wedding. A period piece, there
are serious, romantic and humorous moments, and in this nursery
scene from the beginning of Act Two, young and older family members,
including in-laws, assemble on the Saturday morning.

Set: The nursery: a room that remembers three earlier generations of
children. Period: 1938.

Cast: M3 F4, 1 boy 2 girls.
Nanny Patching, comfortable-looking; 62. Flouncy, golden-curled,
plump, affected; 12. Scrap, small, thin, very shy manner, her mother
died two years previously; 9. Bill, nice looking; 10. Hugh Randolph,
good-looking grandson of Charles and Dora Randolph; 23. Laurel,
his wife, very lovely, fair; 22. Nicholas, attractive son of Charles and
Dora; 35. Margery, fair, pretty and too fat, Flouncy and Bill's mother;
42. Kenneth, pleasant, stoutish, Flouncy and Bill's father; 45. Fenny,
slender, pretty, pleasant unaffected manner; 29.

Playing time: 13 minutes.

---

*The Nursery. A pleasant, sunny room, with plush window-curtains, yellowed white
paint and a faded Caldicott wallpaper depicting John Gilpin's adventures; a room
that remembers three earlier generations of children*

*There is a fireplace R with a high fireguard. Below this is a small service lift. There is
a very large, high toy-cupboard in the R corner of the room with a small step-ladder
near it. RC of the back wall is a big bow-window with a window-seat; a rocking-horse
stands between it and the door to the landing, which is in the L of the back wall. Some
low shelves, piled with books, toys and oddments are on the L of this door. Then, in
the L wall is the door to the night-nurseries, and below this an upright piano. The
furniture includes a large table C, with chairs round it*

It is Saturday morning. Nanny Patching, a comfortable-looking woman of sixty-two, is finishing breakfast with Flouncy, Scrap and Bill. Nanny is above the table, with Scrap on her R and Flouncy on her L. Bill is below Flouncy

Scrap (*holding her mug*) I like mugs. Did they always have mugs in this nursery?
Nanny Always, Miss Scrap.
Bill This is the very same mug that Mummie had, isn't it, Nanny?
Scrap Which mug did my Mummie have?
Nanny Let me see now—some of them got broken, of course. Your mother had a bluebird mug.
Scrap Do you mean it might have been this very one?
Nanny Sure to have been.

Scrap looks at her mug lovingly

Now don't you go thinking about it. Your mother wouldn't want you to brood.
Scrap But I like thinking about it.
Nanny That's enough, dear. Finish your milk.
Bill Oh, hurry up, hurry up. I want to paint. (*He rises*)
Nanny (*restraining him*) No, you don't, Master Bill.

Bill returns to his seat

We say grace in this nursery. "For what we have received may the Lord make us truly thankful. Amen."
Scrap Amen.
Flouncy (*intoning slightly*) Amen.
Bill (*intoning heavily*) Selfridge's.
Scrap Why did you say that?
Bill (*casually*) I always do.
Nanny He's a very naughty boy.
Bill Come on, let's clear the table. (*He takes bread and marmalade to the lift*)
Nanny Careful of that lift, now.

Flouncy takes the teapot and hot-water jug to the lift. Nanny starts to clear on to the tray. Scrap helps Nanny. After Bill has put his things in the lift, he takes the hot-water jug from Flouncy, goes to the cupboard, takes out a cup and fills it

Hugh and Laurel enter from the landing

Hugh Hallo, Nanny. Has he been good?
Nanny I never knew such a good baby. Good-morning, madam.
Laurel Shall we take him for a bit now?
Nanny I'd be glad if you would, I want to run down to the kitchen.

Scrap takes the tray to Flouncy at the lift. Flouncy puts it on the lift, then goes to the window-seat, gets a magazine from the cupboard under it and takes them to the table. Scrap goes back C and helps Nanny fold the tablecloth. Nanny puts the cloth and napkins in the drawer of the table

Laurel (*looking through the night-nursery door*) He's just waking up.

She goes in

Nanny He had a lovely sleep after his bottle.

Hugh goes in after Laurel

The lift is stacked

Bill (*pushing Flouncy away from the lift and putting in the hot-water jug*) Oh! come on, Guinevere.
Nanny (*folding the tablecloth*) Miss Scrap, will you help me?
Bill (*blowing down the speaking-tube*) Good-morning, Cook — how's your varicose veins? ... Really? I'll be down. (*He replaces the whistle in the tube*) She's got her elastic stocking on.

The lift goes down

(*He crosses with his paint-box and the cup of water*) We'd better have the glass too.
Nanny Miss Scrap's rose is in it.
Flouncy I'll throw it out, it's dead. (*She picks the glass up*)
Scrap No, it isn't—not quite. Please don't.
Nanny Leave it alone—you can manage with the cup. (*She puts Flouncy in the chair at the top of the table and moves the chair from up L of the table to up stage of the piano*)
Bill What'll you have, Flouncy? *Fashions*? And I'll have *Country Life*. Choose one for yourself, Scrap.

The children are now seated at the table: Flouncy above, Scrap R, Bill L

Nanny You won't get long for your painting—we'll be going out walking in no time. (*She goes to the night-nursery door*) Mr Hugh——They've gone down. (*Turning*) I'll be back for you children in a quarter of an hour.

She goes off into the night-nursery

Bill (*licking his brush and settling to his painting*) I may be going out with Great-aunt Belle. She wants to know what I said at school.

Scrap (*choosing a magazine*) What *did* you say at school?

Flouncy He said Damn Blast Devil Hell and Strike Me Pink.

Bill (*pushing Flouncy*) You beast, Flouncy. It's my language. I tell it. I said Swelp me, too.

Scrap Swelp you? What does it mean?

Bill Something frightful.

Scrap I don't think much of it. I know a worse word than any of those.

Flouncy You don't.

Bill What is it?

Scrap I couldn't tell you. It's too awful.

Bill Oh, go on, Scrap.

Flouncy She's just pretending.

Scrap I'm not pretending. It's the most terrible word there is. (*She looks round nervously, then whispers hoarsely*) It's District Nurse.

Bill District Nurse? But they put that on gates.

Flouncy You silly baby. Everyone knows what District Nurse means.

Bill It might have a double meaning, Flouncy.

Flouncy Of course it hasn't.

Bill I'm afraid you've got it wrong, Scrap—but I'll find out. I say, Flouncy, you've made this water filthy. You can use any colours you like, Scrap, except the cobalt blue. That's my special colour.

Scrap (*frigidly*) I don't want your beastly cobalt and it *is* an awful word.

Bill All right, all right. I told you I'd find out. I'm putting my brush in my mouth over and over again. I'll probably die.

Voices are heard outside. Margery, Kenneth and Nicholas enter from the landing. Margery goes to Bill, Kenneth to Flouncy, and Nicholas to Scrap

Margery Isn't Nanny taking you for a walk?

Bill Presently. We're just using my new paint-box.

Kenneth I say, that is a beauty.

Flouncy Do you know Scrap, Uncle Nicholas?

Nicholas Yes. I looked in on her last night. (*He looks over Scrap's shoulder*)

Margery Careful, Bill—you're running your trees into your sky.

She takes his brush. There is a mute protest from Bill

There! Just saved it. Look, you want to carry that blob of paint right down——

Margery pushes Bill off his chair and sits. Bill wanders to the piano-stool

Kenneth (*behind Flouncy*) You can't have them all in black. Give them some red buttons—and red heels to their shoes. Here, budge up a bit. (*He sits beside her and paints, gradually edging Flouncy off*)

Nicholas (*over Scrap's book*) Why don't you make that one a zebra?

Scrap Because it's a horse.

Nicholas But you could make it a zebra with some white stripes. Look, we'll use some chinese white. We'll use oodles of chinese white. We'll give him lovely stripes. Come on, Scrap. (*He starts to paint*)

Kenneth (*who has completely edged Flouncy off her chair*) I've given her a jolly old red hat. Why don't you have a red hat, Margery?

Flouncy goes to the rocking-horse

Margery Half a minute, Ken—this is quite difficult.

Nicholas That's marvellous. I used to be awfully good at this. Just a second, Scrap, while I get under his stomach.

He takes Scrap's place. Scrap goes to the arm of the armchair

Kenneth I often think I ought to have gone in for art.

Margery There—I don't think that's too bad. (*She turns the page*) Oh, there's a beauty on the next page.

Bill Mummie, wouldn't you like to play the piano? (*Getting no reply, he goes over to her*) Oh, darling, You've smudged it. You are a clumsy old cow.

Margery (*swinging round on Bill, who springs back*) Bill! Never let me hear you use that word again.

Bill What word? Clumsy?

Margery No. Cow. You must *not* call me a cow.

Bill But you don't mind me calling you a donkey.

Margery I'm not really keen on it. And anyhow, cow's different. You must never call anyone a cow.

Bill Can't I call a cow a cow?

Margery (*to Kenneth*) It's really very difficult.—You can call a cow a cow, but you must never call a lady a cow. Now go and get ready for your walk.

Kenneth. You'll understand when you're older, old chap. It's a sort of double meaning.

Bill Golly—a nice little word like cow. Perhaps you're right, Scrap. (*He looks meaningly at Scrap, who signals to try to stop him, then plants his feet wide apart and looks at the ceiling*) District Nurse. (*Louder*) District Nurse.

Margery Well, what about the district nurse?

Bill Don't you mind me saying it?

Margery Not if it gives you any pleasure. It's very silly, of course.

Bill (*with a gesture*) Told you so, Scrap.

He goes off L into the night-nursery

Margery Run along or you'll keep Nanny waiting.

Scrap and Flouncy follow Bill. Scrap shuts the door after her

Kenneth, how heavily you're breathing.
Kenneth (*sitting back*) I've given the whole bally lot of them red hats.

Dora's voice calls "Margery"

Margery Is that Mother calling?

Fenny enters from the landing and comes to the top of the table

Did I hear Mother?
Fenny I'm afraid so. She wants extra eggs from Malting's Farm.
Margery No, I'm damned if I'll go. (*Rising to the door up* L) There's no car road and it's in a sea of mud. Come on, Ken, we'll slip down the back-stairs and hide in the greenhouse.

Kenneth rises and follows her

Don't give us away, Fenny.

She hustles Kenneth off L

Fenny goes to the shelves L

Nicholas (*rising*) Good old Margery. She always was the champion job-evader. (*He goes over to the window-seat and sits*) I feel very well disposed towards the world.
Fenny (*rummaging on the shelves by the door*) Do you?
Nicholas Wakened up feeling absolutely sunny.
Fenny Good. You were a bit on the morbid side last night.
Nicholas Oh, that's all gone. I lay awake this morning, smelling coffee and bacon being cooked, and felt that things were exactly as they should be. Youth, age, birth, death, the changing seasons—I assure you I had the key to the whole damn works.
Fenny How very useful. (*She crosses to the toy cupboard, pushing the armchair well down by the fire*)
Nicholas Now don't flatten me. One so seldom has these moments of illumination. (*He goes to the rocking-horse and mounts it*) This one seems to be quite lasting, too. Yes, I feel positively glowing with human kindness.

Fenny turns and laughs at him

I wonder why? What are you looking for?
Fenny Some french chalk to make the drawing-room floor slippery.

Nicholas I say, don't overdo it. It's horse's work keeping those Vicarage girls on their feet.

Another laugh from Fenny

Why *will* Mother give dances?

Fenny There'll be three tables of whist.

Nicholas Whist? Can you play whist?

Fenny Certainly. I shall probably have to.

Nicholas Oh no, you're going to dance with me. Does Mother still insist on dance programmes?

Fenny She does. They've got wedding bells on them.

Nicholas Then I shall bag six dances and we'll sit out on the back-stairs.

Fenny Last time I sat out on the back-stairs I got kissed on the ear.

Nicholas Fenny! Who by?

Fenny The curate with the wig.

Nicholas I knew you had a past.

Fenny I know this stuff's somewhere. (*She jumps, trying to see the top shelf*) This is a ridiculous cupboard for a nursery. (*She drags up the step-ladder and mounts it*)

Nicholas It had its uses. The best toys were kept on the top shelf. Here, be careful. (*He gets off the horse*)

Fenny Pooh! You should have seen me washing all this paint yesterday. I'm very nifty on a step-ladder.

Nicholas I got marooned up there for an afternoon, when I was about four.

Fenny How do you mean?

Nicholas Sit on the top.

Fenny sits on the top of the cupboard

The steps were about for spring-cleaning, so up I went—and Cynthia came and moved them—so. (*He moves the steps away*)

Fenny You poor kid. It's quite a long way.

Nicholas "Come down, oh maid, from yonder mountain height."

Fenny Well, give me the steps.

They laugh together

Here, come on, I can't stop dallying here.

Nicholas (*strolling away*) I think I shall go for a walk.

Fenny Oh, come on. All right, I'm going to jump.

Nicholas No—no, Fenny, it's much too far. (*He goes to her and puts his hands up to her waist*) Now you can. (*He jumps her down*) Has the curate with the wig left you with any inhibitions about being kissed on the ear?

Fenny I don't know.

Nicholas Then you should find out. (*He hears sounds in the night-nursery*) On the
back-stairs—remember, it's an assignation.

*He goes back to the table and paints. Fenny puts the armchair straight. Nanny and
the three children come in from the night-nursery, dressed for walking. First Bill,
who goes to the table and washes out his mother's painting. Then Scrap, who goes to
the landing door. Thirdly Nanny, followed by Flouncy*

Nanny Anything you want from the village, miss?
Fenny Yes, Nanny—try to get some french chalk.
Bill Let's go in the woods, Nanny.
Nanny And me with the perambulator? Get along with you.

*She bustles off with the girls. Flouncy and Scrap precede her, Flouncy arranging
her curls with the aid of a mirror from her miniature handbag*

Bill (*pulling Nicholas's arm*) Take us in the woods, Uncle Nick?
Nicholas Will you come, Fenny?
Fenny I'm up to my eyes in jobs.

Nicholas smiles at her, then allows Bill to pull him off

Bill (*as they go*) Come on, come on—we'll give the others the slip.
Nicholas All right. All right.

*Alone, Fenny puts her hands to her cheeks, looking slightly dazed. She goes to the
mirror and looks at herself. Bill comes back*

Bill I want the blackberry basket. (*He gets the basket from the shelves* L, *then comes*
C) Fenny, you do look nice to-day.
Fenny Do I, Bill, do I? I wish I was coming blackberrying.
Bill Never mind. I'll have a dance with you tonight.
Fenny You can have it now, if you like. (*She catches his hands and whirls him
round*)
Bill (*breathless, but pleased*) Oh, Fenny, you are fun. I'll bring you some blackberries
back.

He goes out

FIND ME
by Olwen Wymark

Verity Taylor is a very disturbed child whose family find that they are unable to cope with her unpredictable outbursts and unsocial behaviour. Although very bright with moments of warmth and affection and a sense of wanting to be loved and understood, Verity is moved from a mental home to Holloway Prison and is finally admitted to Broadmoor in 1976 at the age of 20. The play uses a technique of multiple characterization to investigate the personality of Verity and to study her effect on her family and officials. Thus there are Verity I and II, Doctor I and II and two sets of parents to show different facets of character.

Set: A bare stage.

Cast: 11 speaking parts, may be performed by M3 F5.
Verity I Verity II, 11, 12 years in the final sequence. Edward, her father. Jean, her mother. (NB. There are two sets of parents.) Mark, her brother. Nurse. Clerk. Assistant Registrar. Doctor. Doctor II. Miss Everitt, a social worker.

Playing time: 17 minutes.

The stage is bare. Edward, Jean and Verity II stand in a little group in the middle. Verity II is completely blank and seems unaware of her parents' presence. She has a scarf tied over her head. On the raised area upstage sits Verity I hugging herself in her own arms and kneeling

A Nurse comes on to the stage and walks briskly across, passing the Taylor family

Edward Excuse me.
Nurse Yes?
Edward We were told to wait in here but we ...
Nurse Who did you want to see?
Jean We've brought our daughter to be—to be ...
Edward Admitted. (*He clears his throat*) As a patient.

Verity I Dear Mum and Dad, I hope you're all right. If you get a map you can look up Broadmoor and then you will know where this place is. Perhaps you could write to me because I get very lonely here.

Nurse Who sent you in here?

Edward The porter at reception.

Jean We've been waiting nearly half-an-hour.

Nurse I'm sorry. We're very understaffed today, I'm afraid. It's the bank holiday.

Edward Yes.

Nurse He should have sent you straight to Admissions. If you'll just come this way. (*She starts to walk away*)

Edward and Jean both put a hand on Verity II's shoulders to bring her along. Swiftly and without looking at them she ducks out from under their hands and takes a step back. They look helplessly at the Nurse. She goes over to Verity and efficiently takes her hand. Verity neither resists nor looks at her

Come along, dear. Come with me. (*They start to walk and the others follow*) And what's your name, eh?

Verity II turns her head round suddenly and stares very intently into the Nurse's face. She says nothing

Never mind. I expect you'll tell me later.

Jean Verity. Her name's Verity.

Nurse That's a pretty name. Just along here.

The Admissions Clerk comes on in one corner of the stage carrying a chair, sits, starts to write

The Nurse brings the group up

New patient.

Clerk I'll be with you in a moment.

Nurse (*to the Taylors*) All right?

Edward Yes. Thank you.

Nurse (*going off*) Not at all. Bye-bye, Verity.

There is no response from Verity II

The Nurse goes

Verity I There's a ward in this place called Katherine Ward. You go there if you do something bad. They sent me there because I ripped up some lino. It's cold in there.

Clerk (*looking up*) Name?
Edward Taylor. E. J. Taylor.
Clerk Name of patient?
Jean Verity Rose.
Clerk Age?
Edward Eleven years and—five months.
Clerk Date of birth?
Jean February the thirteenth, nineteen fifty-five.
Clerk Name and address of GP?
Edward Well, we ...
Clerk You do have a letter from your doctor, don't you?
Jean He's away. For the bank holiday. We had to find another doctor. (*Pause*) They all seemed to be away. It took such a long time ...
Edward But we do have a doctor's letter, yes.
Clerk I think you'd better see the Assistant Registrar if the letter isn't from your own doctor. Just down that corridor and straight along to the end.

They turn to go. This time Edward carefully takes Verity II's hand. She does not resist and continues to be quite unaware of what is going on

The Assistant Registrar enters with a chair and sits

Jean, Edward and Verity II walk towards him

Verity I Some of the ones here have to sit with no clothes on in a small room. They just sit. Sometimes they throw themselves about.
Registrar Name?
Edward Taylor. E. J. Taylor.
Registrar Patient's name?
Edward Verity Rose.
Registrar Age?
Edward Eleven years and five months.
Registrar Date of birth?
Edward February the thirteenth, nineteen fifty-five.
Registrar Has your daughter been a patient here in the past?
Edward No.
Registrar Or in any other mental hospital?
Jean (*too loudly*) No! (*Awkwardly*) No, she hasn't.

Jean puts an arm round Verity's shoulders. Again Verity II swiftly ducks away, not looking at her

Registrar May I see your doctor's letter?
Edward (*handing it to him*) It isn't actually from our own doctor. He was away.

Jean (*softly, looking into Verity II's blank face*) Verity?

Verity I Oh God high in your heaven, please come and reveal for me. I need you now. Our Father our Father our Father hold me in your hand. It's dark.

Registrar (*reading the letter*) "—severe anti-social behaviour culminating in actions that appear to me to justify hospitalization." Could you give me some details? When did this happen?

Edward Yesterday afternoon and evening. She broke three windows and locked herself into the bathroom and flooded it. She cut off a lot of her hair and she tore up a whole box full of letters and photographs. Just destroyed them utterly and threw them all over the room. Then she got herself dressed up in all sorts of strange clothes and ran out of the house.

Jean We couldn't stop her. She ran so fast. She was screaming and shouting and waving her arms about. We were terrified.

Edward She was missing for seven hours. We went out with friends looking everywhere for her. Then someone saw her knocking over dustbins outside her school and spreading rubbish over the pavement.

Jean (*sadly*) In the dark.

They both look at Verity II, who is totally oblivious

Edward (*continuing with an effort*) They called the police. We'd notified them already of course but—(*pause*)—the police know Verity. They telephoned us. When we got her home she wouldn't speak to us or look at us. She went straight into the kitchen and opened a tin of sardines and covered them in jam. She ate them out of the tin with her fingers.

Jean She wouldn't go to bed. She lay on the floor under the kitchen table all night. When we—when we tried to touch her she kicked and—bit us.

Registrar Hmmmm—yes—yes—I see. There is a history of erratic behaviour?

Edward Yes.

Registrar And no previous psychiatric treatment?

Jean She's been attending the Child Guidance Clinic since she was nine.

Registrar And there have been specific epileptic features?

Edward Yes, she's been on medication for that for over three years now.

Registrar Well now, I think perhaps the best thing is if you go along and see one of our psychiatric staff before we go ahead with Admission. Third corridor on the left and up the stairs. (*He hands back the letter*) If you'll take this to the doctor ...

Jean, Edward and Verity II walk across the stage

Doctor enters, carrying a chair, and sits

They stand in front of him

Verity I Sometimes I feel afraid that I will get lost in the dark maze of corridors here.

Doctor Sorry to keep you waiting so long. Your name is ...

Edward Taylor. E. J. Taylor. (*He hands him the letter*)

Doctor And your daughter's name?

Edward Verity Rose.

Doctor And her age is ...

Jean Eleven years and five months. She was born on February the thirteenth, nineteen fifty-five.

Doctor Has Verity had previous hospital treatment?

Edward No.

Doctor (*reading the letter*) "—to justify hospitalization." Can you tell me what happened?

Jean (*a little desperately*) They've asked us all this before.

Doctor Just for the records.

Edward (*rapidly*) She broke some windows. She cut off a lot of her hair and she flooded the bathroom. She destroyed a box of letters and photographs and she ran away from home dressed in bizarre clothes and screaming. The police brought her back seven hours later.

Doctor I see. Yes. And how are you feeling now, Verity?

Verity II gives no response at all

Jean She hasn't spoken at all since last night.

Doctor Ah. And she's been on drugs for epileptic symptoms for how long?

Edward Three years.

Doctor No previous psychiatric treatment?

Edward She's been going to the Child Guidance Clinic.

Doctor I'd like you to take Verity along to see one of my colleagues who's on the staff for the children's ward. Room One B. You may have to wait a little I'm afraid. It's bank holiday, you see. Just down the corridor and to the left.

A second Doctor comes on bringing a chair and sits

Verity I I have a fear of being alone in a small room.

Verity II moves C. Jean and Edward stand together downstage. The following is very quick

Registrar Date of birth?

Edward February the thirteenth, nineteen fifty-five.

Doctor II What exactly did she do?

Jean Cut off her hair.

Edward Screaming and waving her hands about.

Clerk Previous psychiatric treatment?

Edward Child Guidance.

Doctor I A history of erratic behaviour?
Jean Yes.
Doctor II How long has Verity been having treatment for epilepsy?
Edward Three years.
Registrar Name?
Jean Verity Rose Taylor.
Doctor I How long was she missing from home?
Edward Seven hours.
Clerk Age?
Jean Eleven years and five months.
Doctor II Has Verity been in a mental hospital before?
Edward No.
Registrar If you'll just wait here please.
Clerk Right along to the end of the corridor.
Doctor I May I see your doctor's letter?

Doctor II stands. The others stand at once

Doctor II Yes. Well, I think we can admit Verity into our children's ward.

The Doctors, the Clerk and the Registrar pick up their chairs and carry them over to place them deliberately around Verity II like a cage

The Doctors, Clerk and Registrar go off

Edward and Jean move towards Verity II who stands impassive

Jean Goodbye, Verity.
Edward Goodbye. We'll come and see you soon.

Verity II turns her back on them

Jean and Edward look at each other, then go off

The two Veritys are now facing each other

Verity I Dear whoever you are ...
Verity II (*kneeling and taking up the exact posture of Verity I*) Whoever you are ...

Black-out

Verity I leaves the stage. Another Edward and Jean come on

Verity II stays in the "cage" silently during the following

Jean A year, Edward! She's been in there a whole year and they still can't tell us what's wrong with her. How can they say she's ready to be discharged when she isn't any better? Is she? Do you think she is? Did you think so today?

Edward I know it was bad today, Jean, but last time we visited her she was quite— placid. They said today was a worse day than usual for her. But you have to expect it sometimes.

Jean Last time! She'd just been having that horrible shock treatment last time. I wouldn't have said placid. Confused. Miles away. Like a strange little old woman. Not like a child. Why did they do that to her? It didn't do any good—no good at all.

Edward Jean, they have to try every kind of treatment they can. She has been better—some of the time. And they think if she comes home now she'll settle down.

Jean Why should she? What makes them think that? Look what happened when they let her come home for Christmas ...

Jean goes off

Edward (*going to the side of the stage*) But that was six months ago ...

Verity erupts out from inside the chairs, knocking them over and shouting

Verity II All my presents smell of old socks! Dad! You've been walking all over my Christmas presents with your dirty socks on.

Edward (*coming forward*) Don't be silly, Verity. Of course I haven't.

Verity Doesn't matter. I don't care anyway. I've smashed them all up and thrown them into the dustbin.

Edward Oh Verity ...

Verity Oh Verity! Oh Verity! I'm the underdog female in this family. I know. I know. That's what you all think I am.

Edward That isn't true. You know that isn't true.

Verity Liar liar pants on fire can't get off the telephone wire. (*She points at him. Fiercely*) She wouldn't take me to the zoo today. She took Mark and Nicky but she wouldn't take me.

Edward (*calmly, sensibly*) That's because you were naughty, Verity. You know perfectly well none of us got any sleep last night. How many times did we tell you if you didn't go to bed quietly and stop all that noise you wouldn't be allowed to go to the zoo.

Verity I wanted to play with Nicky. He liked the music. He likes it loud. He loves it. (*She sings the Ying Tong song loudly and runs round Edward pulling at him*)

Edward He needed to sleep, Verity. We all needed to sleep. (*He gets hold of her and quietens her*) Now then, why don't you start to lay the table for tea? They'll be back soon.

Verity (*with dislike*) Oh yes! Another order! (*Suddenly docile*) All right, Dad.

Edward (*gratefully*) Good girl.

Verity II goes off. Mark comes on

Mark Hallo, Dad.
Edward Hallo, Mark. Did you have a good time?
Mark Smashing. They've got a new place for nocturnal animals. They use infra-red
light. I wish you could've seen it.
Edward Well, we'll go again. Where's your mother?
Mark Putting Nicky to bed. He fell asleep on the way home. (*He looks round. Wary*)
Where is she?
Edward Verity? She's in the kitchen.

Jean comes on wearing a cape and scarf

Hallo, darling. All right?
Jean Yes. We had a lovely time. Nicky adored it. (*Pause*) How was she?
Edward Not bad. Not bad at all. She was fine.
Jean Thank goodness. I was worried.
Edward She's just gone to set the table for tea.
Jean (*pleased*) Well then.

Verity comes on, her forearms upraised, blood running down them

Verity (*smiling*) Look! Look!
Jean Oh my God!
Edward Verity, what have you done?
Verity (*giggling*) I've carved myself with the carving fork. (*She licks the blood on
her arms*) Here's two legs of lamb for tea. Here Mark—do you want some? Have
some. Have a bite. Here. (*She goes to Mark pushing her arms at him*)
Mark Get off! Get her off me! (*He rushes over to Jean*) Why are you so stupid? (*He
shouts more and more hysterically*) You spoil everything. Go back to the hospital
where you belong! Leave us alone!
Jean Ssshhhh—Mark—don't.

Edward grabs hold of Verity and wipes off the blood with his handkerchief

Edward (*very controlled*) They're only scratches. Come along with me, Verity, and
we'll put something on them.
Verity (*leaning against him*) All right, Dad.
Edward (*leading her off*) Aren't you a silly girl?
Verity (*breaking violently away from him*) Silly? Silly? I'm not the silly one. I'm not
going back to the hospital. (*She rushes over to Jean*) You can go back there. You

go. (*She starts pulling at Jean's clothes, yanks the scarf off her neck and puts it round her own. Then she pulls off Jean's cape*)

Mark (*pulling Verity away*) Stop that! Stop doing that to Mum! Leave her alone!

Verity You leave me alone! (*She trips him up and he falls. Then she takes her mother's face in her hands and speaks very gently*) See, Mum? I'll wear your clothes and you can wear mine then they'll think you're me. (*Again violent, she tears off her own cardigan and throws it in Jean's face*) Have a good time in the hospital, Verity!

Verity runs off

Edward Quick, Mark. Come with me. We must go after her.

Edward hurries off

Mark Let her go. Let her run away and stay away. I don't care.

Jean (*near to tears*) Mark—please.

Mark I'm sorry, Mum. I'm sorry.

Mark goes off in the opposite direction from Edward

Jean picks up Verity's cardigan and folds it. She hugs it to her heart

Jean I can't bear it. I just can't bear it. (*She walks up stage and puts the cardigan down*)

Miss Everitt, a Social Worker, enters downstage

Miss Everitt Mrs Taylor? I'm Miss Everitt, Social Services.

Jean (*going to her and shaking hands*) How do you do. It was good of you to come. Would you like some tea?

Miss Everitt I can't really stay, I'm afraid. I've got three other house visits this afternoon. I don't know whether I'm coming or going this week. I've been making enquiries since I had your husband's letter. (*Pause*) I'm afraid I've got disappointing news for you.

Jean (*flatly*) You can't find a residential place for Verity.

Miss Everitt I'm so sorry. There just doesn't seem to be a suitable boarding school. It's partly her age. Fourteen seems to be too old for most of the schools and then a lot of them just aren't keen to take on someone so—disruptive.

Jean There must be somewhere she could be taken care of. We've tried. We've tried so hard.

Miss Everitt (*business-like*) I'm sure you have.

Jean This last two years has been like a nightmare. She's been back twice to the children's ward at the hospital. Won't they take her in again?

Miss Everitt I've had a letter from them saying in their view she's no longer in need of hospital care. I understand the last two admissions were because of breakdowns. They don't regard the present situation as an emergency, you see.

Jean It is for us!

Miss Everitt (*hastily*) Her headmistress tells me she's doing quite well at school. Holding her own in the C stream.

Jean It's when she's at home. I used to think it must be our fault—that we were doing something wrong. But they couldn't keep her in the Care Home. She was only there three weeks. And in that Rudolf Steiner Centre last month it was only two days.

Miss Everitt Yes. I saw the report. Inciting the other children to destructive behaviour and vandalism.

Jean I don't think that's fair! All she did was get the children to pull down the curtains in the house and put them on as costumes. They went for a fancy dress march in the streets. (*She laughs slightly*) I should think they had a marvellous time.

Miss Everitt (*reprovingly*) That kind of behaviour can't be contained in a Children's Home.

Jean (*angrily*) But it can in our home, can't it! We're supposed to be able to manage without any sleep, without any peace and quiet—frantic and exhausted all the time. I mean all the time, Miss Everitt! She still runs off, you know. The telephone ringing in the middle of the night. The police calling. Again!

Miss Everitt There are much worse cases than Verity, you know, Mrs Taylor. Though of course I can imagine how difficult it is for you.

Jean Can you? I don't think you can. I don't think anyone could. Miss Everitt, we've got a son trying to take A levels. We've got a four-year-old boy. There's no peace in this house for either of them when she's here.

Miss Everitt She is your child, Mrs Taylor.

Jean (*passionately*) So are they my children! So are they!

Miss Everitt (*slightly cowed*) Well, we'll certainly continue investigating all the possibilities, Mrs Taylor. But I must warn you that there aren't many facilities for a case like this. We just don't have the places or the staff. We all think you and your husband are managing wonderfully well in the circumstances.

Miss Everitt goes

Jean What are we going to do? Dear God, what are we going to do? Managing! Perhaps it would be better for all of us if we couldn't manage. Then they'd have to do something. Maybe if I became an alcoholic ... I could. My God, I think I could sometimes. (*Pause*) When I go next door to Suzanne's some nights and we sit and get a bit tight together on the whisky and talk about all sorts of things and laugh— just for a little while I can forget. The thoughts stop going round and round in my head. The relief of just feeling like an ordinary person. The relief. Supposing when

Miss Everitt Social Services came round today she'd found me dead drunk on the floor. "Dear me, Mrs Taylor, you're not managing wonderfully well today." (*Pause*) Imagine your own child driving you to drink. Your own child that you love. (*Pause*) I don't even know if I do love her. I don't know what I feel. Pity—oh, pity for her. Why did it have to happen? Poor Verity. Poor, poor baby. (*Pause*) But fear too. She seems to like to frighten me—enjoys it. She never does it to Edward. I really think sometimes she hates me. And he's so good to her—so patient and kind. All those holidays he takes her on. He doesn't talk much about them afterwards but I know, I know she crucifies him. And I feel mean and cowardly because I don't go too. (*Pause*) And guilty. Did I do it? Was it my fault? When I was pregnant with her— all those weeks when she was inside me I thought she was so safe. Nothing could hurt her and yet all the time ... Was it me? Did I—contaminate her? Oh God ... (*She stops herself*) She was so beautiful when she was a baby. Even now sometimes when you look at her when she's asleep. When I'm out with her sometimes I wish she was ugly. Deformed or crippled. Something people could *see*. Then they would pity her too. Instead of getting nervous and embarrassed and moving away from us as if we were lepers. Oh God, will nobody help us? Can't anybody help us?

THE GOLDEN PATHWAY ANNUAL
by John Harding and John Burrows

The play tells the story of Michael Peters, a bright boy, from his birth in 1945 until 1968. The son of George and Enid, a typical London working-class couple, Michael is atypical in that he gets to Grammar School and university. His life is portrayed through a series of sketches, some comic, but all with serious overtones. In these two scenes from Act Two disillusionment begins to emerge.

Set: The first scene starts by a painted wall and finishes in a Magistrate's Court, and may be achieved by lighting or positioning; the next scene is at Michael's parents' home. Period: 1966-67.

Cast: M3 F1.
In the original production the parts were played by three actors and one actress as follows: one actor played George Peters, one actor played Michael, one actor played an Irishman, stage navvy, the Magistrate and the Doorman, a bellowing cockney 'You 'orrible little man' ex-drill sergeant with a log on his shoulder. The actress played Enid and Michael's girl friend.

Playing time: 10 minutes.

SCENE A

1966. Paint on a wall or paint on a person but not at the same time. Michael has a lot to learn

Michael and Girl Friend enter with brushes and buckets

Girl Friend What's so special about this wall, Mike?
Michael This is the American Tourist Office. Everyone'll be able to see it here. Put that spare bucket out of sight in the alley.

She puts her bucket off stage and returns

Now, you know what to do, don't you? You start at that end with "Victory to the NLF" and I'll get on with "Death to US Imperialism" at this end. Then we can do "Yanks out of Vietnam" together. OK?

Girl Friend Mike, I love you.
Michael Great.
Girl Friend Give us a kiss.

They kiss

Michael Don't use all the paint. I want to do the ceiling in our kitchen when we've finished, all right?

They begin painting. The paint is mimed. There is singing, off

Girl Friend Mike!
Michael What?
Girl Friend Someone's coming.
Michael Fuzz?
Girl Friend No. It's someone on his own.
Michael Stay in the shadow.

Off-stage crash of foot in bucket

Girl Friend He's fallen over the bucket!
Irishman (*off*) Jesus, Mary and Joseph!

Irishman enters with the lower left leg covered in wet paint. (It's not necessary to actually use wet paint. Some repeatable "cod" effect is required: e.g. a white shoe, white sock, and white turn-up on trouser leg.) He sings "We're all off to Dublin in the Green"

Michael Please be quiet.
Irishman Oh, I'm sorry, sir. Is it a hospital?
Michael No, it's the American Tourist Office. Now be quiet, please. We're working.
Irishman Work's a wonderful thing ... when you can get it. I wonder, sir, could you perhaps spare me, you know, just for a cup of tea and a bite, I haven't eaten ... Ah! Good-evening, miss. I'm sorry to be holding up the work.
Michael We haven't got anything.
Girl Friend We're students from the University.
Irishman God, they work you all hours.
Michael No. This isn't college work.
Irishman You're working nights, to make up the grant? Oh, that's terrible, terrible. It's the Government. I don't know why you don't have the demonstration about it. I can get you the guns.
Michael We're painting the wall with anti-American slogans: "Victory to the NLF", "Death to US Imperialism", "Yanks out of Vietnam".
Irishman Don't you like the Americans?

Michael They're murdering innocent people in South-East Asia.

Irishman Who is it?

Michael Johnson.

Irishman I give up with some people. What's he want to do that for then, the murdering swine?

Girl Friend He's denying the right of the Vietnamese people to decide their own future because what they want conflicts with American financial interests.

Michael He's trying to push people around.

Irishman Right, lads, I'm with you. Give me a brush.

Michael We've only got the two.

Irishman Then step down for a minute, sir, and lend me yours. I'll give the lady a hand.

Girl Friend Go on, Mike. Give him the brush.

Michael He wouldn't know what to write. Anyway, he's pissed.

Girl Friend Go on. It's you that's always saying people are never given the chance to express themselves.

Michael This is serious.

Girl Friend Don't be so pompous.

Michael offers the brush to the Irishman

Michael You know what you're going to write?

Irishman Oh, yes. (*He paints*)

Michael (*reading*) "Up the IRA". I told you! That's not what we agreed on. Give me the brush.

Irishman Sure, it's the same thing. It's us versus them. (*He turns his back to the wall and becomes aware of his white leg*) Oh, he's a comical bloke. We have a slight ideological confliction, and your man here pours paint down my leg! Up the Republic!

He dabs Michael's nose with the brush. The Girl Friend laughs. Michael takes the brush and dabs the Girl Friend. She dabs him back and Michael retaliates. They see the funny side of this and cover one another in paint. The sequence ends with the Girl Friend putting the upturned bucket over Michael's head. The Irishman becomes the Magistrate

The Girl Friend exits

Magistrate Michael Peters, according to the uncontested account of your activities last night given in evidence by PC Grahame, you seem to be an extremely confused young man. You are not unintelligent, but your squalid behaviour, defacing private property with mindless slogans, bringing your girl friend, Miss Smith, into conflict with the law, and your association with common vagrants speaks more of the gutter than the institution of learning of which you are an undergraduate. You have brought nothing but shame upon your university, your school and your parents. In extenuation I have nothing to consider but that this is your first conviction and your youth, though at twenty most young men seem to have found a more responsible attitude to their fellows. May I suggest you sit down and have a long hard think about your future? Do you intend to take advantage of the privileged opportunities society has seen fit to offer you, or will your behaviour give the Law and your Vice-Chancellor no alternative but to send you down in disgrace at some future date? Have you anything to say?

Michael (*still with the bucket over his head*) What I wrote was not mindless.

Magistrate Fined fifteen pounds plus costs.

Michael and the Magistrate exit

SCENE B

1966. New Year's Eve. Michael's parents know something's gone wrong and Enid tries to define it

George and Enid enter

Enid I think I'll go to bed, George.

George No, don't do that, see the New Year in.

Enid I'm tired.

George Come on. It's not long now.

Enid I'm not bothered really.

George You a bit low? Have a drink. Let's both have a drink. Just the two of us. Shall wc? Ycs! (*He gives her a drink*) Get that down you. Here's to us in nineteen sixty-seven.

Enid Here's to us.

George Don't it sound queer, 'sixty-seven? Every New Year's strange at first. Cheer up. It might never happen. Don't you feel well?

Enid I told you, I'm tired.

George Well, we'll only hear Big Ben. Then we'll go to bed. We can't not see the New Year in, can we?

Enid I wonder what Michael's doing.

George You're not drinking.

Enid I wonder what he's doing, George.

George Don't you like it? I think this sherry of mine's turned out rather well.

Enid Why didn't he come home this Christmas?

George Enid, you said you wouldn't go on any more about it.

Enid I'm not going on about it. But I can't stop myself thinking.

George I suppose he wanted to be with his friends.

Enid Aren't we his friends?

George Course we're his friends.

Enid He wanted to be with that girl! That's why he didn't come home.

George It's only natural with someone his age.

Enid Not at Christmas. What if she had a baby? I wouldn't have minded if he'd brought her here even. Did you ever talk to him?

George Michael knows what he's doing. And if he doesn't, there's nothing we can do now. It's his life.

Enid Don't you miss him?

George You know I do.

Enid I miss him.

George We both do.

Enid Sometimes I wonder if we did the right thing, making him go to that school. Sometimes I think he might have been happier doing something else. I feel he hardly knows us now.

George We didn't make him. We tried to help him. Anyway, he didn't have to go. He wanted to go.

Enid What about this girl? What about this going to court? What about the way he looks? And what he says?

George He's only doing what his own click does. That's what people are like.

Enid They don't all get involved with the police. Some of them have got more sense.

George I'll put the telly on. See what old Andy Stewart is doing up the White Heather Club. Shall we have another?

Enid No, I don't want any more. And I don't want the television on. And I don't want to go on pretending everything's all right when it's not. I want you to tell me what's happening. George, answer!

George I don't know what you want to know. Michael's got his own life to lead. He'll be all right.

Enid I'm not talking about Michael. I want to know about us.

George What about us?

Enid What's going to happen to us?

George When?

Enid When we die.

George Enid! I've let you go on and on but I can't take any more of this. You go from one thing to another, anything that comes into your head. You're not talking sense. What do you mean, "when we die"?

Enid I don't know. I've always thought we'd have Michael and now he's gone.

George Hang on. I think that's it. I can hear next-door's television. Happy New Year. (*He kisses her*)

George and Enid exit

IF YOU'RE GLAD I'LL BE FRANK
by Tom Stoppard

These are the opening four scenes of an ingenious play. Frank, a bus driver, dials TIM, the speaking clock, one day only to find it is the voice of Gladys, his long-lost wife. It is set in the 1960s when the telephone service was controlled by the General Post Office (GPO) and had a 'TIM' girl for a speaking clock.

Set: Scenes A and C could be heard and not seen. Scene B at the door of the building that houses all British Telephone Services. Scene D a telephone box. Period: 1960s.
The presentation of these scenes depends on the ingenuity of the director.

Cast: M6 F4, 1 M or F.
Gladys, the TIM girl, or Speaking Clock. Frank, her husband. Porter. Workers at British Telephone Service: Myrtle Trelawney; Mr Mortimer; Mr Courtenay-Smith; Sir John; First Lord of the Post Office, Lord Coot; Beryl, a secretary. Telephone Operator. Ivy, a bus conductress.

Playing time: 9 minutes.

SCENE A

Frank, who turns out to be a bus driver, is dialling "TIM"

Frank T.I.M.

It can't be ...

(*In fearful hope*) It's not ...?

It is! GLADYS!

Gladys At the third stroke it will be eight fifty-nine and twenty seconds ...
(PIP PIP PIP)
... At the third stroke it will be eight fifty-nine and thirty seconds ...
(PIP PIP PIP)
... At the third stroke it will be eight fifty-nine and forty seconds ...
(PIP PIP PIP)
... eight fifty-nine and fifty seconds ...

Frank It's my Gladys!	(PIP PIP PIP)
	Gladys ... nine o'clock precisely.

SCENE B

Traffic noise is heard. Big Ben begins its nine a.m. routine. The noise fades as the interior action starts

Porter Here we go.

Myrtle enters

Morning, Mrs Trelawney.
Myrtle (*gaily*) Hallo, Tommy.

Myrtle passes through

Mortimer enters

Porter Morning, Mr Mortimer.
Mortimer (*tiredly*) Good-morning, Tom.

Mortimer passes through

Courtenay-Smith enters

Porter Good-morning, Mr Courtenay-Smith.
Courtenay-Smith (*vaguely*) Morning, Mr Thompson.

Courtenay-Smith passes through

Sir John enters

Porter Good-morning, Sir John.
Sir John Ah, Thompson.

Sir John passes through

The First Lord of the Post Office enters

Porter Good-morning, my Lord.
First Lord Morning, Tommy. Anything to report?
Porter All on schedule, my Lord.

First Lord Jolly good.

The First Lord passes through to the others

Myrtle Good-morning, your Lordship.
First Lord Good-morning, Mrs Trelawney.
Mortimer Good-morning, my Lord.
First Lord Good-morning, ah, Mortimer.
Courtenay-Smith Good-morning, Lord Coot.
First Lord Good-morning, Mrs Courtenay-Smith.
Sir John What ho, Cooty.

Sir John moves on to his office. Beryl is there

Beryl Good-morning, sir.
First Lord Who are you?
Beryl I'm new.
First Lord New what?
Beryl New secretary, sir—Miss Bligh. They sent me over from Directory Enquiries last night.
First Lord I see. What happened to my old—to Miss—er ...?
Beryl Apparently she cracked, sir, at one fifty-three a.m. precisely, she had her third stroke. I came at once.
First Lord That's the ticket. The Post Office never sleeps. Do you know the form round here?
Beryl Well ...
First Lord Quite simple. I'm the First Lord of the Post Office, of course. I'm responsible for the lot, with special attention to the Telephone Services, which are as follows—write them down—
UMP—dial-the-Test-score.
SUN—dial-the-weather.
POP—dial-a-pop.
BET—dial-the-racing results.
EAT—dial-a-recipe.
GOD—dial-the-Bible-reading—
—for which I take personal responsibility—and so on, with many others, including the most popular and important of them all—TIM—dial-the-speaking-clock. We can't afford to lose track of time, or we'd be lost. Now, you see, we must keep a continuous check on all of them, because if you don't keep an eye on them they slide back. The strain is appalling, and the staffing problems monumental. Shall we start checking, then? To begin with, synchronize our watches, and then check with TIM—ready? I make it just coming up to nine two and forty seconds ...
(PIP PIP PIP)

SCENE C

This follows straight on with the Time signal (PIP PIP PIP) *heard direct, i.e. not through the telephone, as is Gladys now*

Gladys

... At the third stroke it will be nine two and fifty seconds ...
(PIP PIP PIP)
... At the third stroke it will be nine three precisely.
(PIP PIP PIP)

Or, to put it another way, three minutes past nine, precisely, though which nine in particular, I don't say, so what's precise about that ...?

... nine three and ten seconds ...
(PIP PIP PIP)

The point is beginning to be lost on me.
Or rather it is becoming a different point.
Or rather I am beginning to see through it.
Because they think that time is something they invented,
for their own convenience,
and divided up into ticks and tocks
and sixties and twelves and twenty-fours ...
so that they'd know when the Olympic record has been broken,
and when to stop serving dinner in second-class hotels
when the season opens and the betting closes,
when to retire;
when to leave the station,
renew their applications
when their subscriptions have expired;
when time has run out.
So that they'd know how long they lasted,
and pretend that it matters,
and how long they've got,
as if it mattered,
so that they'd know that we know that they know.

That we know, that is.
That they know, of course.
And so on.

Ad infinitum.

I used to say *ad nauseam*
but it goes on long after you feel sick
And I feel sick.
When you look down from a great
    height
you become dizzy. Such depth, such
    distance,
such disappearing tininess so far away,
rushing away,
reducing the life-size to nothing—
it upsets the scale you live by.
Your eyes go first, followed by the
    head,
and if you can't look away you feel
    sick.
And that's my view of time;
and I can't look away.
Dizziness spirals up between my
    stomach and my head
corkscrewing out the stopper
But I'm empty anyway.
I was emptied long ago.

Because it goes on,
this endless dividing up into equal
    parts.
this keeping track—
because time viewed from such
    distance
et cetera
rushing away
reducing the lifespan to nothing
and so on—
The spirit goes first, followed by the
    mind.
And if you can't look away you go
    mad.

(*Faint time clock, 2–3 seconds*)
... nine four and fifty seconds ...
... nine five precisely ...
... nine five and ten seconds ...

Courtenay-Smith (*reading*) "London
and the south-east: dry with sunshine
and a light breeze: continuing for the
rest of the day."

(PIP PIP PIP)

(*Time clock, 2–3 seconds*)
Courtenay-Smith ... nine six
  precisely
(PIP PIP PIP)
... nine six and ten seconds
(PIP PIP PIP)

SCENE **D**

Frank is dialling; he is excited, intense

Myrtle (*reading*) "... cheesy croquet—you mix half a pound of sharp Cheddar
cheese ..."

The ringing tone breaks off and the Operator is heard through the telephone

Frank GPO?
Operator Number, please?
Frank Listen, do all you people work in the same building?
Operator Switchboard. Can I help you?
Frank I want to speak to Gladys Jenkins.
Operator What's the number, please?
Frank She works there—speaking clock.
Operator Do you want to know the time?
Frank No—I want my Gladys! What's her number?
Operator Speaking clock?
Frank Yes.
Operator TIM.
Frank Her *number*.
Operator T—I—M.
Frank I demand to speak to your superior ...
Operator Just a moment, sir, putting you through ...
Gladys (*through the telephone*) ... At the third stroke it will be nine thirteen precisely.
Frank It's all right, Glad—it's me again—Frank! Can you hear me now, Glad? I've
  had a time of it, I can tell you—I must say, you gave me a turn! So that's where you
  got to—Gladys? Give over a minute, love—it's Frank ... Can you hear me, Gladys?
  I know your voice—are they holding you? I'll get you out of there, Gladys—I'll
  speak to the top man—I'll get the wheels turning, Gladys——

Ivy, a bus conductress, breaks in

Ivy Frank!

Frank —but I've got to dash now, love—I'm calling from the terminus and we're due out ...

Ivy Frank *Jenkins*! The passengers are looking at their watches!

Frank Just coming. (*To Gladys*) That was Ivy, my conductress—you don't know Ivy—I'm on a new route now, the fifty-two to Acton. Keep your chin up, Glad. I'll be giving you another ring later. Goodbye, Gladys—Oh, Gladys—what's the time now?

Gladys Nine fourteen precisely ...

Frank Thanks, Glad—oh, *thank* you, Gladys! (*He rings off*)

Ivy Frank—it's nine fourteen—remember the schedule!

Frank Hey, Ivy—I've found her—I've found my Gladys!

KILLERS
by Adam Pernak

Two brothers, Jonathan and David, are both killers: one a murderer of his girlfriend's lover, the other a hero in the Gulf War. These are the final two scenes of the play: in the first the parents, unable to cope with the strain of the situation, finally part, while in the second David at last wins the confidence and support of Jonathan in prison.

Set: A living-room; a prison room. Period: 1991.

Cast: M4 F2.
David, a fighter pilot; 28. Jonathan, his brother, ambitious, successful, now serving a prison sentence; 25. Mr Shand, their working-class father; middle age. Mrs Shand, their mother. Marian, sympathetic neighbour; middle age. Gerald, her husband.

Playing time: 25 minutes.

SCENE A

The Shands' living-room

Mrs Shand stands by the sideboard. Mr Shand sits in the R armchair staring ahead. There are two suitcases by the door

Mr Shand It's stupid. You don't gain anything. Stupid cow.

Mrs Shand You see, that's what's done it.

Mr Shand I don't care what you say. I'm not listening. You're mental. You've got stupid ideas from stupid doctors. I'm not listening to you.

Mrs Shand I wish I could've talked to you about it. I'd've sooner talked to you than total strangers.

Mr Shand You're not coming back. I'll lock the door. You think you're coming back, you can sod it.

Mrs Shand You never listened. You were always too busy.

Mr Shand You've no need to go on about it. I've told you. Shut it! Shut it—you've been told.

Mrs Shand You'll wish you hadn't spoken to me like that.

Mr Shand Belt up.

Pause

Mrs Shand I don't think I'm being unreasonable.

Mr Shand You don't know what to think. You've gone mad. You're worse than that stupid son of yours.

Mrs Shand Anyone'd think he wasn't your son as well.

Mr Shand He's not. This is it—he's had it now. He's a bloody disgrace. He'll never get a civil word from me again. Filthy little bugger. And I don't know why David wastes his time.

Mrs Shand David's gone because he cares.

Mr Shand He's too bloody soft. He wants to toughen up, I thought that bloody war would've toughened him up. He's no better now than when he went. If anything, he's worse. I can't believe this family.

Pause

Mrs Shand I've made you a list. I'll leave it on here. (*She places it on the sideboard*)

Mr Shand You get worse by the minute.

Mrs Shand I think it covers everything.

Mr Shand You've had nothing but patience from me. Not that you bloody deserved it. You don't help yourself. You want to stop being so damned soft. I've no more patience for you.

Mrs Shand I don't know why you should be surprised. I've mentioned it often enough.

Mr Shand Don't think you're bothering me. Sod that. Get gone—see if I care.

Mrs Shand You can't say I didn't warn you.

Pause. Mr Shand remains seriously disgruntled

Mr Shand I'll tell you what it is. It's them bloody neighbours. That's what it is. You're only doing it to get away from them.

Mrs Shand The neighbours have got nothing to do with it.

Mr Shand It's 'cause you're ashamed. You know that they talk about you every time you leave that door, so you're runnin' away.

Mrs Shand Don't be ridiculous.

Mr Shand It's Jonathan, and it's David, and it's them soddin' neighbours, but it's not me.

Mrs Shand Is that what you think? It's just as well I'm leaving then.

Mr Shand It doesn't scare me. Them suitcases. Doesn't bother me.

Mrs Shand Good for you.

Mr Shand It's all talk.

Mrs Shand Is it?
Mr Shand We'll see.

Mrs Shand looks at her watch and puts her overcoat on

You'll not get far. Not on a Sunday. It's Sunday, you know.
Mrs Shand I know what day it is, thank you very much.
Mr Shand Think you're smart. There's no buses on a Sunday.
Mrs Shand I know.
Mr Shand Oh. You're wasting your money on a taxi. They'll charge you double for a Sunday. Or maybe it's treble now, I don't know. Where are you going?

No reply

I don't care. You're totally mad. They'll put you away, wherever you go. (*Slight pause*) I saw that letter from your doctor. About drugs. I think it's disgraceful. You'll end up like a delinquent, out on t'streets. This is the end for you. You've had it now.

Pause

I suppose you'll be back round that prison.
Mrs Shand What makes you think that?
Mr Shand You're in league with him.
Mrs Shand I'm trying to help him.
Mr Shand Another waste of time. He won't even talk to you. Just sits there.
Mrs Shand He can hear me.
Mr Shand You ought to be ashamed. You would be ashamed, if you had a shred of decency about you.
Mrs Shand It's his birthday next week.
Mr Shand Huh! He can forget that.

Doorbell

Mrs Shand (*cheerily*) I'll get it.

She exits to the front door

Mr Shand Bloody visitors. Snoops.
Mrs Shand (*off*) Hallo. You're early. Do you want to come in for a drink?

Gerald and Marian enter, followed by Mrs Shand

Sit down. Shall I take your coats?

Marian No; it's all right.
Mrs Shand Sit down. I'll get some tea—kettle's just boiled.

She exits to the kitchen

Gerald and Marian edge in, wary of Mr Shand, and sit down. Silence

Gerald They're digging that road again. Kept us waiting.

Silence

Marian How's the allotment, Reg?
Mr Shand 'S all right.
Gerald Did you plant those radishes, like I said?
Mr Shand No.
Gerald Oh.
Marian Is David about?
Mr Shand Gone out.
Marian We were hoping to catch him. How is he?
Mr Shand Not so bad. (*He stands, gets his shoes, and starts to put them on*)
Gerald Are you off down the allotment?
Mr Shand Yes.
Gerald What are you on with at the moment?
Mr Shand Lettuces, carrots. All sorts.
Gerald I might have a wander down later.
Mr Shand Please yourself. I can't talk, Gerald, I've a lot to do.
Gerald Ah. Maybe next time then.

Mr Shand stands

Mrs Shand emerges from the kitchen with a tray of tea. She stops

Mrs Shand Are you going out?
Mr Shand Get a couple of hours in; before it goes dark.
Mrs Shand I'll be gone, you know.

He stands, says nothing. She puts the tea down. Marian starts to pour

Marian We had ever such a time getting here. They can't leave that one-way system
     alone.
Mrs Shand Is there anything else you need?

Mr Shand stands in silence

I've left you a list. There's a phone number on there also, but you know Marian's number, don't you?

Silence

Sure you don't want a cup of tea before you go?

No reply

Marian Have some tea, Reg.

Mr Shand looks at his wife

Mr Shand I don't see why other people should interfere.
Mrs Shand If you're referring to Marian, I rang her. And I'm very grateful to her.
Mr Shand There's some things that should be kept private.
Mrs Shand Sometimes things go too far.
Mr Shand Don't think I'll forget this.
Gerald We're only trying to help.
Mr Shand You were no bloody help when you were needed. When it all came out, you were nowhere to be seen.
Marian We didn't want to interfere.
Mr Shand You didn't want to know. You were scared for your name. You treated us like dirt.
Mrs Shand That's not true.
Mr Shand (*angrily*) Don't you bloody start! Bloody hypocrite. The first three weeks we got one visit from these. Just while they saw what a state you were in. Then they didn't want to know.
Mrs Shand As a matter of fact I asked them not to visit. I didn't want anyone to see me.
Mr Shand They didn't want to know. If you'd've asked them, they'd've found an excuse.
Gerald That's not right—that's unfair.
Mr Shand No it's not.
Gerald We've done our bit. When Jean rang, we came right away. You can't say we don't do our bit.
Mr Shand You weren't welcome. You weren't wanted.
Marian We understand your position, Reg. It's very difficult.
Mr Shand I don't want no bloody sympathy, I just want for you to stop interferin'. Wouldn't be so bad if it was genuine.
Marian How can you say that?
Mr Shand I know it. You're all in it together. You've come here ... (*A sudden pause. He looks at his wife, realizing what is happening*) Jean ... Well what am I supposed to say?

Pause

Mrs Shand I think it's too late.

Pause

Marian Do you want us to wait in the car?

A moment

Mrs Shand (*finally*) No. (*She still looks at her husband*)
Mr Shand Right. (*He moves to leave*) I'm off.

He looks to the visitors and registers their phoney expressions

You're pathetic. (*He looks at Mrs Shand*) The lot of you.

Mr Shand exits R

Silence

Marian I've got the spare room ready; you can stay as long as you like.

Pause

Do you know what you're doing yet?

Mrs Shand shakes her head

There's no hurry. Take your time. Stay with us.
Gerald Has she told you the news? I got a job.
Mrs Shand Really?
Gerald It's the same people. They called me back. Couldn't make the orders on time. So they called me back, see.
Mrs Shand Very nice.
Marian It means there'll be more room round the house during the day.

Gerald looks to her, a little disgruntled

Mrs Shand (*her thoughts elsewhere*) He pretends not to. But he knows what it's about.
Marian Yes.
Mrs Shand He'll see about it when I've gone.

Gerald I'm on reduced hours now. And slightly less pay.

Marian I think you're doing the right thing.

Mrs Shand Do you?

Marian If that's what he's like.

Mrs Shand Oh, that was nothing. He's been ranting, raving, thinks it's all my fault.

Marian No.

Mrs Shand It's all got a little bit out of hand.

Marian Well, you're welcome to stay with us for as long as you like.

Gerald Free of charge.

Mrs Shand Thank you.

Pause

Gerald I find it hard to believe it's the same man. He never was very cheerful, but it's a bit much when he's like that. I never did like him much. I always said, didn't I?

Marian We thought things were getting better.

Mrs Shand Not really.

Marian When we last spoke, it seemed to be getting better. He was taking you to the seaside.

Mrs Shand We didn't go.

Marian I must admit, I was a little surprised. We thought things were on the mend. I mean, you can't ignore what's happened, but I thought you were together on it. Men are bastards.

All three are shocked by this

David enters L. *He looks drained, tired. His smile to them is faint and forced*

David! (*She stands and goes to hug him*)

Gerald Welcome home, young man. I want to hear all about it.

David Hallo, Marian. How are you?

Marian Look at you—you've not been sleeping. What are these? Big dark bags.

Mrs Shand How was it?

David (*too forced*) Fine.

Marian I hope you'll make a point of catching up on all that sleep missed. We've heard all about you. There was an article ...

David Yes.

Gerald She bought three copies.

Marian I kept all the cuttings. I've got a big thick scrapbook full. I'll show it to you, and you can tell me the stories.

Mrs Shand Did he see you?

David I'll tell you later.

Marian See who? Did who see you?

Pause

Oh, David, is that where you've been? You're too good. Your first Sunday back.
Gerald I don't get it.
Marian He's been to visit his brother. On his first Sunday back.
Mrs Shand David, there's some tea here. Why don't you come and sit down.
Gerald He's been to see Jonathan? What for?

He is glared at for this

Marian And how was he, David?
David I don't really feel like talking just now.
Mrs Shand Have some tea. (*She hands him a cup*)
David It's very tiring.
Gerald You've been to the prison? On your first Sunday back?
Marian Isn't he an angel?
Mrs Shand Was he talking?
David Oh yes.
Mrs Shand What did he say?
David Plenty.
Mrs Shand Was he pleased to see you?

No reply

Oh. You didn't fight, did you?
David I'll tell you later.
Marian We've heard he's been very difficult.
David (*sharply*) Is it surprising?
Marian No.
Mrs Shand Drink your tea, David. Calm down.
David He's ill, you know.
Mrs Shand I know.
David He needs support, and he needs help.
Mrs Shand I know.
David You've hardly been to see him.
Mrs Shand We have.
David When?
Mrs Shand Last week.
David Well ... (*To the others*) Did you go?

They look at him, shocked

You don't like to.

Marian Think of what he did.
David I know what he did. I've just seen him.
Gerald Nobody could condone what he did. It's too terrible for words.
David He killed a man.

They are shocked

Marian I think I must be old-fashioned, I find all this very difficult.
David It's simple enough.
Gerald It's a wicked business. I don't think we should talk about it.
David If you stop trying to complicate matters.
Gerald I don't think we're doing that.
David I think you are. (*Pause*) What do you think of me?
Gerald What's that?
David How do I compare with Jonathan?
Gerald There is no comparison.
David Oh, I think we could work on one.
Gerald He's a different kind of person. It's a different thing.
David What is?

Pause

Do you realize what I've been doing?

No reply

Do you realize what I've done?

Silence

Marian I was thinking we might get on the road. I don't like driving in the dark.

No reply

Is there anything else to pack?
Mrs Shand No. The cases are there. Would you mind if I had a word alone with David?
Marian We'll wait in the car. Gerald.

She stands. He stands

Gerald, can you manage those cases?

Gerald hesitates to answer

David I'll bring them.

Marian Oh, all right. No problem then. We'll wait in the car. The red one, Jean.

Mrs Shand OK.

Marian Come on, Gerald. Let's make a move now, shall we.

Gerald (*feebly*) See you later, David.

No reply

Gerald and Marian exit

Brief silence

David It surprises me you chose them. Is there no-one else?

Mrs Shand No. (*Pause*) He spoke to you then. I told you what he's like. I don't know how to take him. (*Pause*) Did you tell him about me?

David No.

Mrs Shand What did you talk about?

David Nothing.

Mrs Shand Nothing?

David I hardly said anything. He wasn't in the mood to listen.

Pause

I'm going back. I don't care if it takes the next ten years. I'm going back till I get him to hear me. And then I'm going to tell him precisely what I think.

Mrs Shand And what *do* you think?

Pause

David I think that he needs me ...

Mrs Shand And ...?

No reply. Long pause

David (*standing*) I'll take your cases.

Mrs Shand I have to do this, David. I have to do something—you do understand? Otherwise ... It's going to go on forever.

David I think that you're doing the right thing.

Mrs Shand Do you?

David Yes. I think that you're right. You have to do something.

He lifts the cases and moves to exit R

Black-out

Scene B

The Prison Room. A visit several weeks later

There is a table, slightly L, *and a chair to* L *of this. There is a door* R

Bright Lights come up on David and Jonathan

Jonathan No sharp objects. No knives, bullets, toys and games. Don't bring things. Don't ... don't ... you'll annoy them!
David What's the matter?
Jonathan (*pointing at the door*) We've got men who keep the noise down. Don't yell. Keep quiet. Keep it down, lads, come on now let's keep it down. (*Suddenly*) Alastair Angry in seventy-two ... Alastair Angry ...
David What?
Jonathan (*shouting*) ... KILLED HIMSELF!!

Pause

We've got madmen all around us. Do you realize this is the maximum high security top security highest mental metal prison in all the whole of England? And this is the toughest. Of all England.
David It's not the worst. There are others.

Pause

Jonathan Took a knife in breakfast canteen and hid it in his boot. Then he took it out at two in the morning and sliced away and shouted at us all, 'cause he still had things to say, but he floated away too quick and he didn't have time to say it.

I knew what he wanted to say. He wanted to tell us what it's like when you're dead. He found it out. He was trying to tell us. But he floated away. He got dragged out in a white sheet. They said, "Bloody bloody bloody mess." He's only painted his bloody cell red.

Frigging smelly, I should say!

Filthy's what they thought, but really it was beautiful, 'cause it was natural. That's what they don't get. But I get it. It's natural. What's the problem? They've all got blood to spill. It's all right really.
David I still know you, Jonathan. I know what you're doing.
Jonathan We've got vermin in the khazi. It's out there! Cross your legs, lads!

David laughs, exasperated

David If I stopped coming, you'd only think you'd won. So I keep coming; almost to spite you. You can only keep this up for so long.

Jonathan If Angus is in there, he whistles. I wait for him to stop. If he stops whistling, if he stops, then he's been got. He doesn't even mind. He wants to be got.

David I know from the warden that you know how to behave. Once the visitors have gone, you go right back to being normal.

Jonathan And it's not just him because I'd quite like to be got too. I know I've never seen it, but I know it's there! Killer rat in the khazi—what a way to go! (*He laughs*)

David I remember when you were a boy, at night, you were always too frightened to use the bathroom. You thought that there were monsters in there.

Slight pause. Jonathan deliberately focuses away from him

Dad told you not to be silly. I was the one who had to go in and put the light on for you. Do you remember that? It's not all that long ago.

Pause. Jonathan is rocking on his chair

Jonathan This week's viewer's question comes from Mister Anal Retention of Accrington, Lancashire, who asks: How many times a day does Angus use the khazi? Thank you for your question, Mister Retention, your tie is in the post.

David Yes; you're trying hard today. It's definitely one of your better days. (*Slight pause*) How's the writing? The warden says he found an exercise book of stories you'd——

Jonathan We've got serial killers of every sort here. A man to suit every requirement. Hatchets, screwdrivers, shotguns, hands, feet, hair, teeth ...

David I heard they were very good, these stories. I wondered if maybe you'd let me read them. Can I read them? Would you let me?

Pause

What do you write about? Anything in particular?

No reply

Well actually the warden told me. He said you write about adventures. Children on adventures, making things up, playing at being heroes. Sounds familiar.

Jonathan We're surrounded by it. Bastards who know what's best for us.

David I don't mind you not answering me. It doesn't bother me. So long as you listen, and I know that you're listening, 'cause you never were much good at pretending. Oh, you're trying hard, pretending, but I'm very sorry——

In a swift movement, Jonathan grabs his chair, lifts it, and smashes it to the ground, yelling angrily. He kicks at it. Then he stops, and stands still, breathing heavily

Jonathan Don't nobody be put off now. I am a very mild man. I'm just a little confused.

Silence. He turns to David

I smash a bottle and a little old man who's doing six times life says, "why do you do it?" I say, "I don't know why, and if I did know why I wouldn't tell you, you old weasel-face."
David I know why you break things.
Jonathan And then I say that maybe I do know why. I break things 'cause they're no good and they're there. They shouldn't be there if they're no good. They deserve to be broken. Bastard chair. (*He kicks at the chair*) It's just a shitty wooden chair. (*He kicks it*)
David It is. I couldn't agree more.

Slight pause

Jonathan If there's any justice she'll be dead and buried now. I wanted her crying but that's no good, I want her dead and buried with a metal spike in through her eye and I'd do it myself, and don't think I wouldn't.

Pause

"I can't think of things we did," she said.
David You hurt her too.

Jonathan looks at him and then turns away

Jonathan (*softly*) I've still got a knife.

David is shocked

David Where is it?

Jonathan smirks, knowingly

Jonathan People only get what they deserve. Isn't that true?
David (*earnestly*) Yes.

Pause. Jonathan is feeling uncomfortable, threatened

Jonathan (*suddenly, impatiently*) I've got to get out. I've got things, there are things, I've got, to do. I've got things ... there are things ... (*He looks about him as if searching for the way out*)

David Don't go yet. What about the news? Dad's got a job interview.

Jonathan walks away, towards the L exit

He keeps practising what to say. He's very determined.

Jonathan There's a tournament now and I'm all set to win, it's a certainty I'll win, all set.

David (*trying*) Mum's still at Marian's. She rings him on a Sunday. She says she'll not go back but at least they're speaking now. It's getting better.

Jonathan Angus is a bastard. He's got my book. I've got tactics and he nicks the book from right on my table. He dies, Angus.

David (*losing momentum*) I don't think there's anything else. Mum sends her love. She says to wear your scarf when you're out in the yard. You will remember?

Jonathan Fat Angus. He's fat, Angus.

A long pause

David Why won't you listen? Why?

Jonathan paces, his attention elsewhere

What's the matter with you? Do you want me to hate you? Is that it? All right then, I hate you. All right?

Jonathan still paces

The more that I think about you, the more I give up. And still I come. For three weeks I come here. Three weeks, and all I get is "Angus is a bastard—I've got a tournament". Are you punishing me, Jonathan? Is that it? (*Sadly*) I think you are.

Pause

Why do I come here? Why do I waste my time? Jonathan?—listen to me! (*He moves towards Jonathan*) I want to help you. I'm here because I care. Oh, sod this, I'm sick of saying it. (*He looks straight at Jonathan*) Look at you—you're pathetic. Parading around, self-pitying. Mum's crying, Dad gets spat at in the street, and here's you. Poor sad lonely you. No-one understands you. (*Slight pause*) Do you really think you're the only one? Here's how it is: you killed a man. You killed him, you got locked up for it. He had a weak heart, they cut the sentence, but it was you who did it. (*Slight pause*) What's so bad about that? You think you're hard done by? Think it's unfair? And nobody understands you.

Pause

Were you forced to do it? Were you ordered? (*Angrily*) What about me?

Pause

You feel guilty. You know what you did, but still you can't get close enough to believe it. You need to be punished, you need to suffer, but this punishment, it's not enough. There's still the thought, the image, of the terrible thing you did. (*Slight pause*) People don't know. (*Slight pause*) They tell you what you are ... (*Slight pause*) You know that they're wrong but how can they know when it isn't them? You know what you are. You know what you did. You hear it and see it. (*Slight pause*) Everything you were is gone. And in its place, that one act. The taking of a life. That's it. You're a killer. And it's always going to be there. Until the day you die. (*Slight pause*) Am I right, brother? Is that how you feel?

Jonathan stares at him, his face bearing an expression of relief and sudden understanding. Then, slowly, he extends a hand and takes hold of David's arm. He pulls David to him and the two brothers embrace

Fade to Black-out

LARK RISE
by Keith Dewhurst, from Flora Thompson's trilogy

Flora Thompson grew up in an Oxfordshire hamlet in the 1880s. She was village postmistress for some years before writing the semi-autobiographical trilogy of books *Lark Rise to Candleford* which recorded a disappearing way of life in rural England and became a classic work. The trilogy was adapted by Keith Dewhurst into two plays for the National Theatre and intended to be performed as promenade productions with no distinction between stage and auditorium. *Lark Rise* is the first of these plays and re-enacts the first day of harvest. These two scenes from Act One focus on the early morning, the Timms family and their neighbours. Laura Timms represents Flora Thompson as a ten-year-old girl.

Set: Various interior and exterior settings.
The end house, Laura's home, in the hamlet of Lark Rise, is a focal point, but the acting area includes the street and other cottages in the hamlet. Period: 1880s.

Cast: M5 F4, 1 boy 1 girl.
Laura, small, skinny, dark-eyed, yellow-haired; 10. Edmund, her brother, tall for his age; 8. Emma, their mother, graceful, copper-coloured hair. Old Postie, gloomy, grumpy, flat-footed. Mrs Peverill and Mrs Blaby, villagers. Sharman, ex-army, ill; old. Doctor. Carrier. Grandfather, tall; old. Twister, small, thin-legged, rheumaticky; old. Queenie, his wife, little, wrinkled; old.

Playing time: 11 minutes.

SCENE A

Emma has done her scrubbing and emptied the fireplace which she is now cleaning, watched by Laura and Edmund

Emma See this grate I'm cleaning? Looks done, doesn't it? But you watch. (*She brushes vigorously*) There. That's the secret. Just that bit of extra elbow grease after some folks would consider a thing done.
Laura Oh, Mother! Post, Mother! Here's Old Postie!

Emma and other women come out of their houses. Old Postie is a gloomy, grumpy man with flat feet. He has been forty years on this round and walks with deliberate, rheumatic slowness

Emma Look at him dawdle! You expecting something, Mrs Peverill?
Mrs Peverill No, I b'aint expecting nothing, but I be so yarning.

Old Postie stops and looks through the letters and small parcels

Old Postie (*to the women outside the group of cottages*) No, I ain't got nothing for you, Mrs Peverill. Your young Annie wrote to you only last week. She's got summat else to do, besides sitting down on her arse in the servant's kitchen writin' home all the time.
Mrs Peverill Now I call that real forrard language.
Old Postie Mrs Blaby. Parcel!
Emma Mrs Blaby!
Mrs Blaby (*coming out of her cottage*) It's not summat for me, is it?
Old Postie 'Tis from your Aggie in London. Sent you her best dress, I'll be bound.
Mrs Blaby Well, better be out of the world than out of the fashion, b'ain't that what they say?
Old Postie Oh, there is one for you, Mrs Peverill! And my! Ain't it a thin-roed 'un. Not much time to write to her mother these days. I took a good fat 'un from her to young Chad Gubbins.
Mrs Peverill Oh!—Don't he leave a sting behind him!

Old Postie waddles on. The women return to their homes. Emma takes her mats in with her

Edmund Mother, why are people in Lark Rise so poor?
Emma Poverty's no disgrace, Edmund, but 'tis a great inconvenience.
Laura (*she has seen something in the distance; pointing*) What's that?
Emma Where?
Laura Coming from the turnpike.
Emma Oh yes. I see him. Driving too quick to be the fish cart.
Edmund It's the doctor's gig.
Emma So it is.
Laura Is anybody sick?
Emma If they were we'd have had the gossips round by this time in the morning— and Mrs Beamish hasn't come to her time yet.
Edmund He must be going to Fordlow.
Emma Ay. (*Her mind goes on to the next thing*) Now, Laura, you run round the Rise to poor Mr Sharman, there's a good girl, and ask him could he fancy a bite of cold bacon for his dinner.

Laura goes to the cottage of Sharman who is known as the Major because he served in the army. He is old and ill and has just dressed and with great difficulty dragged his chair to the fire

Laura Mr Sharman! Morning, Mr Sharman.
Sharman Uh? Oh. It's you, Laura.
Laura My mother says, could you fancy a bit of bacon for your dinner?
Sharman I'm cold.
Laura Sun's shining, Mr Sharman.
Sharman I'm cold.

The Doctor and the local Carrier have got out of the gig. They walk past the end house

Emma Morning, Doctor.
Doctor Morning, Mrs Timms.
Emma No trouble, I hope?
Doctor No, no. We've just come for Mr Sharman.
Emma Oh no! (*She knows exactly what they mean*)
Sharman Dunno where I'd be without your mum, Laura.
Laura Would you fancy some bacon?
Sharman I had bacon every day in the army.
Laura What shall I tell her, then?
Sharman I'm cold.
Laura It's coming up very hot, Mr Sharman.

The Doctor and the Carrier march in

Doctor Morning, Major. Come along, now.
Sharman Eh? What?
Doctor It's a nice morning. We've come to take you for a drive.
Sharman A drive? I've not driven nowhere since I left the hospital. Where to?
Doctor Oh, just a drive.
Sharman You'd not put me in the workhouse?
Doctor You'll feel better for the sunshine.
Sharman I won't go. I can look after myself.
Doctor No, you can't, and you've no family to do it for you.
Sharman I'm a soldier. I'll not die in no workhouse.
Doctor Come along, old chap.

They lift Sharman up. He tries to resist but is too weak. They hustle his coat round his shoulders

Sharman Let me be.
Doctor That's the way. Put your shawl on.

As the Doctor and Carrier walk Sharman slowly away the band sings "John Barleycorn"

Song

There were three men come out of the West,
The victory to try,
And these three men they made a vow,
John Barleycorn should die.

They ploughed, they sowed, they harrowed him in,
Throwed clods all on his head,
And these three men rejoicing went,
John Barleycorn was dead.

They rode him round and round the field,
Till they came into a barn,
And there they made a solemn vow,
On little John Barleycorn.

They hired men with the crab tree sticks,
To cut him skin from bone,
But the miller he served him worse than that,
For he ground him between two stones.

Doctor It's all for the best.

Everyone sings

All good gifts around us
Are sent from heaven above,
So thank the Lord, O thank the Lord,
For all His love.

SCENE B

Laura's Grandfather is a tall, old man with snow white hair and beard and blue eyes. He wears an old-fashioned, close-fitting black overcoat and a bowler hat. He moves slowly and painfully because rheumatism is gradually seizing up his joints. He is carrying a gift of freshly cut flowers from his garden

To reach the end house Grandfather must pass Queenie's cottage. Queenie Macey is a little, wrinkled, yellow-faced old woman in a lilac sunbonnet. She is dozing on a chair in the sun

Grandfather Morning, Queenie, and how are you this—fast asleep, God bless her.

Queenie's husband Twister pops up from behind the hedge. He is a small, thin-legged, jackdaw-eyed old fellow dressed in an old velveteen coat that once belonged to a gamekeeper, a peacock's feather stuck in the band of his battered old bowler, and a red and yellow handkerchief knotted under one ear. He, too, has rheumatism and is slowly becoming the slack-witted person that he has often pretended to be. He has a big, open clasp-knife in one hand

Twister Why should God bless her? Why should he? I'll wake 'un up fer 'ee.
Grandfather No need for that, Twister, thank 'ee kindly.
Twister Her be my wife and un'll do what I says.
Grandfather What was you a-doing behind that hedge?
Twister Nothing. I caught a frog. Sun's shining, ain't it?
Grandfather You let that frog go, Twister, d'you hear?
Twister I did. I did let 'un go. But first I cut him front legs off. (*He thinks that this is both daring and funny*)
Grandfather Lord have mercy, Twister. Lord have mercy. (*He walks slowly on*)
Emma (*seeing him, goes to meet him*) Why, Father: you've not walked round the Rise for a week or more.

Grandfather gives her the flowers

Oh, Dad. From your garden? Thank you. It just makes me think, if only I had thirty shillings a week regular I could keep everything so nice and tidy and keep *such* a table.

Grandfather sits painfully. Emma gets a flower jar

Grandfather Poor old Twister, eh? Poor Twister.
Emma There's some thinks he'd be better put away—but there he is, he still goes beating at shoots and he still earns a shilling or two opening farm gates for the brewery salesman's gig.
Grandfather I've known him forty year and he was allus the same. Whatever he dies on, he won't kill hisself with hard work. (*He notices that something is wrong*) Emmie? Emmie, you b'ain't crying, be you?
Emma Oh, Father!

She weeps. Then she hears the children, and pulls herself together

Laura and Edmund come in

Laura Oh, Mother. Mother, they've taken Mr Sharman away.

Emma I know. I saw them.

Grandfather We all saw 'em—except your Granny. She wouldn't look.

Laura Why not? What was she doing?

Grandfather Reading.

Edmund What? What was she reading?

Emma Don't ask questions!

Grandfather Now, Emmie ... She were reading one of those what-d'you-call-'ems, Edmund—novelettes. All about dukes and duchesses. When you say your prayers tonight, ask the Lord to help Mr Sharman.

Edmund D'you ever pray for your old fiddle?

Grandfather My old fiddle?

Edmund Didn't that get taken away?

Laura It had to be sold when Granny was ill.

Grandfather I got five pound for it.

Laura Did you miss it?

Grandfather I did, my maid, more than anything I've ever had to part with, and that's not a little, and I miss it still and always shall. But it went for a good cause and we can't have everything we want in this world. It wouldn't be good for us.

Laura Why not? I'd call it very good for you to have your old fiddle.

Emma Laura. Don't answer back.

Laura It's always money that causes people's troubles.

Emma Laura!

Grandfather If it *were* just money, Laura, life 'ud be simple.

Emma Now then, Laura, here's a penny. You go wait for Jerry Parish and you buy three oranges.

The children are delighted. They rush out

I'm sorry, Father. They've so many questions.

Grandfather They'll find answers in the Bible and their own good time.

Emma How's your rheumatics?

Grandfather Bad.

Emma Is this walk too much for you?

Grandfather gestures. He does not want to admit it easily, but the walk is too far

I'll visit you. You save yourself for your garden.

Grandfather It's run wild since I can't stoop so much. (*Silence*) Your uncle's well. He sends you kind regards.

Emma He's a good man.

Grandfather To send me money? Ay. He is.

Emma But you'd send it to him if you'd prospered.

Grandfather (*watching her*) What about you, Emmie? Do you prosper?

Emma (*shaking her head*) Every year Albert says we'll give notice and move to Candleford. We'll go when we've killed the pig, he says. Then when we've killed the pig he'll say we'll go at Michaelmas. But we won't.

Grandfather Do you want to leave the Rise?

Emma I want him to be happy. I don't want him always coming home late from public houses. (*She almost cries again*) You're good to me, Father. You're so good.

Grandfather Well, you've always brought me your troubles, haven't you?

Emma kneels in front of him: a little girl again. Grandfather smiles and, a bit awkwardly because of his rheumatism, wipes her eyes

Emma Oh, Father ...

Grandfather Sssh ...

Emma I'm sorry. I don't want to flinch. (*She blows her nose*)

Grandfather That's better. That's better. Now, you're going to be my own brave little wench. And remember, my dear, there's one above who knows what's best for us, even though we may not see it ourselves at the time.

Emma kisses him. There is great love between them

Now help me up.

Emma helps him up. It hurts. He smiles ruefully. He starts to go

Emma How long did you have that violin, Father?

Grandfather Oh—fifty-year. It's no use to me now. My fingers is too stiff to play it. (*He seems to be going but turns again*) Of course, when I bought it I was still a sinner. I hadn't seen Jesus, face to face. I were an eggler of course but I didn't have the horse. I walked to buy eggs and carry 'em to market. Oh, I strode out, Emmie. I was a brisk young sinner I can tell you and I'd take my fiddle with me and play it at fairs. Folks 'ud dance and sing all night and I'd laugh and play for 'em all night! (*He shakes his head and walks slowly away to the accompaniment of a lively fiddle tune*)

OTHER PEOPLE
by Geoff Saunders

Andrea, Stephen, Hilary and Duncan share a flat and, given their very different characters, it is no surprise that they do not get on particularly well. The play depicts half an hour in the life of this chaotic, argumentative household on an evening when important issues have arisen: the kitchen, scrupulously cleaned by Hilary, is in a mess again and neither Stephen nor Andrea can pay the rent. Hilary is nearing the end of her patience. This scene, which brings the play to its climax, begins just as Hilary has confronted Stephen about the rent.

Set: A living-room.

Cast: M2 F2.
Andrea, smartly-dressed, neurotic; early 20s. Stephen, scruffy, lazy; early 20s. Hilary, houseproud, efficient, highly-strung; slightly older. Duncan, conservative, meek; early 30s.

Playing time: 11 minutes.

The living-room of the flat shared by Stephen, Andrea, Hilary and Duncan. 6.30 p.m. Winter

The room looks comfortable and warm, though the decor is dated and in need of renewal. The seating — armchairs and a sofa — is mismatched and rather shabby. A stereo unit features prominently, with a small table nearby. There are three doors: these lead to the entrance hall, the kitchen and to the rest of the flat

Stephen and Hilary are on stage. Duncan enters

Duncan I'm going to have a bath, if that's all right. Anyone who wants to use the loo had better do so now.

Stephen Righto. Thanks Duncan, you timed that very well; I was beginning to buckle under the onslaught.

Duncan I'm sorry?

Stephen Hilary's doing her rent–police bit. Part of her Gestapo training.

Stephen exits through the door to the rest of the flat

Hilary See? I turn on my best professionally cheerful manner and what happens? He still gets upset. Damn. (*She pauses*) Would it surprise you, Duncan, that I was Head Girl at school? And a senior prefect before that, library monitor before that and even at primary school, milk monitor? I, and I alone, was allowed to put the straws in the milk bottles and carry the crate round the classroom. I've been an organizer all my life, God alone knows why. My family's completely disorganized. Grandparents, parents, both my brothers, totally hopeless. Late for everything, never looking tidy, never knowing what they're supposed to be doing. All having a wonderful time. And in the middle of it, me, desperately organizing things: meal times, bedtimes, cleaning shoes, worrying, worrying, worrying about having the right dinner money or whether my hair had been brushed enough times. And wanting, more than anything, to be able to let go, have fun, be a mess, be late without caring. But, somewhere in my family's past, a little, miserable organizing gene was introduced into the line, and, having skipped a few generations, blossomed with knobs on in me. I hate it. I hate having red hands because I wash them all the time, I hate the attacks of breathlessness I get if I miss the bus, I hate making myself late for work because I've had to run home and change my ear-rings because they don't co-ordinate with my skirt. I hate it. It drives me mad.

Pause

Duncan I've ... er ... I've written out my rent cheque. You can have it this evening.
Hilary I feel so guilty about Andrea. She needs so much support and I've always been able to give it to her in the past. But tonight — tonight I couldn't. I've had an awful day, Duncan, one of the worst. I've been dumped on all day: "Hilary, can you just do this for me?", "Hilary, can I talk this through with you?" Erica Bisley can't decide whether to have an abortion and spent three quarters of an hour in my office, crying, which is fine, but I was supposed to be able to give her sympathy, help, support, you name it, and deal with the monthly accounting which had to be done by four. To come home and find Andrea doing her drowning puppy routine and getting ready to dump all her problems on me was the last straw. I do feel sorry for her, I even like her, but, tonight, well, I could happily have shoved her in the microwave and run away laughing. Which is an awful thing to think about anyone.

Pause. Duncan looks distinctly uncomfortable

Thank you for having your cheque ready, anyway, Duncan. It's nice that there's one person here I can rely on.

Andrea enters

Which is more than can be said of ——
Andrea Were you talking about me?
Hilary I was about to be phenomenally rude about you, Andrea, but you ruined everything by turning up.
Andrea Oh.
Hilary Never mind. I'm sure another opportunity will present itself. It normally does. At the moment, the most important matter is the rent.
Andrea The rent?
Hilary It's due. I don't suppose you read Mr Craven's letter?
Andrea It had your name on it.
Hilary You lot are hopeless, you really are. Anything from Mr Craven will be for all of us, not just me, it stands to reason. Initiative is dead, long live apathy.
Andrea I can't pay.
Hilary Anyway, if you'd bothered to read his letter, you'd know that he's getting fed up with us constantly being late with the rent and ... what did you say?
Andrea I can't pay it.
Hilary This I don't believe.
Andrea Well, not all of it, anyway. I just don't have enough.
Hilary Oh brilliant. Mr Craven's going to have us all out before you can say "tenancy agreement".
Andrea Out?
Hilary Out. Evicted. On the street. If we don't pay. If *you* don't pay.
Andrea It's not my fault! You can't blame it on me!
Hilary Where's the money gone then, eh? Were you robbed?
Andrea No.
Hilary You're being blackmailed by someone who knows you have a facial hair problem?
Andrea No.
Duncan (*to Andrea*) Do you?
Andrea You keep out of this!
Hilary Duncan, please don't change the subject!
Duncan Sorry.
Hilary Well?

There is a pause. Andrea looks shamefaced

(*Light dawning*) That dress you wore to Katy's party ...
Andrea It was reduced.

Hilary To what?

Andrea Look, Hilary, I was really depressed. I had to cheer myself up somehow. I hadn't stopped crying for two days ——

Hilary As if I don't remember. How much?

Andrea — and I saw it in this shop window and I thought to myself, "That'll cheer me up! I'll buy it, however much it costs."

Hilary Andrea!

Andrea Well, I felt I was worth it!

Duncan It is a very pretty dress.

Hilary Thank you, Duncan. Andrea?

Andrea A hundred and seventy-five pounds.

Hilary And you paid cash.

Andrea (*beginning to cry*) My credit cards were stopped last month. And I'm four hundred pounds over my overdraft limit now.

Hilary You are a stupid, selfish little cow!

Andrea I'm sorry, I'm really sorry. I was so depressed. I had to do something. I know it was silly, but it did cheer me up for a while.

Hilary A couple of drinks would have had the same effect and cost considerably less! My God, you've really achieved classic status this time. One stupid, hideous, tarty ——

Andrea You said you liked it!

Hilary — overpriced little frock and four people get made homeless!

Andrea Don't, please, Hilary, you're hurting me! I'm sorry. I really am. Please forgive me. I'll feel awful if you don't forgive me.

Hilary How can I?

Andrea Duncan, you forgive me, don't you?

Duncan Well, gosh ... of course, Andrea, of course I do. No harm done.

Andrea See, Hilary: Duncan forgives me.

Hilary Oh, does he now. Well, I don't. God, it's all so easy for you isn't it? You spend half your time being a pain and the other half asking to be forgiven for being a pain, which is a pain in itself, and everything's meant to be all right. What you never do is make any bloody effort not to be a pain in the first place; you think that apologizing will make it all better. Until next time. Well, your apologies stink, Andrea. They mean nothing.

Andrea You hate me, don't you? You've always hated me. All of you! You've never even made an effort to like me!

Duncan begins to edge towards the door leading to the rest of the flat

Hilary (*to Andrea*) Well, you've never made any effort to be likeable! (*She sees Duncan moving away*) Where are you going?

Duncan My bath ...

Hilary Stephen's in there! Don't run away, I need a witness!

Duncan Oh, but, er ——

Hilary Stephen's right! You're a complete moral coward!

Andrea Don't be horrible to Duncan!

Hilary Why the hell not?

Andrea He's the only one of you who's ever shown me any kindness.

Hilary Only because he's too bloody frightened of you to say no!

Andrea That's enough, Hilary, please!

Hilary I'm wasting my breath here, I can tell.

Andrea This is just awful, awful! I don't need this in my life! I've been so happy here and now you've ruined it! Ruined it!

Andrea exits through the door to the rest of the flat. There is a considerable pause

Stephen enters

Stephen Good heavens, here's a surprise: Andrea's crying. I'm amazed this flat isn't flooded on a regular basis with her here.

Hilary Duncan, you heard her; she likes you. Could you talk to her about the rent? You work in a bank, after all; surely you know of some way she can sort herself out?

Duncan Well, I'd rather not, actually ... you see ——

Hilary Why not?

Duncan Well, she's so upset, she's very fragile ...

Hilary You saw the letter, Duncan. No rent, no flat. Craven is sick to death of us. Please just talk to her.

Duncan I couldn't; she'd only get more upset. I'm no good at that sort of thing anyway. I prefer not to get involved.

Hilary You are the completest mouse, aren't you? I've never known such a coward!

Duncan It isn't cowardice, not at all. I just happen to believe that it's more ... mature ... to leave people to make up their own minds about things.

Stephen You're mature then, are you Duncan? Is never having an opinion mature? Is never taking responsibility for anything mature? Is running away from any emotional confrontation mature?

Duncan One has to learn to let people live their own lives in their own way.

Stephen You pompous git!

Duncan Was that mature?

Stephen I've never claimed to be mature. In fact, I'm quite glad now that I'm not. If being mature means being a spineless, characterless nonentity like you, I want to be a child forever!

Hilary Don't worry, Stephen, you will. Now, chaps before we get into round two of this fascinating moral debate, can we please discuss the rent problem?

Stephen You're calling a meeting?

Hilary Well, no, not exactly, but we've got to do something haven't we?

Stephen You mean *you've* got to do something. You're taking charge.

Hilary No, not at all.

Stephen Why do you always take charge, eh? Suddenly you're the flat's rent collector and bully, and no-one asked you to be.

Hilary If I didn't do it, who would? Duncan's afraid to ask anyone for so much as a penny, you're too bloody idle and Andrea would probably burst into tears at the thought. It's got to be me.

Stephen But why does anyone have to do it? We're here collectively.

Hilary Not in the political sense.

Stephen All right, no, but ... well, we are all, supposedly, equal: why should one person have to take responsibility for any one task?

Hilary Because if she didn't — note I say she because it's always me, isn't it — if she didn't no-one else would and we'd be out on our ears.

Stephen Typical fascist scare-mongering tactics, those ...

Hilary My God, you can be so stupid sometimes! Mr Craven has every right to throw us out!

Stephen Perhaps he has, but that doesn't give you the right to lord it over everyone else.

Hilary One day you'll stop being clever and start being intelligent; then you'll realize what a prize pillock you've been for the past twenty-odd years. You don't do anything, you just sit about making smart comments and picking holes in other people. You make me sick.

Duncan Hilary!

Hilary (*to Duncan*) And so do you! You may be St Francis of Assisi in terms of maturity but you're positively Neanderthal in every other respect. (*She pauses*) Right, I've had enough of this. I'm going to clear up the kitchen.

Hilary exits into the kitchen. She returns almost immediately

No. I'm not. Why the hell should I?

Duncan No, that's fine, Hilary, I'm happy to do it.

Hilary You didn't make the mess.

Duncan No, but I feel a bit guilty, really; perhaps I should help you out a bit more.

Hilary Great. Now I'm responsible for making people feel guilty. And, Duncan, it's not a case of helping me by clearing up, it's a case of doing your fair share. The sooner you people stop thinking of me as the housekeeper who has, occasionally, to be honoured with help, the better. We are, as Stephen points out, a collective; this should mean but doesn't, as yet, that everything is shared equally, including the cleaning. After all, I can't be the only one who doesn't like living in a pigsty.

Stephen My God, you're terrifying! Mess really offends you, doesn't it? Any kind of disorder offends your tidy middle-class, middle-aged, anally-retentive mind!

Hilary Whose crockery is that on the draining board? And that teapot? I mean, to whom do they actually belong?

Stephen Well, they're mine actually, why?

Hilary Right.

Hilary storms off into the kitchen. A series of crockery smashes is heard, continuing under the following dialogue

(*Off*) Here's some mess for you! Clear this bloody lot up yourself!

Stephen (*rushing to the kitchen door*) What the hell are you doing?

Hilary (*off*) You wanted a mess? Here's a mess! It's all yours!

Stephen That's my stuff you're breaking! Leave it!

Stephen exits into the kitchen

The smashing noises stop; then there is the sound of a very loud slap and a cry from Stephen

Stephen enters from the kitchen, clutching his cheek

She bloody hit me! She's gone mad! Completely mad!

The crashing continues. Hilary is screaming, off, half with joy, half with rage. Stephen stands near the door watching her. Duncan retreats into a corner

Andrea enters

Andrea Oh no, what's happening?

Duncan Hilary's upset. She's smashing up the kitchen.

Andrea Stop it, Hilary! Stop it! You're making me feel awful! I would have washed up, I really would have, but I was so upset I just couldn't. Stop it, Hilary, please stop it! I've said I'm sorry. (*She falls into an armchair and curls up, weeping noisily*) I'm sorry, I'm sorry! Oh, God, I hate you! I hate you! I hate you all!

There are more crashes. Then silence

Hilary, dishevelled and exhausted, emerges from the kitchen and stands wearily in the doorway

The others all look at Hilary

Hilary smiles

PACK OF LIES
by Hugh Whitemore

Based on the true story of the Krogers, an American couple living in London who were convicted of spying for the Russians in 1961, Hugh Whitemore has constructed a powerfully moving fictionalized account of the events leading up to the arrest. The appeal of this play is partly its capture of domesticity and neighbourly friendship in a suburb in 1960s London and partly the conflict of loyalty and betrayal.

The first excerpt establishes the close relationship between the outgoing Helen and her neighbour Barbara, a suburban housewife who finds it hard to form close friendships. Stewart, the MI5 official introduces the background.

Set: The kitchen, hall and sitting-room of a semi-detached house in a London suburb. Period: 1960-61.

Cast: M1 F3.
Stewart, MI5 official; middle age. Barbara, neat, kindly, suburban housewife; late 30s. Helen, tall American, very casual, friendly neighbour; 40s. Julie, Barbara's teenage daughter.

Playing time: 9 minutes.

Stewart enters and addresses the audience. He is in his forties, wearing a raincoat and a dark blue suit. He might be mistaken for an averagely successful provincial solicitor

Stewart Eventually our investigations led us to a street in Ruislip. It was autumn, nineteen-sixty. Ruislip, I should explain, is a suburb of London. It lies to the north-west of the metropolis and is one of the places one drives through on the way to Oxford. That is how I remember it, at any rate: as somewhere glimpsed briefly through car windows, generally at dusk, generally in the rain—neat rows of semi-detached houses; small front gardens, each with its square of lawn and herbaceous border; bay windows; clipped hedges; and every so often, where the downstairs curtains have yet to be drawn, the bluish flickering light of a television set. And that, since all stories have to begin somewhere, is where this particular story began for me—or rather this particular chapter of this particular story, for the case as a

whole has been occupying my attention for several months. It is, by the way, by
and large—true.

The Lights fade

Stewart exits

The Lights come up. Dusk

*Barbara and Helen are coming downstairs. Barbara is carrying a dress; Helen is
wearing an almost-completed dress (some of it is still only pinned together), and
carrying the dress she arrived in*

Helen Where do you want me to go?
Barbara In the sitting-room.
Helen (*going into the sitting-room*) Jesus, it's cold in here. You ought to get central
heating.
Barbara (*switching on the electric fire*) Well, one day.

*Helen drapes her own dress over a chair and positions herself in the centre of the
room*

Helen Okay, what do you want me to do?
Barbara Just stand still. I want to make sure that it fits all right.
Helen God, you're a fast worker.
Barbara I've got to get a move on if it's going to be ready for Christmas. Hold your
arm up. Let me look at the sleeve.
Helen Like this? (*She extends her arm*)
Barbara Yes, that's fine.

*Thus for a moment, Barbara and Helen stand face-to-face, with their arms extended,
almost like ballroom dancers, Helen, realizing this similarity, suddenly grabs Barbara
by the waist and whirls her across the room*

Helen Hey, come on—let's dance!
Barbara (*protesting but laughing*) Stop it, Helen, stop it.
Helen (*singing*) "Shall we dance, pom pom pom pom—Shall we dance deedle-
eedle"—come on.
Barbara (*laughing*) Oh, Helen, you are a fool.
Helen Do you ever go dancing? I never go dancing. I used to love dancing when I
was a girl.
Barbara Where could you dance round here?
Helen We could organize something. Why not? We could have dances in the afternoon.
What are they called? Tea dances. We could have tea dances in Cranley Drive.

Barbara Who'd come?

Helen Lots of people, I bet.

Barbara All the men are at work.

Helen Okay, so we could ask some of the boys from school.

Barbara They're a bit young.

Helen Who cares? They're a good-looking bunch.

Barbara Some of them.

Helen That guy Julie likes—he's really good-looking.

Barbara You mean Malcolm Granger?

Helen Don't you think he's good-looking?

Barbara He's completely irresponsible. Have you seen the way he races around on that motorbike of his? He'll get himself killed one of these days.

Helen If you're worried, tell her.

Barbara I can't.

Helen Why not?

Barbara She thinks I worry about everything.

Helen She's right, you do.

Barbara I try not to.

Helen It's your nature, you can't help it—she knows that, I know that, we all know that. (*She squeezes Barbara's hand comfortingly*) Now, listen, here's what to do if you're worried: you tell her she's too young to go riding about on motorcycles.

Barbara I've told her that already.

Helen Then she won't. She's a good girl. She'll do what you say.

Barbara, unconvinced, says nothing. Helen grins

You know something? Malcolm Granger has a beautiful body. I saw him at the pool last summer. Beautiful! Maybe I should lure him round to the house when Peter goes to one of his antiquarian book sales. What do you think? Shall I introduce him to the more sophisticated charms of an older woman?

Barbara does not respond; she is preoccupied with her anxieties about Julie

Barbara I wish you'd say something to her.

Helen Say what?

Barbara About going on the motorbike.

Helen looks at Barbara

Helen You really are worried.

Barbara Yes, I am.

Helen What can I say?

Barbara She'd listen to you.

Helen What about Bob? Why doesn't he talk to her?

Barbara You know what Bob's like. She can't do a thing wrong as far as he's concerned. (*Brief pause*) Please. There's no-one else I can ask ... Please.

Helen hesitates

Helen Okay.

Barbara (*relieved*) Would you?

Helen Okay, if it'll make you any happier.

Barbara Well, it would.

Helen Okay.

Barbara Thanks. I hate asking.

Helen Don't be silly. (*Deliberately changing the mood*) It's beautiful, this dress—really beautiful. You're such a clever girl, Barbara. You do so many things real good. You've got golden hands.

Barbara What a funny thing to say.

Helen Well, it's true.

Julie opens the front door. She's wearing a raincoat, scarf, and gloves over her school uniform. She carries a satchel

Julie (*calling*) Mum!

Barbara (*calling*) In here, Julie. (*Whispering to Helen*) Don't tell her I asked you to say anything.

Helen Of course I won't. Don't worry.

Julie enters the sitting-room and kisses Barbara

Julie Hallo, Mum. Hallo, Auntie Helen.

Helen Hi, Julie, sweetheart.

Barbara How was choir practice?

Julie Boring. Every year it's the *Messiah*. If only we could do something different. It's so boring doing the same old thing year after year.

Barbara Everything's boring as far as you're concerned.

Julie The dress looks smashing.

Helen Doesn't it? (*She starts to change dresses*)

Barbara It's quite an easy pattern.

Helen Don't be so modest. Be proud. If I could make a dress like this, I'd be really proud of myself.

Barbara You could if you tried.

Helen Honey, I couldn't and you know it. I've got five thumbs and no finesse.

Barbara (*smiling*) Oh, Helen.

Helen It's true. I remember, when I was a kid, one of the farm hands saying to me—

I'd just done something stupid or clumsy or both—and he said, "God help the man you marry, Miss Helen, you may be okay with cattle, but you'll be a disaster in the home."

Barbara Oh, what nonsense.

Helen He was right.

Barbara (*to Julie*) Don't start making yourself comfortable, Julie. Remember: homework first.

Julie Can't I even have a cup of tea?

Barbara Do you know what the time is? Your father will be home in a minute.

Helen Come on, Barbara, give the poor girl a cup of tea.

Barbara You spoil her. (*She gets up and goes to the kitchen*)

Helen Well, why not? (*To Julie*) Hey—I see the folk down the street are having a bonfire party tomorrow. Are you going?

Julie (*dismissively*) Oh no.

She gets up, picks up her satchel, coat, scarf, and gloves, crosses into the hall and into the kitchen, putting her things down on the chair at the table. Helen follows and sits at the table

Helen Too old for fireworks, huh?

Julie I've got better things to do.

Barbara Yes, she's got better things to do—like homework. (*To Julie*) Cake or biscuits?

Julie (*irritated*) Oh, Mum ...! Neither, I *told* you.

Barbara (*to Helen*) Have you heard about this stupid diet?

Julie It's not stupid. Look at Sue Galleyford.

Barbara She's always been a big girl.

Julie Only because she eats so much.

Barbara Well, I think it's ridiculous—someone of your age ...

The telephone rings

Julie I'll go—it's probably Maureen.

Barbara Hang your coat up! How many more times?

Julie Sorry, sorry. (*She picks up her raincoat and goes towards the hall*)

Barbara If it's that insurance man, tell him to ring back later.

Julie Okay. (*She closes the kitchen door. She hangs her raincoat on a peg and then answers the telephone*)

Barbara Would you like a cup of tea?

Helen No thanks, I'd better not.

Barbara makes tea for Julie

Say, whatever happened to the Pearsons?

Barbara The Pearsons ...?

Helen Brian and Betty, down at number twenty-three.

Barbara They're all right, as far as I know.

Helen I've been round there half a dozen times and there's never anyone at home. I just wondered if they're okay.

Julie returns

Julie Who's that?

Helen The Pearsons.

Julie They've gone on holiday. (*To Barbara*) It's for you, Mum.

Helen (*to Julie*) At this time of the year?

Julie Only for a week. They're back tomorrow.

Barbara goes to the door

Barbara (*to Julie*) Who is it?

Julie A man.

Barbara What man?

Julie He didn't say.

Barbara Oh, Julie ... (*She goes into the hall, closing the door. She goes to the telephone*)

Julie pours tea for herself

Julie Do you want some?

Helen No, thanks.

Julie sips her tea; Helen watches her

Well, now, young lady, and how are you today?

Julie Fine.

Helen Good.

Julie (*mock American accent*) Fine and dandy.

Helen Let's hope it stays that way.

Julie (*glancing at Helen*) Why shouldn't it?

Helen You tell me.

Julie turns, frowning, to face Helen

Julie What's the matter, Auntie Helen?

Helen I thought you weren't supposed to go riding about on motorcycles.

Julie Oh.

Helen Yes—oh.

Julie When did you see me?

Helen The other afternoon, with young Mr you-know-who.

Julie Malcolm.

Helen Yes, Malcolm. I thought all that was strictly *verboten*.

Julie He was only bringing me home from school—and he's very careful.

Helen Your momma doesn't think so.

Julie You know what she's like: she worries about everything.

Helen Only because she loves you.

Julie She keeps treating me like a little girl. She doesn't realize that I'm grown up.

Helen looks at Julie; she smiles affectionately

Helen No. No, and I don't suppose she ever will. (*She goes to Julie and kisses her*) Okay, I won't say a word. It'll be our secret. Don't do anything silly, do you hear me?

Julie (*smiling*) I won't. Thanks.

Barbara returns

Barbara Come on, Julie, what about that homework?

Julie (*to Helen, smiling*) See what I mean?

Barbara See what?

Julie Nothing. (*She picks up her cup of tea and goes to the door*) Who was that on the phone?

Barbara Someone for your father.

Julie slings her satchel over her shoulder

Julie 'Bye, Auntie Helen.

Helen 'Bye, sweetheart—work hard.

Julie I will.

Julie exits and goes upstairs

Helen She's a good girl.

Barbara finds Julie's gloves on a chair

Barbara If only she wasn't so untidy.

Helen has now changed back into her clothes

Helen There are worse things in life than being untidy.

Barbara You ought to try living with her. It takes at least half an hour to clear up the mess after she's gone to school: books and clothes all over the place—not to mention all the washing and ironing and mending. She doesn't do a thing for herself, it's disgraceful, really.

Helen Say what you like—she's a good girl and I'm very fond of her.

Barbara glances at Helen, mildly surprised by her uncharacteristically serious tone of voice

Barbara Yes—well, she's very fond of you.

Helen I hope so.

Barbara You know she is.

Helen I guess I do. (*She sighs*) I'd give a lot to have a daughter like Julie. You don't know how lucky you are.

The second scene emphasizes the strain Barbara is under as she tries to maintain normality and sustain a friendly relationship with Helen while coping with the MI5 girls who are using her house as a surveillance post to watch the Krogers.

Cast: F4.
Thelma, sturdily-built ex-regular-Army girl working for MI5; late 20s. Sally, pleasant, middle-class, working for MI5; about 30. Barbara. Helen Kroger.

Playing time: 8 minutes.

The Lights come up. Day

The back door opens and Thelma enters from the garden; she is wearing a crash helmet, goggles, a waterproof cape, and leggings

Thelma Mrs Jackson? It's me. Sally?

Sally walks down the stairs. She is about thirty; pleasant, but rather plain; middle-class. She wears a sweater, skirt and raincoat; she is carrying an umbrella. She goes to the kitchen

Sally You're late.

Thelma I know, sorry. There's been an accident on the Western Avenue and the traffic's murder. (*She takes off her motorcycling gear*) What about that rain—did you see it? I really thought the end of the world had come.

Sally That motorbike of yours makes a hell of a noise. Are you sure Mr Stewart said you could bring it?

Thelma Of course—why not? There are dozens of motorbikes around here. You don't think the Krogers are going to notice one extra, do you? (*Looking around*) Where's Mrs Jackson?

Sally Out shopping.

Thelma Poor thing. I hope she didn't get caught in that storm. (*She drapes her cape and leggings over a chair*) God, I'm dying for a cup of tea. How about you?

Sally No, thanks. I've just had one.

Thelma goes to the sink and fills the electric kettle

Thelma Look, don't worry—I always park the bike round the corner. I park it somewhere different every day—and never outside the house. (*Switching on the kettle*) So what's been happening this morning?

Sally Nothing much—just routine comings and goings.

Thelma As per usual. (*She yawns*) It's going to be a long job, this one.

Sally Do you think so?

Thelma Don't you?

Sally (*shrugging*) I don't know.

Thelma Oh yes—this is a biggie. I can smell it. (*Spooning tea into the pot*) Mr Stewart went to the American Embassy yesterday—twice.

Sally How do you know?

Thelma Sylvia told me. She went out with Bill last night. He was duty driver yesterday, and he told her. Twice in a day! That must mean it's a biggie.

Thelma takes a bottle of milk from the fridge and puts it on the table

Sally Don't leave the milk there. You'll have Mrs Jackson tut-tutting at you.

Thelma (*not understanding*) Why?

Sally She always puts milk in a jug, haven't you noticed? She obviously thinks milk in bottles is common.

Thelma makes no response; she takes the jug from a cupboard and pours the milk into it. Sally watches

Can you imagine what her life must be like? Dusting and washing and ironing and polishing and cooking. God. No wonder she's as dull as she is.

Thelma I like her.

Sally looks at her

Sally Yes, you do, don't you? (*She buttons her raincoat*) She thinks we're going at the end of the week.
Thelma Did she say so?
Sally Sort of. She keeps dropping hints.
Thelma Like what?
Sally "It'll seem strange without you next week", that sort of thing, you know.
Thelma What did you say?
Sally Well, nothing. What could I say?

Thelma sighs, but says nothing; she is standing by the window, waiting for the kettle to boil

Right, then—I'll be off.
Thelma Right.

Sally goes to the back door

Clark Gable died.
Sally Yes, I heard it on the radio.
Thelma I think it's really sad, don't you? No more Clark Gable. Gone forever.

The front door opens. Sally and Thelma swing round, suddenly alert

Barbara enters; she is wearing a raincoat and carrying shopping bags

Mrs Jackson?
Barbara (*closing the front door*) Hallo. What a dreadful morning! Did you see that rain?
Sally Wasn't it awful?
Thelma I thought the end of the world had come. (*She makes the tea*)
Sally At least you didn't get too wet.
Barbara No, I was lucky. Pour me a cup, would you, Thelma? (*Putting the shopping bags on the table*) Those bags weigh a ton.
Sally Is it raining now?
Barbara Not really—but there's more on the way, by the look of it.
Sally I'd better go. (*To Thelma, as she goes to the back door*) I'll see you tomorrow.
Thelma It's Pat tomorrow—I don't come back till Saturday.
Sally Okay, I'll see you then. Bye, Mrs Jackson.
Barbara 'Bye, Sally.
Thelma 'Bye.

Sally exits

Barbara She's a nice girl.

Thelma (*pouring the tea*) Milk and two sugars?
Barbara Yes, please. (*She starts to unload the shopping*) I got some sausages for lunch. Do you like sausages?
Thelma I love them—but you really must stop cooking all these meals for us.
Barbara I'd hardly call sausages a meal.
Thelma Mr Stewart would be furious if he knew.
Barbara Don't tell him, then.
Thelma (*grinning*) Don't worry, I won't.

Barbara takes some tins of food to the store cupboard

(*Giving a cup of tea to Barbara*) Here ...
Barbara Thanks.

Barbara and Thelma sip their tea. Pause

Thelma Clark Gable died, did you know?
Barbara Yes. What was it—a heart attack or something?
Thelma Yes, I think so. Sad isn't it. (*Pause*) Mind you, he wasn't as good as Gregory Peck. Or Richard Burton. I think he's wonderful. Did you see him on TV the other night?
Barbara No.
Thelma He was wonderful. Those eyes. That voice.

The front doorbell rings

Silently, furtively, Thelma gathers her motorcycling gear and hurries upstairs

Barbara waits, tense, until the coast is clear. Then she goes to the front door and opens it

Helen enters

Helen Hi, honey, how are you?
Barbara Helen ...
Helen I've brought this tin back. (*She displays the cake-tin she is carrying, and walks to the kitchen*)
Barbara Oh yes ... thanks. (*She closes the front door and follows Helen*)
Helen Those little cookies were deelicious, Barbara. So light and crisp—yummy! How do you do it?
Barbara Oh—just a knack.
Helen Some knack. (*She turns, smiling, to Barbara*) So how's life? Is everything okay?

Barbara Yes, fine.

Helen How's Julie? I haven't seen her for ages.

Barbara She's fine—um ... working hard.

Helen Come to that, I haven't seen you either. You gave me those cookies on Monday, and here we are—it's Thursday. (*Mock-accusingly*) Have you been avoiding me, Barbara?

Barbara (*a stab of alarm*) Have I what?

Helen A joke, dear—I was joking.

Barbara Sorry, I didn't hear what you said.

Helen You're not mad at me, are you?

Barbara What?

Helen Well, are you?

Barbara No, no, of course not. I've been a bit busy, that's all.

Helen Busy doing what?

Barbara Oh, nothing much.

Helen Busy doing nothing much ...?

Barbara Well, you know how it is.

Helen (*lightly*) No, I don't. I'm beginning to feel like the girl in the bad breath commercial. (*She smiles*)

No response from Barbara

How's the dress coming along?

Barbara The dress ...?

Helen My party dress.

Barbara Almost finished. Ready next week.

Helen Terrific! (*Glancing at the empty cups on the table*) Hey, what's all this?

Barbara What's all what?

Helen Two cups of tea on the kitchen table. Don't tell me you've got a lover hiding away upstairs.

Barbara Oh dear—fancy that. I haven't even washed up yet. (*Quickly plunging the cups into the sink*) Isn't that awful?

Helen (*staring at Barbara*) Are you sure you're all right, honey? You look kinda pale.

Barbara No, it's nothing, just a headache.

Helen Take a pill.

Barbara I have.

Helen Take another pill.

Barbara Yes, all right.

Helen I'll go get you one, shall I?

Barbara No, please ...

Helen You know me; pills and potions keep me going. I'll run upstairs and see what you've got.

Barbara It's all right, Helen. Please don't fuss!

Helen frowns, startled by Barbara's irritability

Helen Fuss ...?
Barbara I'm sorry, I'm sorry. I didn't mean to be rude.
Helen You be just as rude as you like, honey. I mean, jeeze, if you can't shout at friends, who can you shout at?
Barbara I didn't mean to shout. I'm sorry.

Helen goes to Barbara and takes her by the hand

Helen Look, I'll tell you what. Why don't you put your feet up, go to bed—read a book or something, huh?
Barbara Yes, perhaps I will.
Helen It'll only make things worse if you try to keep going.
Barbara Yes.
Helen How about some magazines—Would you like some magazines?
Barbara No, please—I don't feel like reading.
Helen Are you sure?
Barbara (*nodding*) I think I'd rather just go to sleep.
Helen Okay, you know best.

Helen goes to the front door; Barbara follows

Now look—if there's anything I can do—and I mean anything ...
Barbara That's very kind of you, Helen.
Helen Well, for God's sake—what are friends for? (*She smiles at Barbara*) You take care of yourself.
Barbara You too.
Helen Go right upstairs and have a good long rest.
Barbara Yes, I will.
Helen Good girl. See you tomorrow. *Ciao.*

Helen opens the front door and goes out

Barbara closes the front door. She shuts her eyes and leans back against the wall. Suddenly, she feels the bile rising in her throat; she runs to the kitchen and vomits into the sink

Thelma walks down the stairs; she pauses halfway

Thelma Mrs Jackson ...?

No response

   Are you all right, Mrs Jackson?
Barbara Leave me alone—just leave me alone!

THE PASSING-OUT PARADE
by Anne Valery

It is 1944 in the Auxiliary Territorial Service Barrack Room at an Army Base in Pontefract, Yorkshire. An assortment of characters, the new ATS recruits, are enduring the early days of training with humour, homesickness and camaraderie. But, as we see in this scene from Act One, their relationships also produce conflict and drama, due in part to the class divisions between Howard and Smith-Jenkins and the rest of the girls. ('Stacking', a way of folding bedding, and 'boning', a method of polishing shoes, are Army terminology. A 'button stick' hooked behind the buttons on the uniform so that cleaning fluid did not get into the cloth when the buttons were polished.)

Set: An Army barrack room in the Second World War. Period: early 1944.

Cast: F9.
Corporal Segraves, kindly but with authority; 38. Sally Stokes, an ill-used orphan and devout Catholic; about 18. Private Lil, a Cockney 'old soldier'; early 20s. Anne Howard, upper middle-class; 18. Diana Smith-Jenkins, upper middle-class, very sophisticated; 18. Maureen Crab, suburban Londoner; 22. 'Basher' Beasley, North Country; late 20s. Val Davis, Jewish, East End of London; early 20s. Sergeant Joyce Pickering, from Worcestershire; 40s.

Playing time: 17 minutes.

Segraves enters with letters and parcels

Segraves Right, you horrible lot, let's have a touch of the tranquil morts — dead quiet, to the uninitiated. Post!

General excitement. Lil is expectant. Beasley takes a pill

Stokes—one. Howard—two. Beasley—letter, parcel. Crab—three. Jenkins—parcel. And I hope you're all resilient, because Sergeant Pickering's raring to go for an inspection of room *and* person. And as you've not yet learnt how to stack, it's *making* beds. (*She inspects the beds*)

Stokes sits at the table and reads her letter

Stokes (*reading*) "Dear Child, Your mother has asked me to write this letter for her. She wishes to thank you for the ten shillings and to tell you she lit a candle to our Blessed Lady. You'll be sorry to hear that The Home was hit, though the good Lord saw fit to spare us. Minnie Simpson—who I believe was a special friend of yours—is now working at your old job as scullery maid. She sends the enclosed handkerchief, which she embroidered in the rest period. We all pray for you daily, that you may remain in the path of obedience in which you were raised. May God keep you. Reverend Mother. P.S. Father O'Brian wishes to remind you of the penance you were given." (*She strokes the handkerchief, in tears*)

Jenkins and Howard laugh at a private joke

Segraves Jenkins! Howard! Get on with it.
Howard Sorry, Corporal.
Jenkins (*to Howard*) Haven't you heard? *Here* sorry's not enough.

Lil looks respectfully at Jenkins

Segraves I'll deal with you later. (*She goes to Lil's bed*) Very neat. Very neat indeed! No bulges. No irregularities!
Crab (*reading her letter*) "Darling Maureen, Praise the Lord and pass the ammunition, Dad's gone off on one of his trips. For what it's worth I enclose a photo he turned up. And guess what? Yours Truly has a new blouse—don't ask, no coupons. And hands off. It's pink satin with buttons like tiny bows; so think of me at the social Saturday. Mr Johnson sends his regards, as always! From your ever-loving Mum, Elsie."
Segraves (*at Crab's bed*) Crab—no pyjamas lingering. And let's see if you've polished your insteps.

Crab lifts her foot

(*To the room in general*) And remember, if any of you are bright enough to make driver, boot studs are polished ditto. (*To Davis*) Somehow, I don't think you've used your button stick on that. (*She points to a buckle*)
Beasley (*reading her letter*) "Hallo, Pal, I'm sending you—you know what—separate! Our Bett's been rehoused at number seventeen, but she still suffers from them sweats. As Gran says: Hitler's such a little fidget! Went to Eighth Airforce dance with Chuck Kaminski. And guess what: it were one nylon afore and one after as per usual. That's all for now, so keep your legs crossed and maybe this'll find you as it leaves me. Some hope! Your ever loving Pal, Blanche."
Segraves (*going to Beasley's bed*) What's this then—Digging for Victory?
Beasley It's noble, is that!

Segraves Not the word I would have chosen. Now remember, Girls—don't let me down.

Segraves exits

Howard (*reading her letter*) "Darling, thank you for your very amusing letter. Poor Uncle Charles was rather shocked, bless him, and said to be sure to tell you that a chap sticks by her unit. Take care and wrap up in this ghastly wind. We're very proud of you. All my love, Mummy. P.S. Some fondant creams, and a pound to help out."

Jenkins stares at a card—without expression

Jenkins (*reading the card*) "Ordered by Major Smith Jenkins—Fortnum and Mason." (*She examines the contents of the parcel*) Dundee Cake, Senior Service, tortoiseshell cigarette-holder and matching case.

Lil polishes her shoes, the polish bubbling on the stove. Crab is looking at her father's photograph. Davis goes to Lil

Davis What you doing?
Lil Boning! (*Taking off Pickering*) "i.e.: rubbing in with said handle of said toothbrush, not forgetting bubbling polish what soaks in easier"!

Howard takes her shoes to the table and copies Lil

Davis (*to Lil*) Know it all, don't yer?
Lil (*flatly*) Not always. (*Talking without thinking, because she is watching Howard*) My Johnny used to say he got such a shine on his that if he got 'em under my skirt, he could see me twat.
Davis So who's Johnny?
Lil Forget it.

Lil walks to Howard at the table, bumping into Beasley, who drops her bottle of pills. Lil has always been rude to Howard, or ignored her

(*Friendly*) Hey, Howard—got a light?
Howard (*happily surprised*) Yes. Yes, of course.

Howard runs to her bed and fetches her matches. Jenkins turns away in disgust. Lil backs to the table and takes Howard's shoes, holding them behind her back

Lil (*taking a light*) Ta.
Howard Any time—mate.

Howard turns at Beasley's shout—she has grabbed Crab's photograph out of her hand. Lil backs to her locker and puts Howard's shoes inside

Beasley Hey Crab, I thought you said yer dad weren't in Forces? Oh my Gawd, he's a ruddy Blackshirt!

The room is still—horrified. Crab grabs her photograph

Crab Yes well—that was in thirty-seven. And Mosley's not all wrong you know. Did a lot of good, all things considered.
Jenkins Name one?
Lil (*liking Jenkins*) Yer, go on.

Lil walks towards Crab, menacingly. Crab backs to her bed

Crab Well—take Edgware.
Lil No thanks.
Crab It was a nice place before them German yids came! No, I mean it. Swamped us, they did. Couldn't even get into Lipton's for them "zitting" and "zatting" and holding us up. It was ...

Segraves enters

Segraves Ten-Shun!

Pickering enters like a thunderbolt

The Girls stand to attention by their beds on which their clothes and kit are laid out

Pickering Morning, Corporal Segraves.
Segraves Morning, Sergeant Pickering.
Pickering Right, my lovelies. Ready for The Off, are we?

Pickering paces the room starting with Stokes. Segraves follows with a clipboard. Crab starts to tie her tie

(*Kindly*) Careful of that collar, Stokes. (*To Davis*) Hair on collar, Davis. (*To Crab*) And when a sergeant enters the room you stand to attention, whatever your disorder. Understood? (*She looks at her face*) And you can wipe that muck off. (*To Lil*) Not bad. Not bad at all. (*She moves to Beasley's bed*) What's this, then? The church stall attacked by mice? Re-do it! Well, well, I can see none of you lot worked in window display——

Lil coughs

— with the exception of Private Lil. When Corporal Segraves says an inspection, she means—(*to Segraves*)—if I'm not mistaken—a well-made bed, unimaginative and sticking to the book. Not something wooshed through a wind tunnel. (*At Howard's bed*) Very neat. Very neat indeed. A pity about the shoes!

Howard (*looking at her feet*) Shoes? But—but they *were* there, Sergeant. (*She points to the table*)

Pickering But they're not now, are they?

Howard No, Sergeant.

Pickering (*moving to Jenkins's bed*) Walked off on their own, have they? Well, if they don't strut right back again, you can report to the Charge Room for loss of Army Issue. Am I getting to you?

Howard Yes, Sergeant.

Pickering (*to Jenkins*) It'll pass. (*To the Girls*) Could be worse, I suppose. (*She catches sight of a bottle of cider by Crab's bed, and fumes*) In all my years in His Majesty's Service, hundreds—nay, thousands of girls have passed through my hands, and I have never seen such *horrible havoc* as I have in this room. Never! (*She picks up the bottle and gives it to Segraves*)

Pickering exits, speaking as she goes

(*Off*) I just hope Company F will cheer me up. (*Bellowing*) Morning, Corporal Smithers.

Segraves (*furiously*) As—you—were!

Segraves gives the bottle to Stokes and exits

Lil Don't say I didn't warn you.

Lil lights a cigarette as Howard stalks downstage

Howard (*quoting Lil back at her*) So who's an "officer-licking slut" now?

Stunned silence

Lil Yer what?

Howard You heard me. *You pinched my shoes.*

Lil Why should I pinch 'em?

Howard I don't know. But I bloody well know where they are. (*Before Lil can stop her, she dives into Lil's locker and pulls out her shoes, which she throws at Lil*)

Lil It were only a joke!

Howard You bastard! You rotten filthy little bastard!

The Girls go rigid. Lil swings round, her face haggard with venom

Lil Nobody, but nobody calls me *that*, mate.

Lil hits Howard across the face and follows through with a stomach punch. Howard buckles. They roll towards the stove, fighting viciously. The Girls are stunned, except for Jenkins who shouts: "Go it, Howard." At the stove, Lil mounts Howard's back and hits it with a lump of coal. Howard goes berserk. She kicks Lil off, leaps up and by mistake hits Beasley—who is trying to separate them—before grabbing Lil's arm and pushing it up her back. Lil screams. Everyone except Jenkins protests. The fight is very nasty. Beasley collapses on her bed

Howard You thieving little bitch. Well you can damn well apologize. (*She pushes Lil's arm*) Now!
Lil Up yours. Christ, you'll break it.
Howard That's right. So—are you sorry?
Lil Sod off.
Howard (*pushing further*) Come along.
Lil Ahhhhhh! OK. OK.
Howard And apologize.
Lil (*through her teeth*) Sorry I'm sure.
Howard That's more like it.

They stagger to their feet holding on to each other. They are panting and exhausted. Stokes creeps back to her bed, frightened

Lil (*sarcastically*) Going to nark, are we?
Howard What?
Lil Tell Pickering?
Howard You must be joking.
Lil Yes, well ... (*She grins*) You look terrible.
Howard (*grinning*) I see you've managed to keep in your curlers.
Lil Take more than you to shift that bloody lot! Give it to you, Howard; for a four-foot nothing you can't half pack a wallop.
Howard For an old campaigner, you're not so dusty either.
Lil Not, am I? (*She nurses her arm*) And don't you ever call me that name again, do you hear me?
Howard What name?
Lil You know.
Howard You mean "bastard"?

The Girls mutter. Howard realizes the implication. Where they come from, it is the final and all-too-often accurate description

Oh! Yes. Of course. Gosh I'm sorry. No, *honestly*, I—really I am.
Lil Yeah, well—you forgets the shoes and we'll say no more. OK?

Howard OK! Shake on it?

A pause. Lil wipes her hands on her skirt. Howard copies. With great dignity, they hold out their hands

> *Jenkins, believing Howard has betrayed her class and dignity, goes out, slamming the door*

Howard's hand drops as she watches Jenkins. Then she turns back to Lil. She has made up her mind. She holds out her hand, and they shake

Lil (*ruffling Howard's hair*) Thirsty work, punch-ups.
Howard You're telling me.
Lil Right then, drinks on me in the N.A.A.F.I. So come on, let's get cracking.

They turn to leave and see Beasley lying—eyes closed, hands on her stomach

'Ere, you all right?
Beasley Bloody delirious!
Howard You don't look all right—does she, Lil?
Crab (*moving forward*) Know what, I think she's got a bun in the oven! (*To Beasley*) You have, haven't you?
Beasley What if I have?
Crab Told you!
Howard Oh my God—I hit her! Lil, I hit her! (*To Beasley*) Look, don't move. Don't do anything, I'll fetch the M.O.
Beasley You'll do no such thing!
Lil (*understanding*) Howard—leave it.
Howard But she'll ...
Lil *Leave it*, I say.
Howard But she might have a miscarriage!
Beasley I should be so lucky!
Crab I knew you were. All those pills.
Lil Me sis tried 'em, and now she's got little Sid, bless him.
Howard But if they don't work?
Beasley (*getting up*) Oh Gawd—*in case*, stupid. T'otherwise it's your friendly back street abortionist, *if* I saves the ready.
Howard But that's *dangerous*.
Beasley And if you don't belt up, I'll be.
Stokes But you mustn't. You really mustn't.

Beasley works herself up into a fury

Beasley Don't *you* bloody start.

Stokes It's a mortal sin.
Beasley (*standing*) No more than murder ...

Crab goes to Stokes and leads her back to her bed

Crab Come on, love. It's none of our business.
Beasley Too bloody right.
Lil Beasley? What about the M.O.?
Beasley He's not pregnant, is he?
Lil We get a check-up before leave.
Beasley (*horrified*) Oh God. Can't win, can I? (*To Lil*) I'm five months gone.

The Girls are horrified

Lil Why'd you join then?
Beasley Street were noticing. What'll I do? (*Trying to smile*) As actress said to ... (*She cannot continue*)
Lil Hold on—I've got a glimmer!
Beasley Leave it alone.
Lil No listen. There were a girl in our lot—you know, before ... And she were carrying.
Beasley Bully for her.
Lil No, listen. 'Cos it might work, it just bloody might. I mean, the M.O., he's pretty doddery, in't he? And he's four-eyes, right?
Beasley (*angrily*) The suspense is killing me!
Lil Hold yer hat! Anyway this girl—the one in pod ...
Beasley *I know which one!*
Lil Yeah well—she told the M.O. she had the curse!
Beasley Don't talk daft!
Lil Straight up! It's like this 'ere Psychologic Warefare, see. You puts it in the head. I mean, there she stood bold as a brass Buddha. (*Indicating a round stomach*) S.T. like the Cenotaph, complaining she got sort-of blown up with wind when it were on her. And guess what? She got a chitty for Syrup of Figs!
Howard (*eager to make amends*) If you starved till leave, you could look a *bit* thinner.
Lil And go on taking them pills.
Howard Just in case!
Beasley (*excitedly*) By heck it might work! I mean you never knows yer luck, do yer?
Howard Gin!
Lil Hey—mother's ruin!
Howard It'd have to be an *awful* lot.
Beasley Yer breaking my heart! Yippee! N.A.A.F.I. here we come!

Jubilantly, the Girls leave

Stokes remains, sitting facing the wall

  Crab returns

Crab Coming, pet?

Stokes shakes her head

  Nothing you can do.
Stokes I can pray.
Crab You're a funny one.
Stokes Poor little baby.
Crab What about Beasley, then. Who'll look after her?
Stokes Our Lord.
Crab Try telling her that ... so come on, we're missing out on good drinking time.
Stokes I mustn't.
Crab (*angrily*) For Christ's sake.
Stokes Yes. For His sake.
Crab (*irritated*) Can't win, can I? Look ... (*She searches around*) I mean, let's face
  it, even Jesus had a tipple now and again.

Stokes nods

  And you do have it at Confession.
Stokes (*smiling*) Communion.
Crab There you go then. So come on—be a mate.
Stokes (*amazed*) Me?
Crab Who else?
Stokes *Your* mate?
Crab Why not—I likes you.

Crab holds out her hand. Stokes takes it

The Lights fade to Black-out

THE ROSES OF EYAM
by Don Taylor

Based on a true story of 1666 the play tells of a village stricken with plague that resolves to isolate itself to try to contain the spread of the disease. Despite conflict between the present rector, Mompesson, and his Noncomformist predecessor, Stanley, the two form an uncomfortable alliance to minister to the courageous villagers facing tragedy.

Set: A representation of the Derbyshire village of Eyam.
In a central position is a large Saxon cross, with an open area around it, including the cottage. Period: 1666.

Cast: M22 F18. (Many of these are non-speaking, but are part of the crowd of villagers.)
William Mompesson, Rector of Eyam; mid 20s. The Bedlam, tall, thin, mental defective, dressed in rags, stoops, limps, wears a small silver bell round his neck; 20. Thomas Stanley, former Rector of Eyam, imposing white-haired Puritan preacher; 50s. Richard Sydall. Mrs Sydall, his wife. Ellen, their daughter; 18. Emmot, their daughter; 20. Catherine Mompesson, William's wife. Rowland Torre, from the next village, Emmot's boyfriend. Edward Thornley; 55. Isaac Thornley, his father; 80. Andrew Merril and Old Unwin, two querulous, lively men; about 80.William Torre; 44. Edytha Torre, his mother; 65. The Torre family: Humphrey, 75; Frances, 17; John, 27; Thomas, 18; Alice, 42. Marshall Howe, enormous, tall. William Hancock, John's brother; 38. Mrs Hancock and John Hancock, husband and wife; middle age. Alice Hancock, their daughter; 25. Elizabeth Hancock, her sister; 20. Frances Frith, 44. George Frith, her husband; 50. Elizabeth, his sister; 44. Frith children: Mary, 25; Francis, 23; Anne, 20; Thomas, 19. John and Deborah Wilson, 35 and 40. Rowland and George Mower, 45 and 30. Elizabeth Swanne, 20. Lydia Chapman, 42. Mrs Cooper.

Playing time: 29 minutes.

The church bell is tolling slowly, and the stage is empty

Over this sound we hear a cackle and hooting of laughter, and the tinkle of the Bedlam's bell. He enters L, *still hooting and cackling, and bouncing up and down on his bent legs*

Bedlam I seen it, I seen it! (*He whispers, as though a secret*) Three new graves, open in the churchyard. I laughed and danced, but they sent me away. They don't think it's funny: putting a man in a hole.

Four villagers enter up C, *hooded in black, carrying a coffin. They make slowly* DL

Bedlam stands down C *with his back to the audience, and turns his head*

They've got Peter Halksworth in that long box.

He walks over and looks. The bearers take no notice

They've nailed him in. In case he changes his mind.

A second similar cortège enters up R, *followed by a third down* R, *both crossing* DL

The Bedlam dances over, weaving between them

They've put Thomas Thorpe in that one, because he didn't wake up this morning when they shook him. And in that one his wife Mary. Just because her toes went black. They owned a shop. But last night a white cricket sang at the back door, and this morning the shutters are closed.

The cortèges exit. As the last goes off, the bell stops

They've stopped all the music, and planted them in the earth. Perhaps they think they'll grow, like flowers.

Mompesson enters briskly down L, *walking up* C

Bedlam Mister!
Mompesson I'm sorry, boy, I'm in a hurry ...
Bedlam Can I come with you?
Mompesson Not now, I must see Mrs Sydall's daughter.
Bedlam I been playing in the grass by the church.
Mompesson I know, you mustn't play there.
Bedlam I seen four graves.
Mompesson Three you mean.
Bedlam No, four. There's one all grass, not open yet.

Mompesson looks at him curiously for a moment, then becomes brisk again

Mompesson There's no time now, boy. Tell me your dreams another day.

Mompesson exits up C

Bedlam shouts after him, his words gradually becoming terrified

Bedlam And I seen another one, and another, and another, all in a line, and black buds on all the trees, and a forest of crosses growing up the street, and over the river and all across the valley, till it's all thick and dark, no more people, just big black trees ...!

He is alone on stage

Nobody listens to the madboy.

The Bedlam runs off, his bell tinkling

The Lights cross-fade to the cottage area up R *and we see a tableau. The only furniture is a bed. On it lies Sarah Sydall. By the bed Stanley kneels in prayer. Mrs Sydall, Richard, Ellen and Emmot stand with their backs to the audience. There is a knock at the door. Richard Sydall opens it. No-one else moves*

Mompesson enters

Mompesson I'm sorry to be so long, I was delayed at the ... (*He stops as he sees the girl*)

Stanley rises from his knees and covers her with the sheet. He then turns to Mompesson

When did she die?
Richard Sydall Ten minutes ago. She got ill during the night.
Stanley I'm sorry, sir, to have had to kneel in your place. But the prayer of an exile is better than no prayer at all. God's blessing to all here.
Richard Sydall Amen.
All Sydalls Amen.
Mrs Sydall Thank you, Mr Stanley.

Stanley exits through the cottage door

Mompesson I'm sorry I was not here ...
Richard Sydall We have enough sorrow of our own, Rector. We don't need yours.
Mompesson I will make it my business to see the carpenter and make the necessary arrangements.
Richard Sydall Too late again, Rector. My son John is there now.
Mompesson Then there is nothing more I can do.

Richard Sydall No sir, nothing.

Pause, as Richard looks at him

Mompesson Don't look at me like Judas, Mr Sydall. My business was at the Thorpes',
   and as sadly urgent as yours.
Richard Sydall Tom Thorpe died last night.
Mompesson And so did Mary this morning.
Mrs Sydall No, not Mary ...
Mompesson There were two children left alone.
Mrs Sydall Are they all right?
Mompesson My wife is with them. Tell me, did she, Sarah, did she go out last
   night?
Mrs Sydall Only to Mrs Cooper's yesterday afternoon, to take a parcel for me.
Mompesson Oh. I see.
Mrs Sydall Why is it, Rector? What sin have we committed?
Mompesson God—has his reasons.
Richard Sydall For six people, in a few days, like this? My Sarah didn't know the
   meaning of wrongdoing. And look at her child's face, covered in filthy black scabs!
Mompesson God's mercy to this stricken house.
Richard Sydall Ay. He ignored our prayers last night, so perhaps he'll listen to us
   this morning.

Mompesson looks at them for a moment and then goes out into the street

*The Lights cross-fade, leaving the cottage in darkness. Stanley is sitting on the pedestal
of the cross with a Bible in his hands, reading. Mompesson sees him. Then walks past
him down L. Then stops, and turns*

Mompesson Mr Stanley.

Stanley puts away his book, looks up and says nothing

   I'd like to talk to you.
Stanley There's nothing to say, sir. You were not there, and I took your place, for
   which I have apologized.
Mompesson No, no, not that. We are both servants of the same God ...
Stanley Untrue, sir. I have spent my life fighting against everything you stand for. I
   have been beaten but I have not been humiliated, nor have I betrayed myself.
Mompesson Mr Stanley ...
Stanley Talking to you is unfair, Mompesson. It opens wounds in my side which
   you are too young to know about. It's better to keep silent. Good-afternoon.

*Stanley begins to go down R. Mompesson is at a loss. Stanley is just leaving when he
calls*

Mompesson You know what it is, don't you!

Stanley stops dead then turns

Stanley Yes, I know what it is.

Mompesson You know what the black scabs mean.

Stanley Plague.

Mompesson They had it in London this year, people were dying a thousand a week.

Stanley Yes.

Mompesson What are we going to do?

Stanley What do you mean?

Mompesson We must make some plan together.

Stanley You may do as you please. I shall do nothing.

Mompesson Nothing? You must help me, Stanley, or more people will die.

Stanley Do you know nothing at all but what you have read in books? When God sends the plague into a house the Angel of Death takes residence. When he leaves, he leaves a tomb. Do you understand?

Mompesson Is there no cure?

Stanley You can lance the boils when they first appear; you can make them drink hot water. If the boils turn black, the best thing you can do is to take a spade and start digging.

Mompesson Is that all?

Stanley I have told you all I know. You are the rector now. You won't want advice from an outlaw and a beggar.

Mompesson There are houses here where even death won't make me welcome ... It isn't long since these were your people. They haven't changed.

Stanley But I have, and now they are yours. You must do as you choose.

Mompesson I choose to ask your help ... I'm a stranger here, a young man, and I find it hard—to make myself loved. You are older—perhaps wiser than I am ... Don't look at me like that, Stanley, people are dying who might have lived, and all I ask is your counsel ...

Stanley Listen to me, Mompesson, you are not my judge passing sentence ...

Mompesson That was never in my mind ...

Stanley I gave these people fifteen years of service; every morsel of my precious God they had at my hands, I gave my love, and they took it and returned no thanks. There is none left now, sir, I am empty. When the King returned there was more than one loyal cheer, and many prayers of thanksgiving. Seeing that has blinded me—I gave them the hard discipline of God's service ...

Mompesson They need now his mercy.

Stanley Let them seek it on their knees then.

Mompesson Is there nothing we can do together? I have been called for in three houses already this morning, and the day isn't ended yet. I shall need all one man's strength.

Stanley "As thy days, so shall thy strength be."

Mompesson Is that all you can offer?

Stanley Do you expect riches from a beggar? (*He walks towards the exit, then stops and turns*) If you tell them to stay in their houses, you will have done all you can do.

Mompesson I shall pray for them, Stanley. I shall pray till my heart bursts!

Stanley Yes, pray. I prayed when my hour came, but my prayer wasn't answered. This hour is yours.

Stanley exits R. *Catherine enters* L

Catherine Where have you been?

Mompesson At the Sydalls'. Their daughter is dead.

Catherine The same way?

Mompesson Yes. What about the Thorpe children?

Catherine I persuaded their aunt to take them in. She looked at them as though they were lepers. I'm tired now.

Mompesson Soon the villagers will know. Every door will be bolted then.

Catherine What are we going to do? It may be us next.

Mompesson You mustn't say that.

Catherine Don't be frightened for me. They say the plague only takes the strong.

Mompesson You must keep away from the infected houses.

Catherine My place is where you are. If you must be there, I must be with you.

Mompesson I feel so helpless. As though a great wheel has started to roll, and I am left watching. Nothing is as I planned it. Three days ago I thought it best to leave here.

Catherine And now?

Mompesson I saw it so clearly, but it wasn't this. I was to be the great preacher, with a tongue like a whip! But these are good people, their worst sin a missed service on Sunday, or a day late in bed. My weapons are useless, and my insufficiency is left naked. Now I must be their father, and I don't know how to begin.

Catherine With love. They will need love.

Mompesson Many of them hate me. Catherine, I haven't the words to do it ...

Catherine Love doesn't need words.

Mompesson I shall *make* them love me, I shall *make* them. Even if I must kiss their black sores to do it. Stanley thinks I will crumble, but if God wants me here, I shall stay at his bidding.

Catherine You may not be loved yet, but already you are needed.

Mompesson But I wanted to fight. Here there is no enemy I can see.

Catherine There may be no enemy, but there is a battle for sure. Are you running, or do you stand?

Mompesson I stand.

Mompesson and Catherine exit L

The church bell begins to toll slowly

A large crowd of villagers begins to appear. All the Hancocks, Friths, Thornleys, John and Deborah Wilson, Elizabeth Swanne, Lydia Chapman, Rowland and George Mower, Howe, Unwin and Merril

The bell continues, and they all group themselves round the mid-stage L *rostra, as if watching a funeral off* L. *The bell ceases*

Almost at once the Torres begin to enter, all except Scythe, who is dead. They have black cloaks over their dresses. Edytha and Humphrey are first, followed by Frances, John and Thomas, and finally William and Alice. As they appear, the crowd stumbles and shuffles away leaving a clear way to the exit. The Torres stop and gather in a group round William, the tallest. The younger ones are frightened. There is silence for a moment

Edward Thornley Pass on to your house, William Torre, and stay there.

William Torre Why do you draw back?

Edward Thornley The earth's still soft on your son's coffin.

William Torre You were my friends yesterday. Now the streets are empty when I pass.

Edward Thornley We want to stay alive.

William Torre Will I kill you?

He moves towards them, hands outstretched. They all stumble away

Yesterday my son was living. Two weeks ago you were dancing to his pipes at the wake. God's hand came into my house with no warning and took my son. For all your drawing back, it can come as easily into yours. What happens then? Will all neighbours be strangers?

There is no reaction. He shouts

Draw back then now. Your turn will come!

Edytha Torre Come home, son. Leave them.

All the Torres begin to go together. Just before they exit, William shouts again, in a terrible, grief-stricken voice

William Torre Your turn will come!

The Torres exit

The crowd begins to disperse. Edward Thornley jumps on to the pedestal of the cross and shouts to them

Edward Thornley Don't go, listen to me!

The crowd ceases its murmur and listens

Something terrible is happening in our village. One month ago, George Vicars died, with black scabs on his face and chest. Since then ten more people have died the same way, the last today. Now, are we blind, or children, or what?

William Hancock What can we do? People are dying and nobody knows why.

Francis Frith The Rector told Mrs Cooper it's a strange fever from Africa.

Edward Thornley You may believe that if you like. But I'll tell you what I think.

Howe Listen to the oracle!

A burst of laughter from the villagers. Edward Thornley shouts above it

Edward Thornley It's the plague!

The laughter ceases. There is a moment's silence. Then a frightened chatter begins as people start to move off in all directions

Don't run away like sheep when the dog barks! Listen to me if you want to stay alive!

Elizabeth Frith If it's the plague we can't do anything.

Mrs Hancock How do you get it?

John Wilson It's a clammy invisible mist in the air.

George Frith You take it in with your breath. You can't do anything about it.

Frances Frith You must carry flowers pinned to your breast. The sweet smell drives it away.

Mrs Hancock Is that what they do in London?

John Hancock In London they run away to the country!

Edward Thornley If we panic like this we are all dead men.

George Frith What can we do?

Mrs Hancock We can't do anything, oh God, save us all!

Edward Thornley We can act like reasonable Christian men. We can pray to God, and we can take care.

John Wilson What do you mean?

Edward Thornley No-one must go near the infected houses, nor touch, nor speak to, nor even look at anyone from them. We must shut ourselves inside our own families till the danger is over.

George Frith How can we? There's work to be done.

Edward Thornley Do you want to live? It may be your parents, or your own wife and child. If you want to live you must avoid them all like lepers. The dead must be buried by nearest kin, no stranger must see them.

William Hancock That's sacrilege, Edward Thornley.

Edward Thornley Is it sacrilege to shield your neighbour? If we don't, it will be all over the village within a month, and we won't be able to stop it. But if we act now, before it can get a hold——

Unwin You won't stop it that way.

Edward Thornley If you've nothing better to say, old man, you can keep quiet.

Unwin I've plenty to say. I've seen it all before.

George Frith You've seen it?

Unwin Old men have long memories. You remember it, Isaac Thornley, and you, Andrew Merril. Curbar in thirty-two!

Isaac Thornley Ah, before the war.

Merril A lot of people died there that autumn.

Unwin Nearly fifty of them.

George Frith Fifty!

Edward Thornley Now do you believe me? Go home, and keep yourselves to yourselves.

The crowd begins to disperse during the next section, till Howe, Unwin, Merril and Isaac Thornley are left alone

Unwin Do you remember Frank Rowley, Merril?

Isaac Thornley He were a big man.

Merril Ay. Bigger than you, Marshall Howe.

Howe What happened to him?

As Unwin begins to tell the story, groups of villagers listen to parts of it, and then leave, frightened by what they have heard

Unwin There were eight in that family. Over in Curbar it was, not ten miles away. There was him and his father and mother.

Merril And his wife and four children, wasn't it?

Unwin His wife got it first.

Merril Then his father and his two sons, and then his mother. All of them dead inside a week.

Unwin He had to bury them with his own hands, no-one else would come near them.

Merril He dragged them to their graves in a field, feet first, with a bit of rope.

Unwin Till there was only him left, and his twin little girls. Six years old they were.

Howe And did they survive?

Unwin Survive? You're as bad as young Thornley you are.

Merril The plague's a glutton. It keeps eating till it goes bust.

Unwin The morning after his mother died, he felt ill, hot and thirsty, with a headache.

Merril Frank Rowley were a big man, Marshall Howe. Bigger than you are.

Isaac Thornley Too big for six-year-olds to carry.

Merril Ay.

Unwin So he went again to the field where his family lay sleeping, and he took his spade and some straw, and he dug his sixth grave that week. And when he'd finished, he lined it with straw. The bed must be comfortable that's going to hold you forever.

Merril Then he laid himself down on the straw in the hole, and waited for God to release him.

Unwin He waited all that day, and all night in his delirium.

Isaac Thornley He were a big man, you see.

Unwin And when he saw the sun rise on the next day, he closed his eyes and died.

Howe And the two children?

Merril Died a few days later.

Unwin And were left for the crows to peck at.

Howe And it's here now, like a hawk above the village, waiting to swoop.

Unwin And I'll tell you why all those people died.

Howe Do I need telling?

Unwin They died because they were weak and afraid. Because they were all waiting to die, and as soon as they got a headache they gave up, that's why! You need willpower—(*he taps his head*)—in here. Like I've got!

Merril You're talking rubbish, Unwin.

Isaac Thornley You had the clap when you were a lad, I remember.

Unwin I've had everything I have, plague, smallpox, and the big pox, too, I've had the lot!

Merril Ay, more than once, too.

Unwin I'll tell you something, Marshall Howe, and you, Merril.

Howe Tell me, Solomon.

Unwin When you wake up one morning and your head's aching and your tongue's like a dry washleather, you say to yourself, "I've got a headache, and I need a drink", no more. And you'll live out all the days God sends, mark my words.

Howe I'll remember that.

Rowland Torre enters and makes his way across the stage towards the cottage area

Merril Where do you think you're going, Rowland Torre?

Rowland A carrier came to our farm this morning, and he brought bad news.

Merril Oh ah. He would.

Rowland Is it true, then?

Unwin Bad news always is.

Rowland About Sarah?

Howe You're out of date. That was a week ago.

Unwin Six more are dead since then.

Rowland What? What about Emmot? Is Emmot all right?

Unwin Don't ask us, boy. Nobody's been near that house for a week. I wouldn't give you much for her chances.

Merril Nor any of that family.
Howe Nor you, if you go there.
Rowland I must go.
Howe Don't be a fool, Rowland. There's a long life waiting for you at home.

But Rowland ignores them and moves quickly off

Merril Come back, madman!
Howe You might just as well dam the sea.
Unwin So much for young Thornley. I told him what his taking care would come to.
Merril He'll take it back to Middleton, that's what he'll do.
Unwin People are like rivers. As long as the moon shines they will flow together. Nothing can stop them.
Howe Well. We can only wait now.
Unwin And see who goes next.

Unwin grins at Merril, and they all go off in opposite directions

Cross-fade to the cottage area, where Richard Sydall is standing by the fire, wrapped in a blanket

Rowland enters

Richard Sydall turns to him

Richard Sydall Go away.
Rowland It's me, Mr Sydall.
Richard Sydall I said go away.
Rowland I came to say how sorry I am about ...
Richard Sydall Yes, thank you, now go.
Rowland Where's Emmot?
Richard Sydall She's in there.
Rowland Is she all right?
Richard (*shouting*) Yes, she's all right, now go!
Rowland I want to see her.
Richard Sydall You can't see her today.
Rowland Why? Are you all right, you're shivering.
Richard Sydall Are you blind, boy? Don't come near me!

Rowland stops, horrified

I've got the plague. Get out of here!
Rowland I'm not frightened.

Richard Sydall You may be frightened or not, son. But I've got a boil coming here on my cheek. It will go hard soon, and then black. By tomorrow I shall be dead.

Rowland Don't say that! Look, I'm sure you'll be better soon ...

Richard Sydall Go away and leave me in peace! There's a good lad. I want to die like a man, not like a child.

Rowland You don't look too bad ...

Richard Sydall You fool! I've been sitting here all morning turning myself to stone. Now you come, sturdy as a tree, and tell me I'll be all right ... Go away! (*He begins to cry, trying hard not to*)

Rowland I'm sorry.

Mrs Sydall enters and crouches down beside her husband, holding him

Mrs Sydall Haven't you seen enough yet? Go away.

Rowland turns and is going, when Emmot's voice is heard calling off. He stops and turns

Emmot (*off*) Rowland, can you hear me?

Rowland Yes, Emmot, I can hear you.

Emmot (*off*) I can't come in to see you. I must stay in here with John and Ellen and the twins till Father is better.

Rowland Yes.

Emmot (*off*) You mustn't come here again, Rowland.

Rowland What? Emmot, I must see you!

Emmot (*off*) The door will be bolted.

Rowland I can see you at the window. We can talk through the shutters.

Emmot (*off*) No, you can't. I want you to, Rowland, but it's too dangerous.

Rowland When will I see you again?

Emmot (*off*) I don't know. I don't know.

Rowland It's no good, Emmot, danger or not, I'll break the door down!

Emmot (*off*) Rowland, please ...

Rowland What?

Emmot (*off*) If you promise you won't come back, I'll see you on Sunday afternoon. On the slope above Cussy Dell, you know it there?

Rowland I know it, yes.

Emmot (*off*) Promise me, Rowland, you won't come back into the village!

Rowland All right, Emmot, I promise ...

Emmot (*off*) I'll see you on Sunday. God willing.

Rowland Emmot! Emmot! (*He bangs the door again*)

Mrs Sydall Must she burst her heart with crying before you'll go?

Rowland God be with you, then.

Mrs Sydall Ay. We have need of him here.

Rowland moves to the door. As he gets there Richard Sydall begins to groan in agony. Mrs Sydall cuddles him and whispers words of comfort which we do not hear. Rowland is watching. She looks at him, and he sees for the first time that she is streaming tears

(*Sobbing*) Go away.

Rowland goes out of the door and off

The Lights dim out in the cottage area and come up on the main area. Music is heard. The Lights become hard and brilliant

The Bedlam enters, turning in circles, and holding up his hands, as though catching snowflakes

Bedlam Snow—snow—snow—I'm going to build a snowman for Christmas. I'll make him big and strong, like Marshall Howe, with a hat and a clay pipe, and a stick in his hand. He'll be all right while it stays freezing. But when it gets warmer, his face will go black and dirty, and he'll get old, and when the sun comes out again, I'll watch him melt away to a little pool of dirty water. Then he'll be all gone, and there'll be nothing left except his hat and his clay pipe and his stick, and I expect I'll wonder why I bothered to make him at all. (*He looks very sad for a second. Then he bends down, scrabbling in the snow and making noises*)

Rowland Torre enters

Hallo, mister. I'm going to build a snowman.
Rowland What are you doing up here? You'll get cold in those rags.
Bedlam I don't feel the cold. Are you going to help me?
Rowland Not today. I'm waiting for someone. Go back and play in the village.
Bedlam I seen you here before.
Rowland Yes.
Bedlam Every Sunday, in the afternoon. For a long time.
Rowland Six weeks.
Bedlam I don't like it in the village now.
Rowland Why?
Bedlam Everybody keeps crying. And they shoo me away when I dance.
Rowland Has anyone else died?
Bedlam Buzzz, buz, buzzzzz.
Rowland Do you understand? Have more people been dying?
Bedlam Can I have your hat for my snowman?
Rowland Do you know Emmot Sydall?
Bedlam I don't understand names.
Rowland You know the cottage, nearly opposite the church gate ...?

Bedlam They make boxes in that house.

Rowland Boxes?

Bedlam They make a box, and then they take it as a present for the black-man in the church. Then they go back and make another one. I seen them.

Rowland Listen carefully, boy. Tell me, which one have you seen?

Bedlam I don't understand names.

Emmot appears up c. She is white faced and ill looking, and her clothes are beginning to look ragged and uncared for. Throughout this scene she speaks as though very tired

Emmot Rowland ...

Rowland Emmot ...! All right, boy, go and build your snowman. Here's a penny for you.

Bedlam I haven't had a penny for a long time. I'd throw it in the brook and watch it roll, but it's frozen up.

The Bedlam runs off

Rowland Emmot, are you all right ...? (*He makes to go to her*)

Emmot No, don't come near me! Stay where you are and we can talk.

Rowland You are all right, aren't you? You look so ...

Emmot Don't worry, Rowland, I haven't had the plague yet.

Rowland Don't say it like that, Emmot. You'll be all right now the winter's come. It's too cold.

Emmot I suppose it must be winter now.

Rowland It's nearly Christmas!

Emmot Christmas ...

Rowland We killed the geese yesterday, and there'll be fruit cakes and puddings. You must bring up your whole family.

Emmot My family ...?

Rowland Emmot ...?

Emmot I said I'd come and see you that Sunday.

Rowland I came every week.

Emmot I saw you across the Dell.

Rowland Why didn't you come?

She lowers her head

Tell me, Emmot. (*He moves towards her*)

Emmot No, stay where you are!

She looks up, and the expression on her face stops him dead in his tracks

Father died on the Sunday night. The day after you came. Mother made us stay in the other room, and we heard him crying. It's an indescribable noise, Rowland, a grown man dying: like a baby sobbing, except that it's low and deep. Mother wouldn't let us see him. The carpenter left a coffin outside the door, but he wouldn't come in. My mother had to do it all herself, even the nails. We stayed in during the week after the funeral, and it seemed all right. I was going to come and see you when I promised. Then on Saturday night, John got ill—my little brother John, and on Sunday morning Ellen was ill, too. John died at dinnertime on Sunday, and Ellen on Monday morning. I saw it all the time. My mother couldn't manage two by herself. She kept crying and saying, "I'm sorry, Emmot, but you've got to help me with them". We stayed in the next week, too. There were other people dying in the village. Some of your cousins Torre, I think, but I don't know who. We just saw the coffins going past the window. The next Saturday—a week to the day, both the baby twins got ill. Only two, they didn't have any idea what was happening, except that it hurt. Elizabeth died on the Sunday. It seemed as though Alice was getting better, but on Tuesday night she died, too. Then there was just my mother and me. Every day we sat opposite each other at the table, always on the same chairs, waiting for the first sign which of us would be the next. Which would have to bury the other. We've been sitting like that for three weeks. But nothing has happened. Others are dying, but we pray that God has finished with us. We've been in the house all that time. Today is the first time I've been out since Alice was buried. We've been sitting there, all day, every day, listening to the church bell. It's a month since Alice died now, and it seemed as safe as it ever will be. So I came. That's why I haven't been before, Rowland.

There is nothing Rowland can say. They are still at a distance. Agonized, he makes a swift movement to her, and embraces her before she can object. She struggles

Rowland, no, you mustn't ...
Rowland Who says I mustn't ...
Emmot I've been living with the plague for two months, it must be all over me, in my clothes and hair ...

He kisses her on the mouth. She struggles for a moment, then relaxes

Rowland There. If anything happens now, it happens to both of us.
Emmot You shouldn't have done that, Rowland.
Rowland Shhhhhh ...

He kisses her again

Come away with me, Emmot, back to the farm where it's safe.
Emmot No. (*She breaks a little away from him*)

Rowland No? Why not ...?

Emmot I can't leave my mother alone ... Anyway, they say in the village the cold weather will end it all.

Rowland Why take the risk? Come with me.

Emmot I can't, Rowland. I might bring it with me.

Rowland Does that matter, if we're together?

Emmot Your family might think so.

Rowland They'll welcome you.

Emmot No, Rowland, I must stay with my mother. Then perhaps, when it's safe ... The rector will look after us. I think he and his wife must be saints. They've been to every house that's been visited, every day, saying prayers and comforting the relatives ... I must go now—Mother will be frightened if I'm not back soon. She doesn't like being alone any more.

Rowland When will I see you again? Next week here? Or shall I come down with you?

Emmot No, you mustn't do that. Perhaps next week.

Rowland Next week.

Emmot Yes ... Goodbye, Rowland. Pray for us.

Rowland Emmot ...

Emmot That's all you can do.

Emmot turns, and walks slowly off

Rowland I must be mad to let her go back.

TRAFFORD TANZI
by Claire Luckham

Tanzi's story, from babyhood to marriage, is told with humour and originality in the form of a comedy wrestling contest. As Round One finishes Mum is the Champion. In Round Two Tanzi meets the challenge of school.

Set: A wrestling ring.
The original production of Trafford Tanzi was presented in-the-round with the wrestling ring as the central focal point. When not directly involved in the action the actors remained in the ringside area and encouraged audience participation.

Cast: M3 F3.
The Referee, also plays Dr Grope, the school psychiatrist. Tanzi's Mum. Tanzi's Dad. Platinum Sue, Tanzi's friend. Trafford Tanzi, a schoolgirl; 6, then 11, then 16. Dean Rebel, a professional wrestler, calls from outside the ring.

Playing time: 12 minutes.

The wrestling ring

The cast are in the ringside area. The Referee climbs into the ring and takes a microphone from one of the corner posts. He uses it for all official announcements

Ref Ladies and gentlemen: the winner in Round One, Mum. A big hand for Mum please, showing us all how to do it. Thank you.

Mum takes a bow

Round Two. Can I have the contestants for Round Two, please? In the red corner, Trafford Tanzi. In the blue corner, Platinum Sue. Girls, come here.

They come to the centre, the Ref turns his back on Tanzi and chats up Sue

Now listen, I want nothing you're going to be ashamed of after. No scratching, hair pulling, biting, agreed?

Sue Yes, Mr Referee.

Ref Good girl.

Tanzi Aren't you gonna ask me then?

Ref Yeah, when you can wriggle your arse like that. Tanzi is at school. She's six years old. Just six. Seconds away, Round Two.

Bell. Tanzi holds her hand out to shake hands. Sue takes it down to the ground and stamps on it

Tanzi Fwaugh, fwaugh.

Tanzi returns to her corner, comes back with a lollipop. She offers it to Sue. Sue takes it and "Irish whips" her. Tanzi gets up Sue points in the air. Tanzi looks up. Sue "claims" her leg. Tanzi "break falls"

Ref One ... er ... two ... er ... three ... er ...

Sue   One, two-koo, three-ee,
                           Tanzi hit rock bottom,
                           She tried to knock the champion out,
                           But found her chance was rotten.

Tanzi Why can't we be friends, I want to be friends.

Sue Because we can't.

Tanzi But why?

Sue Me mam says we can't, so there. You've got a snotty nose and dirty knees. You're a tomboy. Only play boys' games. I play house and all the girls' games. You're a slut, so there.

Tanzi I will play if you want.

Sue I can't. Your mouth's dirty.

Tanzi It's not.

Sue You swear.

Tanzi I don't.

Sue You do.

Tanzi Don't.

Sue Do.

Tanzi Don't.

Sue Do.

Tanzi Well, what do I say then?

Sue I don't know. But me mam says you do, so there.

Tanzi Well, what's swearing then?

Sue Well ... dirty words.

Tanzi You don't kno-ow, you don't kno-ow.

Sue I do. I do. I do.

Tanzi I do because me mam tells me dad not to, so there.

Sue Oo, what's he say? Go on. Tell us.

Tanzi Promise to be friends.
Sue I might. Yes. Go on. Go on.
Tanzi Well, in the morning when he can't find his socks he says, "Bloody Hell!"
Sue Ooh!

They both run round the ring yelling "Bloody Hell" and "Poo-poo-poo" etc.

Tanzi And I know that's swearing 'cos me mam tells me dad to stop fucking swearing.
Sue Oo! Oo! Bloody Hell! Fucking swearing!

They play pat-a-cake through this next:

Sue ⎫ *(together)* Salami, salami,
Tanzi ⎭ All the boys is barmy,
Sla-ate, sla-ate,
All the girls is grea-eat!

Tanzi slaps the Ref on the last one

Tanzi 'Ey, 'ey, 'ey, we could have a gang.
Sue What for?
Tanzi Fighting the boys.
Sue Girls don't fight, me mam says so.
Dean *(outside the ring)* That's it, you tell her, Sue.
Sue Ooh! Ooh! I will! I'll tell on her. I'll tell our miss on you. You've been swearing.
Tanzi But ... but we're friends, you said.
Sue I can't. Me mam says I can't. And, and Miss'll send you up to Head Miss and you'll get the slipper for fighting and swearing, so there.

Tanzi tries not to cry. She grabs a dolly off Sue and pulls its arms and legs off and stamps on it

Sue She's got my dolly! She's got my dolly!
Ref Now, Miss, calm down, calm down ...

Bell

The bell's gone. Round Two to Platinum Sue.
Sue Piece of cake. *(She climbs out of the ring)*
Ref And as for you, my girl, watch it, or I'll have to issue you with a public warning. You wash your mouth out with soap and water, we want none of that filthy language in ...

Tanzi has been swilling her mouth round. She spits the content on to the Ref

You ... you ...

Dad No, no. You're getting it all wrong. She's getting it all wrong. My little girl wasn't like that at all. She was, she was (*he takes the microphone*) beautiful.

Mum plays a violin and the Ref dons a pair of headphones and reads "The Sporting Life" as Dad speaks

> Tanzi, Tanzi; buttercups and Tanzi,
> She was so beautiful as she grew;
> Little frocks and cotton socks, pretty as a chocolate box,
> My little girl with her eyes of blue.

Ref Thank you, thank you, Tanzi's Dad. Ladies and gentlemen, Round Three, Tanzi meets the school psychiatrist. In the red corner Trafford Tanzi. She is now eleven, she's eleven years old. In the blue corner ... oh, excuse me, it's me.

He hands the microphone to Mum and hastily changes into Dr Grope. Sue assists, dressed as a Nurse

Mum In the blue corner, the school psychiatrist, Doctor Grope. Seconds away ... Round Three.

Bell. Grope gets Tanzi in a "head lock"

Grope Aha. Got you. Name?
Tanzi What?
Grope Name, stupid. What's yours?
Tanzi Tanzi.
Grope Tanzi what? (*Stamp*)
Tanzi Tanzi.
Grope Yes, but Tanzi what? (*Stamp*) Your second name.

Grope turns away from Mum who is reffing for this round and gouges Tanzi's eye

I've got to send in a psychiatrist's report — (*he runs her face along the top rope*) — on why Tanzi whatever-your-name-is can't read. (*He stamps again and drops her on the floor*)
Tanzi Green.
Grope (*putting his knee in her back and pulling her up by her cheeks*) I should think you are.
Tanzi That's me name.
Grope (*changing to a "nerve hold" and bringing her to her feet*) Oho, how green was my valley, eh?
Dad (*outside the ring*) Stop him, love, that's our name too.
Mum Shush.

Grope (*walking across the ring with "nerve hold"*) Joke, girl. Laugh.

Grope tightens his hold: Tanzi screams

Haven't you got a sense of humour? No greens is good greens, what? I never used to like my greens at school either.

Tanzi breaks free and takes a swing at him. He grabs her lower lip and forces her up on tiptoe

Temper, temper. Naughty, naughty. We're never going to find out why you don't read if you carry on like this. Right.

Grope signals for Sue to hold up a reading card which has a daft picture and "Jane helps Mum wash the dishes" written underneath. He changes back to the "nerve grip"

I'd like you to look at this card. Now what do you see? (*He applies pressure*)
Tanzi (*shrieking*) A girl ...
Grope Yes. And what is the girl called? (*Pressure*)
Tanzi Jane. Jane ... Jane. Jane.
Grope Quite right. Good, very good. Mustn't stint on the praise. (*He pats her on the head and then "rabbit punches" her to her knees*) Now, Tanzi, pay attention, what's the next word? (*"Nerve hold" and pressure*)
Tanzi Helps. Helps. Helps. Helps.
Grope Very, very good. Now ... (*Pressure*)
Tanzi Mum!
Grope Oh, did you hear that? I'm beginning to wonder if they've sent me the right girl. Let's have a look at your teeth. (*He forces her mouth open*) Never mind. (*He takes her nose and lifts her to her feet by it*) Now, Tanzi, I want you to be a clever girl and do all the rest in one go. (*He slaps the hand holding her nose*) Come on, don't be shy.
Tanzi (*reading*) Dig for gold.
Grope Excellent, I ... what? Wait a minute. (*Reading*) "Wash the dishes." What did you say? Say it for me.
Tanzi Dig for gold. (*She "Irish whips" him*) Discover the source of the Nile. Fly to the moon. (*"Monkey climb" on him*) That's it, that's what Jane helps her mummy to do. Take meteoric readings of the stars.

She throws him at the ropes and attempts a "tomahawk chop" as he comes off them but he "grope ducks" and puts "nerve hold" back on her

Grope Now then, my girl, I can see that we've got some learning to do. (*He changes the hold to a "headlock" and throttles her with his left hand*)

Dad (*outside the ring*) Mum, Mum, he's got her by the throat.

Grope changes his hold

Mum Are you choking her?

Grope Would I? I'm the school psychiatrist, I'm just teaching her to read. (*He starts throttling her again*)

Tanzi No, ow, yes, "Jane helps Mum wash the dishes".

Grope (*throwing her down and stamping on her*) Ja, ja, that is right, Jane help Mum vash ze dishes. Oh. (*He changes back to the Ref*)

Mum The winner in Round Three. Doctor Grope.

Dad (*climbing into the ring*) You know what you are, don't you?

Ref Jealous, are we?

Dad A bleeding great bully.

Mum Break it up, break it up. My husband was always supporting Tanzi. Until she came home from school one time.

Tanzi Mum ...

Mum She says ...

Tanzi Can I have a career?

Mum Well! I thought ... I'll let her dad sort it out.

Ref Ladies and gentlemen, Round Four. Tanzi is sweet sixteen. (*He wiggles his hips*)

Tanzi wolf-whistles

Watch it, you. In the blue corner — watch you don't let her get away with anything — Tanzi's Dad.

Tanzi Come on, you great pudding, you're holding up the action.

Dad Action, did you say? She wants some action. I'll give you action and all. Ready?

Ref Seconds away, Round Four.

Bell. Dad and Tanzi circle

Dad (*as they do*) You're late, where've you been?

Tanzi Same as every night, at school ...

They change direction

Dad Answer me, my girl, I haven't come back early from the pub to hear you say at school. Come on, out with it.

"Ref's hold"

Tanzi It's the truth ...

Dad (*putting Tanzi in a "backhammer"*) Pull the other one. I'm ...
Tanzi (*reversing "backhammer" on him*) Listen. I can't work here because me
mam ——
Dad (*reversing "backhammer" on Tanzi*) — has the telly on all the time and you
can't concentrate. I've heard it all before. (*He stamps and forces it higher*)
Tanzi It's true.
Dad (*forcing her down on to the floor throughout this*) I'll tell you whether it's true
or not, my girl. You can't pull the wool over my eyes like you can your poor old
mum. Do you hear me? (*He stamps on her elbow*) A career!
Tanzi But, Dad ...
Dad And don't you "but, Dad" me either. I know where you've been going after
school, don't think I don't. Girls! (*"Crutch hold" and lifts her up into an "aeroplane
spin"*) What else is there for them to do except to go sneaking around in the dark
with the lads. Disgusting, I call it. Makes me all hot inside thinking about it. In the
back alleys, round the back of the garages. On the railway banks. Never mind they
give you those badges: "I don't play on the railway." No. But we do, don't we? (*He
has overdone the "spin" and now staggers to his knees*) I've seen you waiting
outside the Gents at Oxford Road Station and ...

*He throws her off with a "body slam", retreats into a corner and splashes. Tanzi rolls
out from under it. Dad lies prone*

Ooh-er ... Tanzi ... how can you do it to your poor old dad.
Tanzi (*going to him*) Dad, Dad, I didn't mean to upset you.
Dad (*grabbing her foot and bringing her down; "Ankle lock"*) There, I knew it!
Filth. You've been having filth.
Tanzi No, no, Dad.
Dad (*applying pressure to various "leglocks"*)Say yes, will you, girl? Say yes and
put me out of my misery. Tell you what, say yes and I'll forget all about you
wanting a career. Right? Give you fifty quid. Fifty notes, to spend on yourself. Get
the lot. Nice outfit, make-up. Get yourself a decent feller. One that'll want to marry
you, not fiddle about with you up them back alleys. Come on. It's all your mum
and dad ever wanted.
Tanzi But it would be the same as up them alleys except I'd be married.

Tanzi tries to raise her head through this next but Dad keeps slamming it back

I don't want to get married.

Slam

I want me independence.

Slam

I want a career.

Slam

I want to be somebody!

Slam

Dad Somebody! A slut, the way you're going on. A wife is somebody, isn't she? Are you saying your mother isn't somebody? Somebody? Marriage is the best career money can buy.

Tanzi I want some exams.

Dad (*trying to turn her into a "Boston Crab"*) Filthy bits of paper! Right! You want exams. You pay for 'em. (*"Boston Crab"*) You earn your own living. See how you like that. (*He sits back*)

Ref Do you submit?

Tanzi Yes, yes, yes.

Bell. Dad gets off and parades. Tanzi bursts into tears

TRELAWNY OF THE 'WELLS'
by Arthur Wing Pinero

'A Comedietta' set in 1860. The pretty young actress, Rose Trelawny, has fallen in love with Arthur Gower and goes to visit his home where grandfather, Sir William Gower and his sister, Miss Trafalgar Gower, rule the household. Rose finds it impossible to cope with the formalities and sorely misses the happy, casual life of her theatrical companions.

Set: A spacious drawing-room. Period: early 1860s.

Cast: M4 F3.
Rose Trelawny, an actress of the 'Wells' theatre; 19. Vice-Chancellor Sir William Gower. Arthur Gower, his grandson, engaged to Rose. Clara de Fœnix, his granddaughter; 19. Miss Trafalgar Gower, Sir William's sister. Captain de Fœnix, Clara's husband, an example of a heavily bewhiskered swell of the period; 27. Charles, a manservant in plush and powder, he wears luxuriant whiskers.

Playing time: 18 minutes.

The scene represents a spacious drawing-room in Sir William Gower's house in Cavendish Square. The walls are sombre in tone, the ceiling dingy, the hangings, though rich, are faded, and altogether the appearance of the room is solemn, formal, and depressing

The lamps are lighted, but the curtains are not drawn, and outside the windows it is twilight

Sir William Gower is seated, R of LC table, asleep. A newspaper is over his head, concealing his face. Miss Trafalgar Gower is sitting at the farther end of the couch L, also asleep and with a newspaper over her head. At the lower end of this couch sits Mrs de Fœnix—Clara—a young lady of nineteen, with a "married" air. She is engaged upon some crochet work. On the other side of the stage, on the L of RC table, Rose is seated, wearing the look of a boredom which has reached the stony stage. On the couch up L Arthur sits, gazing at his boots, his hands in his pockets. On the R of this couch stands Captain de Fœnix. He is leaning against the wall, his mouth open, his head thrown back, and his eyes closed. De Fœnix is a young man of seven-and-

twenty—an example of the heavily whiskered "swell" of the period. Everybody is in dinner-dress. After a moment or two, Arthur rises and tiptoes down to Rose. Clara raises a warning finger and says "Hush!" He nods to her, in assent

Arthur (*on Rose's* L, *in a whisper*) Quiet, isn't it?

Rose (*to him, in a whisper*) Quiet! Arthur——! (*Clutching his arm*) Oh, this dreadful half-hour after dinner, every, *every* evening!

Arthur (*creeping across to* R, *looking cautiously at sleepers, and sitting on the* R *of* RC *table*) Grandfather and Aunt Trafalgar must wake up soon. They're longer than usual tonight.

Rose (*to him, across the table*) Your sister Clara, over there, (*she looks over her right shoulder, towards Clara*) and Captain de Fœnix—when they were courting, did they have to go through this?

Arthur (*with a nod*) Yes.

Rose And now that they are married, they still endure it!

Arthur Yes.

Rose And we, when *we* are married, Arthur, shall *we*——?

Arthur Yes. I suppose so.

Rose (*passing her hand across her brow*) Phe—ew!

De Fœnix, fast asleep, is now swaying, and in danger of toppling over. Clara grasps the situation and rises

Clara (*in a guttural whisper*) Ah, Frederick! no, no, no!

Rose ⎫
Arthur ⎭ (*turning in their chairs; together*) Eh—what—? Ah—h—h—h!

As Clara reaches her husband, he lurches forward into her arms

De Fœnix (*his eyes bolting*) Oh! who——?

Clara Frederick dear, wake!

De Fœnix (*dazed*) How did this occur?

Clara You were tottering, and I caught you.

De Fœnix (*collecting his senses*) I wemember. I placed myself in an upwight position, dearwest, to prewent myself dozing.

Clara (*sinking on to the couch up* C) How you alarmed me!

Seeing that Rose is laughing, de Fœnix comes down to her

De Fœnix (*in a low voice*) Might have been a vevy serwious accident, Miss Trelawny.

Rose (*seating herself on the footstool*) Never mind. (*Pointing to the chair she has vacated*) Sit down and talk.

He glances at the old people and shakes his head

(*Piteously*) Oh, do, do, do! do sit down, and let us all have a jolly whisper.

He sits

Thank you, Captain Fred. Go on! tell me something—anything; something about the military——

De Fœnix (*again looking at the old people, then wagging his finger at Rose*) I know; you want to get me into a wow. (*Settling himself into his chair*) Howwid girl!

Rose (*despairingly*) Oh—h—h!

There is a brief pause and then the sound of a street-organ, playing in the distance, is heard. The air is "Ever of Thee"

Hark! (*Excitedly*) Hark!

Clara

Arthur } (*together*) Hush!

De Fœnix

Rose (*heedlessly*) The song I sang in "The Pedlar"—"The Pedlar of Marseilles!" The song that used to make you cry, Arthur——!

They attempt vainly to hush her down

(*Dramatically, in hoarse whispers*) And then Raphael enters—comes on to the bridge. The music continues, softly. "Raphael, why have you kept me waiting? Man, do you wish to break my heart—(*thumping her breast*) a woman's hear— r—rt, Raphael?"

Sir William and Miss Gower suddenly whip off their newspapers and sit erect. Miss Gower wakes first. She folds the newspaper precisely and puts it on sofa; Sir William throws his behind the chair. Sir William is a grim, bullet-headed old gentleman of about seventy; Miss Gower a spare, prim lady, of gentle manners, verging upon sixty. They stare at each other for a moment, silently

Sir William What a hideous riot, Trafalgar!

Miss Gower Rose dear, I hope I have been mistaken—but through my sleep I fancied I could hear you shrieking at the top of your voice.

Sir William gets on to his feet; all rise, except Rose, who remains seated sullenly. Sir William goes C; Arthur, with a look of horror on finding the old people awake, clasps his hands

Sir William (*emphatically*) Trafalgar, it is becoming impossible for you and me to obtain repose. (*Turning his head sharply*) Ha! is not that a street-organ? (*To Miss Gower*) An organ?

Miss Gower Undoubtedly. An organ in the Square, at this hour of the evening—
singularly out of place!

Sir William (*looking round*) Well, well, well, does no-one stir?

Rose (*under her breath*) Oh, don't stop it! (*She clasps her hands*)

Clara goes out quickly, up R

With a great show of activity, Arthur and de Fœnix hurry up the stage RC *and, when there, do nothing*

Sir William (*coming upon Rose and peering down at her*) What are ye upon the
floor for, my dear? (*He looks around*) Have we no cheers? (*To Miss Gower—
producing his snuff-box*) Do we lack cheers here, Trafalgar? (*Goes* C)

Miss Gower (*crossing to Rose*) My dear Rose! (*Raising her*) Come, come, come,
this is quite out of place! Young ladies do not crouch and huddle upon the ground—
do they, William?

Sir William (*taking snuff*) A moment ago I should have hazarded the opinion that
they do not. (*Chuckling unpleasantly*) He, he, he! (*Goes over to* LC)

Clara returns. The organ-music ceases abruptly

Clara (*coming to Sir William,* LC) Charles was just running out to stop the organ
when I reached the hall, Grandpa.

Sir William (*going up to her and looking her full in the face*) Ye'd surely no intention,
Clara, of venturing, yourself, into the public street—the open Square——?

Clara (C *faintly*) I meant only to wave at the man from the door——

Miss Gower (RC) Oh, Clara, that would hardly have been in place!

Sir William (*raising his hands*) In mercy's name, Trafalgar, what *is* befalling my
household?

Miss Gower (*bursting into tears*) Oh, William——!

*Rose and Clara exchange looks and creep away and join the others up the stage.
Rose goes up* R *of table, Clara up* RC. *This group looks apprehensively at the Gowers.
Miss Gower totters to Sir William and drops her head upon his breast*

Sir William (*down* LC) Tut, tut, tut, tut!

Miss Gower (*aside to him, between her sobs*) I—I—I—I know what is in your
mind.

Sir William (*drawing a long breath*) Ah—h—h—h!

Miss Gower Oh, my dear brother, be patient!

Sir William Patient!

Miss Gower Forgive me; I should have said hopeful. Be hopeful that I shall yet
succeed in ameliorating the disturbing conditions which are affecting us so cruelly.

Sir William Ye never will, Trafalgar; *I've* tried.

Miss Gower Oh, do not despond already! I feel sure there are good ingredients in Rose's character. (*Clinging to him*) In time, William, we shall shape her to be a fitting wife for our rash and unfortunate Arthur——

He shakes his head

In time, William, in time!

Sir William (*soothing her*) Well, well, well! (*He crosses to* RC) There, there, there! (*Turns to her*) At least, my dear sister, I am perfectly aweer that I possess in you the woman above all others whose example should compel such a transformation.

Miss Gower (*throwing her arms about his neck*) Oh, brother, what a compliment——!

Sir William Tut, tut, tut!

He throws her arms off, and she gets back a step to R. *He turns and goes up* C. *The group at back suddenly turn and face up stage; he looks at them, then turns again to Miss Gower*

And now, before Charles sets the card-table, don't you think we had better—eh, Trafalgar?

Miss Gower (*coming to him*) Yes, yes—our disagreeable duty.

All heads turn

Let us discharge it.

Sir William crosses to R, *taking snuff. Miss Gower goes up* RC *and holds out her hand to Rose, who takes it. There is a look of horror from all, they stare anxiously at Sir William*

(*To Rose*) Rose dear, be seated. (*She goes over to the chair* R *of it—to everybody*) The Vice-Chancellor has something to say to us. Let us all be seated.

There is consternation among the young people. All sit—Sir William L *of* RC *table, Miss Gower on his right hand, at the other side of the table; Rose in the chair* R *of* LC *table; Arthur on the couch* L; *and Clara and de Fœnix on the couch up* C. *Sir William puts the snuff-box on the table*

Sir William (*peering about him*) Are ye seated?

Everybody Yes.

Sir William What I desire to say is this. When Miss Trelawny took up her residence here, it was thought proper, in the peculiar circumstances of the case, that you, Arthur—(*pointing a finger at Arthur*) you——

Arthur Yes, sir.

Sir William That you should remove yourself to the establishment of your sister
Clara and her husband in Holles Street, round the corner——

Arthur Yes, sir.

Clara Yes, Grandpa.

De Fœnix Certainly, Sir William.

Sir William Taking your food in this house, and spending other certain hours here,
under the surveillance of your great-aunt Trafalgar. (*He takes her hand across
table*)

Miss Gower Yes, William.

Sir William This was considered to be a decorous, and, towards Miss Trelawny, a
highly respectful, course to pursue.

Arthur Yes, sir.

Miss Gower Any other course would have been out of place.

Sir William And yet—(*again extending a finger at Arthur*) what is this that is
reported to me? (*He turns his chair to him*)

Arthur I don't know, sir.

Sir William I hear that ye have on several occasions, at night, after having quitted
this house with Captain and Mrs de Fœnix, been seen on the other side of the way,
your back against the railings, gazing up at Miss Trelawny's window; and that you
have remained in that position for a considerable space of time. Is this true, sir?

Sir William and Miss Gower exchange looks

Rose (*boldly*) Yes, Sir William.

Sir William I venture to put a question to my grandson, Miss Trelawny.

Arthur Yes sir, it is quite true.

Sir William Then, sir, let me acqueent you that these are not the manners, nor the
practices, of a gentleman.

Arthur No, sir?

Sir William No, sir, they are the manners, and the practices, of a Troubadour.

Miss Gower A troubadour in Cavendish Square! Quite out of place!

Arthur I—I'm very sorry, sir; I—I never looked at it in that light.

Sir William (*snuffing*) Ah—h—h—h! ho! pi—i—i—sh!

Arthur But at the same time, sir, I daresay—of course I don't speak from precise
knowledge—but I daresay there were a good many—a good many——

Sir William Good many—what, sir?

Arthur A good many very respectable troubadours, sir——

Rose (*starting to her feet, heroically and defiantly*) And what I wish to say, Sir
William, is this. I wish to avow (*her arms extended*), to declare before the world
(*she turns up stage, her arms still extended*), that Arthur and I have had many
lengthy interviews while he has been stationed against those railings over there;
(*pointing* L) I murmuring to him softly from my bedroom window, he responding
in tremulous whispers——

During Rose's speech, Arthur looks at her with amazement, then buries his face in his hands, while Sir William and Miss Gower exchange looks—Sir William struggles to his feet

Sir William You—you tell me such things——!

All rise except Arthur. Miss Gower gets to the front of the table and Sir William gives her his right hand, but is looking steadily at Arthur

Miss Gower The Square, in which we have resided for years! Our neighbours——!
Sir William (*shaking a trembling hand at Arthur*) The—the character of my house——!
Arthur (*rising, with a petulant stamp of his foot*) Again I am extremely sorry, sir— but these are the only confidential conversations Rose and I now enjoy.
Sir William (*turning upon Clara and de Fœnix*) And you, (*he goes up* c *a little*) Captain de Fœnix—an officer and a gentleman! And you, Clara! This could scarcely have been without your cognizance, without, perhaps, your approval——!

Miss Gower, going up R *agrees in dumb show. Captain and Mrs de Fœnix shrink away towards* L

Charles enters, door up R, *carrying two branch candlesticks with lighted candles. Charles is in plush and powder and wears luxuriant whiskers*

Charles (*up* RC) The cawd-table, Sir William?
Miss Gower (*agitatedly—crossing to Sir William*) Yes, yes, by all means, Charles; the card-table, as usual.

Charles carries the candlesticks to the table

(*To Sir William*) A rubber will comfort you, soothe you——

Sir William and Miss Gower seat themselves upon the couch up c, *she with her arm through his, affectionately. Clara and de Fœnix get behind the screen; their scared faces are seen occasionally over the top of it. Charles brings the card-table from* L *to* LC, *opens it and arranges it, placing four chairs, which he collects from different parts of the room, round the table. Then he brings down the candles from table* LC, *and also cards and a bag of counters, to the card-table. Rose crosses to* RC, *followed by Arthur. They talk in rapid undertones*

Rose Infamous! Infamous!
Arthur (*on her* L) Be calm, Rose dear, be calm!
Rose Tyrannical! Diabolical! I cannot endure it.

She throws herself into the chair R of RC table. He stands behind her, apprehensively, endeavouring to calm her

Arthur (*over her shoulder*) They mean well, dearest——
Rose (*hysterically*) Well! ha, ha, ha!
Arthur (*above the table*) But they are rather old-fashioned people ——
Rose Old fashioned! — they belong to the time when men and women were put to the torture. I am being tortured — mentally tortured ——
Arthur (*behind the RC table*) They have not many more years in this world —
Rose Nor I, at this rate, many more months. (*She turns to look up at Arthur*) They are killing me — like Agnes in *The Spectre of St Ives*. She expires in the fourth act, as I shall die in Cavendish Square, painfully, of no recognized disorder ——

The two appear above the screen

Arthur And anything we can do to make them happy ——
Rose To make the Vice-Chancellor happy! I won't try! I will not! He's a fiend, a vampire ——!
Arthur Oh, hush!
Rose (*snatching up Sir William's snuff-box which he has left upon the table*) His snuff-box! (*Rising and going to R, she opens box*) I wish I could poison his snuff, as Lucrezia Borgia would have done. (*Turns sharply to Arthur, who is R of table*) She would have removed him within two hours of my arrival — I mean, her arrival. (*Opening the snuff-box and mimicking Sir William*) And here he sits and lectures me, and dictates to me! To Miss Trelawny! (*Long snort, and stamp of foot*) "I venture to put a question to my grandson, Miss Trelawny!" Ha, ha! (*Taking a pinch of snuff thoughtlessly but vigorously*) "Yah-h-h-h! Pish!" (*Comes down a little towards table*) "Have we no cheers? Do we lack cheers here, Trafalgar?" (*Suddenly*) Oh ——!
Arthur What have you done?
Rose (*in suspense, replacing the snuff-box L of table*) The snuff——!
Arthur Rose dear! (*He gives her his handkerchief*)
Rose (*putting her handkerchief to her nose, and rising*) Ah——!

Charles, having prepared the card-table, and arranged the candlesticks upon it, has withdrawn

Miss Gower and Sir William now rise

Miss Gower The table is prepared, William.

She comes down C followed by Sir William

Arthur, I assume you would prefer to sit and contemplate Rose——?
Arthur Thank you, Aunt.

Rose sneezes violently, and is led away, helplessly, by Arthur to up RC. *Sir William looks surprised and annoyed*

Miss Gower (*to Rose*) Oh, my dear child! (*Looking around*) Where are Frederick and Clara?
Clara
De Fœnix } (*together, appearing from behind the screen, shamefacedly*) Here.

The intending players cut the pack, and seat themselves. Sir William sits upstage, Captain de Fœnix facing him, Miss Gower on the R *of the table and Clara on the* L. *Clara cuts. Captain de Foenix deals*

Arthur (*whilst this is going on, to Rose*) Are you in pain, dearest? Rose!
Rose Agony!
Arthur Pinch your upper lip——

She sneezes twice, loudly, and sinks back upon the couch UC

Sir William (*rising—testily*) Sssh! sssh! sssh! This is to be whist, I hope.
Miss Gower Rose, Rose! young ladies do not sneeze quite so continuously.

De Fœnix is dealing

Sir William (*leaning over table—with gusto*) I will thank you, Captain de Fœnix, to exercise your intelligence this evening to its furthest limit.
De Fœnix I'll twy, sir. (*He gets as far away in his chair from Sir William as possible, with his feet behind the back of the chair*)
Sir William (*laughing unpleasantly*) He, he, he! Last night, sir——
Clara Poor Frederick had toothache last night, Grandpa.
Sir William (*tartly*) Whist is whist, Clara, and toothache is toothache.

Clara, frightened, pushes her chair back slightly

We will endeavour to keep the two things distinct, if you please. He, he!
Miss Gower Your interruption was hardly in place, Clara dear — ah!

The deal is finished

De Fœnix Hey! what——?
Miss Gower A misdeal.
Clara (*faintly*) Oh, Frederick!
Sir William (*partly rising*) Captain de Fœnix!
De Fœnix I—I'm fwightfully gwieved, sir—— (*Some business with chair*)

*The cards are re-dealt by Miss Gower. Rose now gives way to a violent paroxysm of
sneezing. Sir William rises and goes up* C

Miss Gower William——!

The players rise

Sir William (*angrily—to the players*) Is this whist, may I ask?

They sit

   (*Standing*) Miss Trelawny——
Rose (*weakly*) I—I think I had better—what d'ye call it?—withdraw for a few
   moments.
Sir William (*sitting again*) Do so.

   Rose disappears up R

*Arthur is leaving the room with her, but pauses and looks cautiously at the players
before going*

Miss Gower (*sharply*) Arthur! where are you going?
Arthur (*returning promptly*) I beg your pardon, Aunt.
Miss Gower Really, Arthur——!
Sir William (*rapping upon the table*) Tsch, tsch, tsch!
Miss Gower Forgive me, William.

*They play. Sir William leads. The others play quickly, and the trick is taken by Clara,
who leads the second card quickly; and this Miss Gower trumps*

Sir William (*intent upon his cards*) My snuff-box, Arthur; be so obleeging as to
   search for it.
Arthur (*brightly*) I'll bring it to you, sir. It is on the——
Sir William Keep your voice down, sir. We are playing—(*emphatically throwing
   down a card, as fourth player*) whist. Mine.
Miss Gower (*picking up the trick*) No, William.
Sir William (*glaring*) No!
Miss Gower I played a trump.
De Fœnix Yes, sir, Aunt Trafalgar played a trump—the seven——
Sir William I will not trouble you, Captain de Fœnix, to echo Miss Gower's
   information.
De Fœnix Vevy sowwy, sir.
Miss Gower (*gently*) It *was a little* out of place, Frederick.
Sir William Sssh! whist.

Miss Gower leads. Arthur is now on Sir William's R, with the snuff-box

(*To Arthur*) Eh? what? (*Taking the snuff-box*) Oh, thank ye. Much obleeged, much obleeged.

Arthur walks away to RC and picks up a book. Sir William turns in his chair, watching Arthur

Miss Gower You to play, William. (*A pause*) William, dear——?

She also turns, following the direction of his gaze. Laying down his cards, he leaves the card-table and goes over to Arthur slowly. Those at the card-table look on apprehensively

Sir William (*in a queer voice*) Arthur.
Arthur (*shutting his book*) Excuse me, Grandfather.
Sir William Ye—ye're a troublesome young man, Arthur.
Arthur I—I don't mean to be one, sir.
Sir William As your poor father was, before ye. And if you are fool enough to marry, and to beget children, doubtless your son will follow the same course. (*Taking snuff*) Y—y—yes, but I shall be dead 'n' gone by that time, it's likely. Ah—h—h—h! pi—i—i—sh! I shall be sitting in the Court Above by that time——

From the adjoining room, down R, comes the sound of Rose's voice singing "Ever of Thee" to the piano. There is great consternation at the card-table. Captain and Clara de Fœnix rise quietly and get more L. They all rise. Miss Gower gets over to RC as Sir William crosses back to card-table. Arthur is moving towards the folding-doors

(*Detaining him—quietly*) No, no, let her go on, I beg. Let her continue. (*Returning to the card-table, with deadly calmness*) We will suspend our game while this young lady performs her operas.
Miss Gower (*taking his arm*) William——!
Sir William (*in the same tone*) I fear this is no longer a comfortable home for ye, Trafalgar; no longer the home for a gentlewoman. I apprehend that in these days my house approaches somewhat closely to a Pandemonium. (*Suddenly taking up the cards, in a fury, and flinging them across the room over his head*) And this is whist—whist——!

Clara and de Fœnix stand together LC. Arthur pushes open the upper part of the folding-doors

Arthur Rose! Stop! Rose!

The song ceases and Rose appears

Rose (*at the folding-doors*) Did anyone call?

Arthur (*above* RC *table*) You have upset my grandfather.

Miss Gower (C) Miss Trelawny, how—how dare you do anything so—so out of place?

Rose (*advancing to below* RC *table and pointing off* R) There's a piano in there, Miss Gower.

Miss Gower You are acquainted with the rule of this household—no music when the Vice-Chancellor is within doors.

Rose (*below table* R) But there are so many rules. One of them is that you may not sneeze.

Miss Gower (C) Ha! you must never answer——

Rose No, that's another rule.

Miss Gower Oh, for shame!

Arthur (*up by chair* RC) You see, Aunt, Rose is young, and—and—you make no allowance for her, give her no chance——

Miss Gower Great heaven! What is this you are charging me with?

Arthur I don't think the "rules" of this house are fair to Rose! Oh, I must say it— they are horribly unfair!

Miss Gower (*clinging to Sir William*) Brother!

Sir William Trafalgar! (*Putting her aside to* LC *and advancing to Arthur*) Oh, indeed, sir! And so you deliberately accuse your great-aunt of acting towards ye and Miss Trelawny *malâ fide*——

Arthur Grandfather, what I intended to——

Sir William I will afford ye the opportunity of explaining what ye intended to convey, downstairs, (*pointing down*) at once, in the library. (*He points again*)

A general shudder

Obleege me by following me, sir. (*To Clara and de Fœnix*) Captain de Fœnix——

He comes down a little—Captain de Fœnix starts violently on being addressed

I see no prospect of any further social relaxation this evening. You and Clara will do me the favour of attending in the hall, in readiness to take this young man back to Holles Street. (*Going up and giving his arm to Miss Gower*) My dear sister—— (*To Arthur*) Now, sir.

Sir William and Miss Gower go out up R. *Arthur comes to Rose and kisses her*

Arthur Good-night, dearest. Oh, good-night! Oh, Rose——!

Sir William (*outside the door*) Mr Arthur Gower!

Arthur I am coming, sir——

He goes out quickly up R

De Fœnix (*approaching Rose and taking her hand sympathetically*) Haw——! I— weally—haw!——

Rose Yes, I know what you would say. Thank you, Captain Fred.

Captain de Fœnix goes up near door R

Clara (*coming across quickly and embracing Rose*) Never mind! We will continue to let Arthur out at night as usual. I am a married woman! (*joining de Fœnix*) and a married woman will turn, if you tread upon her often enough——!

De Fœnix and Clara depart

Rose (*pacing the room up* C, *then down and round card-table to up* LC, *shaking her hands in the air desperately*) Oh—h—h! ah—h—h!

The upper part of the folding-doors opens, and Charles appears

Charles (*mysteriously*) Miss Rose——

Rose What——?

Charles (*advancing to up* RC) I see Sir William h'and the rest descend the stairs. I 'ave been awaitin' the chawnce of 'andin' you this, Miss Rose.

He produces a dirty scrap of paper, wet and limp, with writing upon it, and gives it to her

Rose (*handling it daintily*) Oh, it's damp!——

Charles Yes, miss; a little gentle shower 'ave been takin' place h'outside—'eat spots, Cook says.

Rose (*coming down* LC, *reading*) Ah! from some of my friends.

Charles (*behind his hand*) Perfesshunnal, Miss Rose? (*He gets near table* RC)

Rose (*intent upon the note*) Yes—yes——

Charles I was reprimandin' the organ, miss, when I observed them lollin' (*he jerks his thumb towards* L) against the square railin's examinin' h'our premises, and they wentured for to beckon me. An egstremely h'affable party, miss. (*Hiding his face*) Ho! one of them caused me to laff!

Rose (*excitedly*) They want to speak to me—(*referring to the note*) to impart something to me, of an important nature. Oh, Charles, I know not what to do. (*She goes up* C *and walks to and fro*)

Charles (*right hand on table, right leg across his* L, *languishingly*) Whatever friends may loll against them railin's h'opposite, Miss Rose, you 'ave one true friend in this 'ouse—(*touches his breast*) Chawles Gibbons——

Rose (*nodding*) Thank you, Charles. Mr Briggs, the butler, is sleeping out tonight, isn't he? (*She comes down* C)

Charles Yes, miss, he 'ave leave to sleep at his sister's. I 'appen to know he 'ave gone to Cremorne.

Rose Then, when Sir William and Miss Gower have retired, do you think you could let me go forth; and wait at the front door while I run across and grant my friends a hurried interview?

Charles Suttingly, miss.

Rose If it reaches the ears of Sir William, or Miss Gower, you would lose your place, Charles!

Charles (*haughtily*) I'm aweer, miss; but Sir William was egstremely rood to me dooring dinner, over that mis'ap to the ontray——

A bell rings violently

S'william!

He goes out up R

The rain is heard pattering against the window-panes. Rose goes from one window to another, looking out. It is now almost black outside the windows

Rose (*discovering her friends*) Ah! yes, yes! ha—h—h—h!

She snatches an antimacassar from a chair and, jumping on to the couch L, *waves it frantically to those outside*

The dears! the darlings! the faithful creatures——!

VISITING HOUR
by Richard Harris

This scene from a full-length play *Visiting Hour* is entitled 'Show Business' and follows the satirical vagaries of a TV crew filming a documentary on the first quadruple transplant in an NHS hospital.

Set: A hospital ward.

Cast: M5 F9, may be played by M2 F4.
Naomi, transplant surgeon. Fiona, black, very attractive, TV journalist. Darbon, transplant patient; elderly. Maureen/Woman Critic/2nd Reader, may be played by one actress. Julia/Daughter/Mother/Reader, may be played by one actress. Male Nurse/Son-in-law/Father/Critic, may be played by one actor.

Playing time: 30 minutes.

SHOW BUSINESS

Hospital noises which fade. Silence for a moment and then Fiona's voice

Fiona Bums. Bums bums bums! All right all right we'll go again — my fault — sorry about the language and here we go and Operating Theatre, St Leonard's Hospital, May Fifteenth.

Fiona's head and shoulders are illuminated in a square of light — as though it's a television screen. She is black, very attractive, very well-dressed, and is holding a stick mike

(*Immediately*) Ten years ago, in this very theatre, Naomi Strelitz was a junior doctor assisting at her first operation. Today, she is one of our country's leading transplant surgeons.

Her spotlight goes out as, at the same time, a second, similar spotlight illuminates Naomi's head and shoulders. She is wearing operating gown and hat, has her gloved hands raised palms towards her. She is well-versed in media technique

Naomi Hallo.

The spotlight goes out

(*Immediately*) All right?
Fiona Super.

An area lights up and we see Naomi, Fiona, Julia and Maureen. Maureen has a small ENG camera on her shoulder. Julia has a sound boom and various other bits and pieces of sound and lighting equipment. Fiona is checking her face in a large mirror. Naomi is carefully taking off the hat and gloves

Naomi Can someone help me off with this gown?
Fiona Be a love, Jules.

Julia somewhat gracelessly helps Naomi out of the gown

Maureen Where to now?
Fiona (*referring to her clipboard*) Umm ... straight to the ward I think. (*To Julia*) It is all cleared with Sister, is it, Jules?

Julia gives her a hard look

Yes, of course — sorry.

By now Naomi is out of the gown: she is very attractive and well-groomed. She takes the mirror from Fiona and checks her hair in it during the following

Naomi How much longer will you be needing me this morning?
Fiona Oh — half an hour should cover it wouldn't you say, Maureen?
Maureen Depends how fast the lighting and sound department can get her arse into gear.

Julia looks up hatefully from her lamps

Julia Slag.
Maureen Slut.
Naomi (*giving the mirror to Julia*) I'll have to follow you on — I've got a few calls to make.
Fiona No problem — (*her professional smile*) — the patients must come first.
Naomi What? Oh — no — telephone calls — my stupid secretary has double-booked a lunch appointment.

Naomi exits briskly

Maureen Tough titty.

Julia holds up the gown and mask

Julia Are these theirs or wardrobe?

The area goes to a Black-out. The Lights come up on the UL *bed*

A Male Nurse enters and pulls back the curtains to reveal the UL *bed which contains Mr Darbon. The Nurse exits*

Mr Darbon lies, slightly propped up in the bed. He is an elderly man who has dozed off listening to the hospital radio programme on his headphones, while at the same time taking oxygen through nasal prongs

Fiona enters the ward, being filmed by Maureen and sound-recorded on the boom by Julia

Fiona This ... is the Peter Smethurst Wing. So-called after the first surgeon to perform a heart transplant here at Saint Leonard's Hospital. Each of the patients in this wing is either recovering from, or about to undergo, intensive surgery. Each of them has either looked, or is looking, into the face of death. Nothing unusual about that, you might say. But for one of them, there is a place in medical history. OK that's that one — happy Maureen, happy everyone? — let's move on then, shall we? (*She moves to the bedside. Bending down to him*) Mr — (*she checks the clipboard*) — Darbon?

No response. She sighs, looks around for help, almost prods him, but instead raises one of the earpieces — delicately, as though fearing infection

Fiona Boyce, Mr Darbon —WTV.

His eyes open and he smiles at her. During the following, Maureen moves around the bed, looking for the best camera angles, while Julia sets up her bits and pieces: a spotlight, etc.

Darbon Is that the time then, is it?
Fiona Good-morning.
Darbon Only you never know nowadays, do you?
Fiona Sorry?
Darbon It was just the same last time I was in.
Fiona Fiona *Boyce*, Mr Darbon — WTV.
Darbon (*face lighting up*) I know you.

Fiona Good.

Darbon I thought you was Basket Making but you're not, are you?

Fiona (*beaming*) Sorry — no.

Darbon No, course you're not — you're the one from Ear, Nose and Froat. Open wide. (*He opens his mouth wide*)

Fiona Hasn't anyone — spoken to you?

Darbon All done? (*He clamps his mouth shut and adjust his headphones*) You're very kind. You're all very kind, you people. (*He points to the headphones*) Tell you who you don't hear a lot of lately: Elsie and Doris Waters.

Fiona (*long suffering*) I'm from the television, Mr Darbon. We're doing a programme about you. About your operation. Someone should have spoken to you.

The Male Nurse enters L

Nurse — someone was supposed to speak to him.

Nurse They did. I did — we all did. It's whether he was listening.

Seeing the Nurse, Darbon gives a big thumbs-up and a smile

You drift, don't you, Walter?

Darbon I tell you another one — Ronny Ronalde.

Nurse You're right there, Walter. (*To Fiona*) One minute he's right on the ball, next minute he's miles away. Years away.

Fiona Look — sorry — but I've got a crew waiting out there and we're on an incredibly tight schedule — I need his permission.

Nurse (*raising one of the earpieces*) They want you to go on television, Walter — they want to make you famous.

Darbon Yes I know, the lady spoke to me about it yesterday. Very nice. (*He goes back to his radio listening*)

Nurse (*to Fiona*) See what I mean?

Fiona Thank you. So we can, er ... (*She mimes "come in"*)

Nurse (*spreading his hands*) Whatever you want — that's what they said.

Fiona (*calling and indicating*) OK crew, here we go!

Nurse You won't be needing me, will you?

Fiona (*her big smile*) I'll give you a shout if we do, OK? (*The smile changes to a look of meaningful intimacy; squeezing his forearm*) Thanks for all your help. (*Immediately turning to Maureen*) What I thought was: start with a wide angle from here ... (*And she continues describing to Maureen how she sees the camera shots*)

Nurse (*leaning close to Darbon*) I'll come back later for your autograph, all right, Walter?

Darbon gives him his smile and thumbs-up

The Nurse exits R

Fiona You don't like it.

Maureen If I came from here, I could get what's-his-name and the equipment and some of the window.

Fiona Outside which life goes on as per ... much better — *much* better.

Maureen I'll need some light to balance up.

Fiona OK, Jules?

Julia gives her a hard look and sets up the spotlight tripod as Fiona smiles down at Darbon and continues

All we'll be doing this morning, Mr — er — Darbon — is a couple of small inserts —the main stuff will be done in the operating theatre when you'll be ... so you won't ... OK? (*But she is already assuming the proposed camera angle*) What would be nice would be if we could find someone to lounge around out there — don't you think, Maureen? Between this window and the blue Fiesta with the roof-rack — say a young couple — having a kiss or a sandwich or something. (*And, to Darbon*) Oh, and in case you're wondering —we won't be shooting in sequence and the cutaway shots will be picked up later back at base — OK?

Darbon gives the thumbs-up

(*To Maureen*) It's a pity he doesn't look more — ill.

Maureen Have a word with the make-up department — she makes everything look like a corpse.

Julia Oh yes, very funny, ha ha.

Fiona If only he looked a bit more — blue or something.

Maureen We might be able to tweak some in later.

Fiona (*squeezing her forearm*) Be super if you could.

The Nurse enters

Nurse Everything OK?

Fiona Super.

He is about to go

Oh Nurse ... (*She links arms with him and guides him away to speak intimately*) What surprises me is how ... well, how well he looks.

Nurse Oh yeah?

Fiona I have to think in terms of visual impact, you see.

Nurse Oh yeah?

Fiona How he looks before the operation ... and how he looks after it.
Nurse If there is an after it.
Fiona I was wondering about that thing sticking out of his nose.
Nurse That's his oxygen, his lungs are dodgy.
Fiona Could he not be wearing one of those — (*she mimes*) — mask things?
Nurse You want him to wear a mask.
Fiona They look so much more ... I mean unless it ... ?
Nurse If that's what you want. (*He goes to Darbon*) They want you to wear a mask,
    Walter — it makes you look prettier.

*Darbon gives him the thumbs-up and the Nurse exchanges a clear plastic mask for
the nasal prongs during the following*

Fiona There's nothing else you can attach to him, is there? Tubes or something?
Nurse They're already attached.
Fiona Well if they could be — arranged — so that they're in shot.
Nurse They want to see your tubes, Walter.

Darbon says something behind the mask

Fiona Sorry?
Nurse He said his brother was on the buses.
Fiona Oh — right.

*She gives a thumbs-up to Darbon who gives one back. During the following the
Nurse adjusts the bed clothing so that the various tubes leading from the instruments
are more visible*

Naomi enters. She looks somewhat pre-occupied

Naomi Look, something's cropped up — (*she switches on the bedside smile for
    Darbon*) — good-morning, Mr Darbon, lovely to see you — (*and switches it straight
    off again*) — so if we can make this as brief as possible — thank you.
Fiona No problem.
Naomi OK, where would you like me?
Fiona Bedside — in the chair — chair please, Jules ...

In fetching the chair, Julia has to squeeze past Maureen

Julia (*icily*) Excuse me.
Maureen Oh yes — I was forgetting the size of the hips.
Julia Slag.
Maureen Slut.

Nurse (*to Fiona, of Julia and Maureen*) What's with those two?
Fiona Lovers' tiff.
Nurse Oh. Oh.

Julia arranges the chair and Naomi sits

Naomi Left profile, please. (*She shows her left profile*)
Fiona OK, Jules? And a little closer d' you think, Maureen? Yes, a tidge closer,
  please, Jules. That's fine.
Naomi How's the make-up?
Maureen Make-up.
Fiona Make-up, please Jules.

Julia gives Naomi a quick powdering

  I'll just knock off a quick wildtrack. (*She takes up her stick mike*) Wildtrack number
  — (*she checks against clipboard*) — fourteen and here we go and ...

A spotlight on Darbon as she continues directly

  Walter Darbon will be the first patient in this country to undergo a quadruple
  transplant operation. Heart, lungs, liver, and kidney — and cut!

The spotlight goes out

Naomi So it's just a simple two-shot of me breaking the news to him, is it?
Maureen That's what it says on the schedule.
Fiona (*to Naomi*) All we've time for, I'm afraid.
Naomi Cries out for a couple of BCU's.
Fiona We'll probably cheat some in later.
Naomi And he's going to be lying back like that, is he?
Fiona What have you in mind?
Naomi Because if he is, all we're going to see of me is the back of my head.

*She turns her head to look directly at Darbon and prove her point. Darbon gives her
his thumbs-up*

Fiona Good point.
Naomi Unless that's what all you want to see — the back of my head.

*She shows it again. And again Darbon gives her the thumbs-up. Julia has set her
lights up and plugged them into the power pack. She turns them on. Darbon stares
into them*

Julia Ask her how that is.

Fiona looks to Maureen

Maureen It'll do.
Nurse Not in the patient's eyes, please.

Julia turns the spotlight on to Naomi

Naomi (*irritably*) Well?
Maureen Can we sit him forward?
Fiona Jules ...
Nurse Uh-uh — I'll do it. (*To Naomi*) You want him forward more.
Naomi Just for half a minute — thank you, Nurse.
Nurse You're going for a ride, Walter. (*He starts cranking up the bed*)

Darbon gives the thumbs up

Fiona All right, Maureen?
Nurse Say when.
Naomi (*leaning into Darbon*) Small suggestion, Mr Darbon — when you look at
me — not in the eyes — at the right ear — OK?

He gives her the thumbs-up and says something behind the mask

What was that?
Nurse He says his brother-in-law worked for Kodak. Just after the war.
Naomi (*to Darbon*) Well you'll know all about these things then, won't you? I can
see I shall have to watch my step. (*She "smiles" but angles the chair a little more
forward*)
Maureen (*looking through the camera*) When.

The Nurse stops cranking. Darbon is in an almost-upright position

Nurse OK?
Fiona OK, Maureen?
Maureen Lights.
Fiona Lights please, Jules.

Julia turns the lights

(*To the Nurse, indicating for him to get out of the shot*) If you could umm ... (*She
grips his forearm briefly*) Thank you. (*To Naomi*) If we could have a little sound
check ... ?

Naomi Eenie meenie minee mo, catch a .... testing, testing, one two three, testing.
Fiona OK, Jules?

Julia is crouching "out of shot" with the microphone, and looking at the control box

Julia OK for sound.
Maureen What about *him*?
Naomi There won't be any need for him to say anything, will there? All he has to do
is react, surely?
Fiona *(leaning into Darbon)* We're going to take a picture of Mrs Strelitz telling
you about your operation. All you need do is look like you understand. That's quite
clear, isn't it?

Darbon says something behind the mask

Sorry?
Nurse He said heart, lungs, liver and bacon.

Darbon gives the thumbs-up

Fiona OK, everyone? Record.
Maureen Running ... *(But)* What about the headphones?
Fiona Strike the headphones.

Julia sighs and takes off Darbon's headphones and gets back into position

OK, Maureen; OK, everyone? *(She leans close to the microphone)* Interior Ward
May Fifteenth — *(and ducks out of shot)* — and — action!

Naomi and Darbon are highlighted and Naomi swings smoothly into action

Naomi Well, Mr Darbon — Walter — it's been a long wait for both of us ... but at
last I can give you the good news: we have a donor for you and it's all systems go
tomorrow morning.

*She takes one of Darbon's hands and squeezes it emotionally. Darbon says something
behind the mask*

Fiona And cut!

The camera lights go out

Super.
Naomi All right?

Fiona Super.
Naomi What was that he said?
Nurse He said "very nice".
Maureen We can get rid of it in the edit.
Fiona OK, let's set up for the alternative — OK, Jules?
Naomi Mirror please.

Julia passes her the mirror and checks her equipment during the following

Nurse (*quietly to Fiona*) I didn't know they were operating on him tomorrow.
Fiona No, no, they're not — we're getting it now to save time later.
Julia OK!
Maureen Hoo-ray.
Fiona Record.
Maureen Running.

Fiona leans into the microphone which Julia is holding and Naomi and Darbon are highlighted again

Fiona Interior Ward May Fifteenth Alternative — (*ducking out of shot*) — and action!
Naomi (*swinging into action again*) Bad news again I'm afraid, Walter. We've lost our donor — yes I know, old chap — but I won't give up, I promise you ... I won't give up.

She takes Darbon's hand in exactly the same way as before and he mumbles something behind the mask

Fiona And cut!

The highlights go out

　　Super.
Naomi All right?
Fiona Super.
Naomi What was that he said?
Nurse He said, "very nice".
Maureen We can get rid of it in the edit. (*She puts down the camera*)
Fiona (*looking at the clipboard*) OK what's next?
Maureen (*pointing to her watch*) Coffee.
Fiona Ah — yes — right.

Maureen is already making towards the exit

　　(*Calling somewhat impotently after her*) If you could umm ...

Julia is on her way out

Um ... five minutes — OK, Jules?

Maureen and Julia exit separately

Nurse All right if he has his music back?
Fiona What? Oh — yes — fine.

The Nurse puts the headphones back on Darbon

Sorry about this. (*She tries a smile*) Union Rules, OK? (*Immediately serious again*)
What we *can* do — what I'd *like* to do ...
Naomi (*to the Nurse, suddenly*) All right if I use the phone?
Nurse Certainly.

Naomi exits, leaving Fiona feeling a bit of a chump

Fiona She's terribly busy of course. Well, you all are. All you people. I really do
think you deserve every penny you get — well, you probably saw that feature I did
on it.
Nurse (*lowering the angle of the bed*) You know what *she's* worried about, don't
you? Fisher.
Fiona Fisher?
Nurse Fisher. Over at the Gladstone.
Fiona Fisher. Oh — *Fisher* — the one who did the heart and lung transplant on that
ten-month-old Armenian child ...
Nurse Six-month-old Turkish child.
Fiona What about him? Sorry.
Nurse (*jerking his head towards the door*) She's got word that he's lining up a
quadruple.

A spotlight illuminates Naomi's head and shoulders, using the telephone

Naomi (*shouting*) He's what? He's bloody *what*?

The Spotlight goes out on Naomi

Fiona (*sensing a story*) How d' you mean: got word?
Nurse They've both done the triple, right? Heart, lungs and liver. And they're both
desperate to be first with the quadruple.

A spotlight, as though a TV screen, illuminates a Woman holding a newspaper

Woman (*reading*) "A Woman's Place Is In The Operating Theatre — Top Surgeon Speaks."

A second similar spotlight illuminates another Woman holding a newspaper

2nd Woman (*reading*) "Transplant Surgeon In Midnight Mercy Dash."

The spotlights go out on the two Women

Nurse (*continuing straight on*) Now then — she's got her recipient — Walter here — *and* a potential donor ... he's got his recipient but he's still looking for his donor — but now it's coming through the grapevine that he might have found one.
Fiona So what we have ... is a race to see who can stick the scalpel in first.
Nurse (*to Darbon*) You're her South Pole, aren't you, Walter?

Darbon gives him the thumbs-up and says something behind the mask

Fiona What did he say?
Nurse He said, "very nice".

Naomi enters, pre-occupied

Fiona and the Nurse exchange a look

Naomi Sorry.
Fiona Problems?
Naomi Problems? No — just ... where were we?
Nurse I'll be in my office. (*He makes to go*)
Naomi Nurse ... there might be a call for me — let me know as soon as it comes through, will you?
Nurse *Certainly*, Mrs Strelitz.

The Nurse exits

Fiona and Naomi sit either side of the bed, ignoring Darbon who will look from one to the other as they speak

Fiona What I'd like to do is get in a few wildtracks, OK? Voice-overs we can use as and when ——
Naomi Yes, yes, I have done this sort of thing before, you know.
Fiona (*an edge*) Yes, of course you have — sorry.
Naomi Just let's ... (*She indicates "get on with it"*)

By now Fiona has her stick mike which she will shove back and forth across Darbon as she refers to her clipboard

Fiona If you could sum up the present situation *vis-à-vis* the donor — OK? And ... (*She indicates for Naomi to begin, holding the mike out to her*)

Naomi (*immediately leaning across to Darbon*) The donor — the victim of a motor-cycle accident — has been on a life-support machine for the past three weeks ...

Fiona Don't think we should be too specific about the date — sorry — and I think we said "unfortunate victim". OK? And ... (*She indicates "go"*)

Naomi The donor — the unfortunate victim of a motor-cycle accident — is at present on a life-support machine and, sadly, with no hope, barring miracle, of physical recovery. Tests for brain death are carried out at regular intervals. (*To Fiona directly*) I understand you've already spoken to the next-of-kin.

Fiona Yesterday.

Spotlights, in the form of TV screens, illuminate the next of kin: Mother and Father. She wears hat and spectacles, he wears a trilby hat

Father We spent a long time thinking about this, but we are now agreed: when our son is pronounced brain-dead, his organs may be used as necessary.

Mother It's what he would have wanted.

Father If our son's death means that others may benefit, then his mother and I ——

Fiona (*voice over*) Cut!

The spotlights go out on the Mother and Father

And you've no idea when that will be?

Naomi God only knows what's keeping him going. But no: there's nothing I can do until they officially pull the plug on him — then it's all stations go — and that can't come soon enough, I can tell you.

Fiona (*of Darbon*) For him you mean?

Naomi What? Oh — him — yes — of course. This bit is all off the record, I take it?

Fiona Oh yes, absolutely.

Darbon says something behind his mask. They both look at him

How ill *is* he?

Naomi Well you've only go to look at his record — or better still, speak to his daughter and her husband.

Spotlights illuminate the Son-in-law and Daughter. The Son-in-law wears a moustache and spectacles, the Daughter wears a headscarf

Daughter He's been steadily going downhill ever since Mum died.

Son-in-law They're all right as long as they're together ...

Daughter But as soon as one goes ...

Son-in-law Like your clutch, really — as soon as your clutch goes, pound to a penny you can say goodbye to your gearbox.

Daughter Since he came to live with us he's been in hospital five times.

Son-in-law First his pacemaker.

Daughter Then that bag thing.

Son-in-law Then they gave him a new hip.

Daughter Then a new leg.

Son-in-law He's got more plastic in him than a box of Lego.

Daughter Last time they operated on him, they wanted him to sign this form donating his body to medical science.

Son-in-law He refused on the grounds that most of it wasn't his body anyway.

The spotlights go out on the Son-in-law and Daughter. The Nurse enters

Nurse Mrs Strelitz — (*miming*) phone.
Naomi Right. *Right.*

Naomi exits quickly

The Nurse is about to go

Fiona Nurse ... you will er, you will keep me informed, won't you?
Nurse (*jerking his head towards the door*) You mean ...
Fiona It *is* in the public interest.
Nurse (*an edge*) Oh — yes — right — *right.*

She squeezes his forearm and gives him the meaningful look

Fiona Thank you.

The Nurse exits

Fiona looks towards the other door, then at her watch, then sees Darbon looking at her and raises one of his earpieces

Sorry about this — coffee break — shouldn't be much longer.

He gives her the thumbs-up and she lowers his earpiece and takes up the stick mike

What I'll do is knock off a few more wildtracks for the talking heads sequence. (*She refers to her clipboard and sits on the bed alongside Darbon*) OK here we go, intro, talking heads and — "Mrs Strelitz, what would you say to those people who argue that operations such as this are a complete waste of time?"

Spotlight illuminates Naomi

Naomi I'd say piss off. (*But*) Can we go again, please?

The spotlight goes out and another spotlight illuminates the Critic who wears horn-rimmed spectacles

Critic The surgical unit is given a budget which enables the team to do x number of operations — an operation like this will mop up the surgical budget for the entire year.

The spotlight goes out and another spotlight illuminates Naomi

Naomi Hospitals compete as service providers. If this operation is a success then it will attract more patients, which means more money.

The spotlight goes out as another spotlight illuminates the Daughter

Daughter I said to her: yes I see that, Doctor, but the thing is — what's the point of giving him a new heart if his liver is on the blink? So they give him a new liver and his bladder goes bust. Give my father a new heart and he could be wetting the bed for another ten years and I'm not sure that I could stand it.

Another spotlight illuminates the Critic

Critic. All right, let's be perfectly frank: keeping this man alive is simply not cost-effective.

A spotlight illuminates Naomi

Naomi The fundamental object of the medical profession is the relief of suffering and the preservation of life.

A spotlight illuminates a Woman Critic

Woman Critic Medical advancement has made it possible to keep a dying person alive almost indefinitely. Death no longer occurs — it is managed!

Daughter Someone has to die though, don't they? Even if it's just so they can borrow a part or two to get someone else going.

Naomi The boundaries of medial science are being pushed back further and further and we — this man and I — are the trail blazers!

Darbon gives the thumbs-up sign

The spotlights go out on Naomi, the Critic, the Daughter and the Woman Critic

Maureen and Julia enter

Julia (*entering*) I never said that.
Maureen Well what did you say?
Julia All I said was, look what the Wicked Fairy has done to Bonnie Langford.
Maureen Meaning what?
Julie Meaning that beige is not your colour.
Maureen It was not beige, it was puce.
Julie Could've fooled *me*.
Maureen Slut.
Julia Slag.
Maureen Where are we? (*She's already setting up her camera*)
Fiona (*referring to the clipboard*) Shot ... twenty-seven — the personal statement.

Maureen directs the camera at Darbon

Maureen You want him like that, do you?
Fiona Umm, no, sitting up.
Maureen Props!
Julia The nurse is supposed to do it.
Fiona Yes, you're absolutely right, Jules, but the nurse is, er, doing something for me. So, umm, OK?

Julia scowls and cranks the bed the wrong way so that Darbon is completely flat. Julia realizes her mistake and cranks the other way, so that he is levered upright — too upright, in fact

(*Removing Darbon's headphones*) What I'd like you to do, Mr Darbon, is just say a few words — your personal message — just in case you don't surv—— is there anything particular you'd like to say — under the circumstances?

Darbon nods and gives the thumbs-up

Fire away, then.
Julia I'm not ready, I'm not ready.
Maureen Always the drama queen.
Fiona Just a rehearsal, Jules, OK? OK, Mr Darbon? Keep a time check, will you, Jules — and — record.
Maureen Running.
Fiona Action. (*She points to him*)

Darbon starts to talk behind the mask

Maureen Sound!
Julia It's not me, it's the mask!
Maureen Typical — strike the mask!

Julia removes the oxygen mask

Fiona (*to Darbon*) Just for a jiffy — OK, everyone? And ... (*She points at Darbon*)
Darbon When I was a very young lad, I used to watch my father shaving. He used
to stand there at the sink with just his trousers and singlet on. Lathering up.
Leathering his cut-throat. One morning I noticed these three hairs. These three
hairs, sticking out the top of his shoulder. Three black hairs sticking out of his
white skin. (*He touches his own shoulder*) I hated my father for those hairs. I hated
him. Twenty years later and I'm shaving and suddenly I look in the mirror and
there they are. Three — black — hairs. (*He lapses into silence*)
Fiona That's it, is it?

The Nurse enters, L, briskly

Nurse (*not unhappily*) It's happened.

*Throughout the following, and unseen by the others, Darbon will become short of
breath and grope to find the oxygen mask*

Fiona (*going to the Nurse*) What?
Nurse Fisher's done a deal with the next-of-kin and the *News of the World*.

Fiona doesn't seem to understand

He's nicked her donor!

A tiny moment as it sinks in

Fiona OK, team — Plan B!

Fiona, Maureen and Julia swing into action, collecting up their gear

Naomi enters L, furious

Naomi Shit! (*She makes to exit* DR)
Fiona Go, Mo, go!

*Fiona is thrusting the stick mike under Naomi's nose and Maureen quickly gets into
camera position and films*

Mrs Strelitz — how do you feel now that you have lost out on the opportunity to perform the first ——
Naomi (*still on the move*) I have no comment, no comment.
Fiona I'm sure our viewers would ——
Naomi Piss off.

Naomi exits DR

Fiona immediately swings her mike, followed by Maureen and camera, on the Nurse

Fiona Nurse Littlejohn — you were one of the first to hear the news that ——
Nurse You don't really think I'm going to discuss that *here*, do you? God you make me laugh, you people. (*He turns on his heel and makes for the door but stops*) Come through into my office — I can sit at my desk, miming an urgent phone call or the like.

The Nurse starts to exit L, *followed by Fiona and Maureen and Julia, who is now laden down with her equipment*

(*As he goes*) What I suggest is you start on the wall chart and then pull back to big close-up me in heavy foreground ... and you'd better do something about my eyelashes, they photograph something terrible.

They have all gone

Maureen (*off*) Make-up!
Julia (*off*) Lights!
Fiona (*off*) Action!

Silence after whirl of activity, and then we become aware of the sound of Darbon's laboured breathing as he gropes for the mask, pulling it towards him by the tube as though pulling in a fish. He gets it to his mouth and sucks in air. A moment. Then he removes the mask

Darbon Oh well ... that's show business. (*He puts the mask back on his mouth and closes his eyes*)

The sound of hospital noises comes up as the Lights fade slowly in on him, and then to a Black-out

VIVAT! VIVAT REGINA!
by Robert Bolt

This play develops the well-known story of Mary Queen of Scots and Queen Elizabeth realistically and powerfully, the scenes switching from England to Scotland. In these two scenes, the contrast and complexity of emotions are projected with mounting drama.

Set: The Courts of England and Scotland. Period: sixteenth century.

Cast: M8 F2. Extras.
Elizabeth I of England, personable, wilful, highly strung. William Cecil, reasonable, courteous, ruthless. Lord Morton, seasoned and at ease in every kind of villainy. Mary Queen of Scots, overbred, refined and passionate, intelligent, brave. Claud Nau, gentle, bachelor, learned, anxious, utterly upright; elderly. David Rizzio, likeable hedonist, affectionate and sceptical, precarious. Lord Bothwell, shrewd, coarse-natured, irresponsible, a law unto himself. Henry Stuart, Lord Darnley, tall, athletic, good looking. Ruthven and Lindsey, lords in league with Morton. Court Ladies attending Mary. Lords with Morton.

Playing time: 20 minutes.

Elizabeth enters at speed, Cecil after. She checks. He is diffident and soothing

Cecil (*placating*) Your Grace of course may marry whom you will.
Elizabeth Oh ...! You are full of news this morning, sir.
Cecil Within what's reasonable. And this petition, which your loving Commons most respectfully present——
Elizabeth —is no petition, but an admonition! I am admonished, by the Commons, to marry—now. Not when I would, nay, nor to whom I would, but to one of these that they have named, and get a child by him—and now!
Cecil The Princes they have named they have enquired into most ...
Elizabeth Enquired, sir? Are they kennelmen and I their breeding bitch?
Cecil You are their mistress, madam, and this country's Queen.
Elizabeth In this I am no more than any other woman, Cecil. And I tell you that I have no mind, nor heart, to marry now.

Cecil Your Grace, it would be very prudent, now. The Queen of Scots expects a
  child.
Elizabeth (*alert*) How do you know?
Cecil I have it from Lord Morton, madam.
Elizabeth He has written?
Cecil He is here, Your Grace.
Elizabeth Fetch him.

Cecil gestures quietly off stage

  Morton enters

  Is this true?
Morton Yes, Your Grace.
Elizabeth She has not announced it.
Morton No doubt she expects to make some use of the announcement.
Cecil She'd be a fool if she did not expect to make some use of it. It is a useful thing.
Elizabeth If it is so.
Morton I have it from a friend who is a friend of a close lady-friend of Signor
  Rizzio.

Elizabeth picks up the petition thoughtfully

Elizabeth Is he still close friends with your Queen?
Morton He's been no more than that since she was married. But he is still that. It's
  true enough, Your Grace.
Elizabeth I thought that Mary and her husband were no longer bed-fellows.
Morton They're not, not since he took to whores. But they were busy bed-fellows at
  first.

*Cecil looks at Elizabeth, expecting her to follow the main issue. But she is looking
down and now looks up*

Elizabeth It's true, is it, that he has taken up with whores?
Morton Oh ay, and common brothel whores at that.
Elizabeth Why?
Morton He's a king in a brothel. In Council he's a clown. She boxed his ears and
  sent him packing from the Council in the end.
Elizabeth She boxed his ears?
Morton She all but pitched him off his seat.
Elizabeth (*with a shrug*) No wonder then he took to whores.
Morton Her wits go out the window when she's in a rage. And she was in a hellish
  rage. He showed so cocky and so daft, you see, so brainless—overbearing, and so
  greedy for his own. And she, then, was in love with him.

Elizabeth She never was in love with him.

Morton Oh, yes, she was, Your Grace.

Elizabeth She was infatuated.

Morton Your Grace may call it what you like. I saw it. She hung upon him like a pedlar's bag. And sometimes when they danced, she had a look upon her face, that showed as much of her as if she had been naked ... (*He is lost for a moment*) No woman ever looked at me like that ...

Cecil coughs. Morton comes to

She's three months gone.

Cecil And she is nightly on her knees, Your Grace, and praying for a son. And praying for her son to be a wise and potent Prince. Of Scotland and of England, too. As he is like to be, and soon, Your Grace, unless Your Gr...

Elizabeth Enough, enough, I am not blind. (*She looks at the petition*) This is not ill-considered neither. But here they name three Catholic Princes and three Protestants. (*She puts down the petition*) And if I go courting any one of these, I lose the love of one half of my people.

Cecil Your Grace may find that one half of your Court is paying court in Edinburgh presently.

She looks at him

Elizabeth ... Do you pay court in Edinburgh?

Cecil No, madam, I do not.

Elizabeth The time may come. Meanwhile tell the Commons that we will not marry, yet, but that we thank them for their care. And will remit some portion of the taxes due to us this coming year. I go a-courting with my people, Cecil. (*She moves to go*)

Cecil (*irritated and anxious*) And the son that she is praying for?

Elizabeth Why, on your knees, good William, and pray for it to be a girl. Three Queens on the run should finish any country.

She goes, leaving Cecil perplexed

Morton That lassie has a long head on her shoulders.

Cecil (*preoccupied*) Yes—the problem is to keep it there.

Morton Well, that may be a problem for us all, quite soon.

Cecil It will.

He looks at Morton, who says nothing

So what do you intend to do, Lord Morton?

Morton (*with a wolfish grin*) Me, Master Cecil? D'you really want to know?
Cecil Perhaps not. Good-day to you, Lord Morton. (*He moves to go*)
Morton Good-day to you.

Cecil goes

You creepy wee creature.

The Scots Lords enter

Morton turns and joins them

The Ladies, Rizzio and Nau enter opposite. A fanfare sounds and Mary enters

They all bow. She mounts to the upper level and addresses the Lords, smiling graciously

Mary My lords, we have assembled you to hear a happy thing. You were right
  melancholy wedding guests, but now I think you will rejoice. My lords, we are
  with child.
Morton And why should we rejoice at that?
Mary Because you are loyal Scots.
Morton Ay, we are Scots. And we should have a Scottish King.
Mary If God grants me a son, you'll have a Scottish King.
Morton His mother for a start is French.

Mary turns away impatiently, but then turns back

Mary My father bore the blood of Bruce. And I was born at Lithgow Castle. When
  I was five years old I do confess I went away to France and got my breeding there.
  Forgive me, it was an error of my youth. If my manner is offensive so be it and
  good-night. I can do no more. It is not for myself I ask your loyalty. My child, on
  whose behalf I do demand your loyalty, will be both born and bred in Edinburgh—
  and fully Scots as you.
Morton And will he so?
Mary By parentage it's true he'll be a little French on one side and a little English on
  the other ...
Morton And will he so? By parentage?
Mary I do not think I understand you, sir.
Morton I think you do. Where is Lord Darnley?
Mary I do not know, sir, where he is.
Morton It's odd that he's not here.
Mary It's very odd. I did desire him to be here.
Morton What means his being elsewhere then?
Mary I cannot guess his meanings, but by Heaven I will come at yours.

Morton My meaning is the same as his. And you can come at it in any pub in Edinburgh. This child, my lords, will be a little French on one side, ay, but on the other—(*he glares at Rizzio*)—half Italian!

Mary raises a hand as though to strike him, controls herself, and turns away

Rizzio My lords, I swear by all the saints ...!
Mary What? Will you protest it? Lord Morton, leave us. You infect the air.

Morton and the Lords bow and go

Mary turns

Well, Claud, I have tried the patient way ...
Rizzio ... Maria. (*He points warningly*)

Mary turns to find that Bothwell has lingered and stands now looking at her. She is a bit startled

Mary Lord Bothwell.
Bothwell (*bowing gravely*) Your Grace.
Mary What do you want?
Bothwell A private audience.
Mary Private? Why so?
Bothwell Don't be frightened.
Mary Frightened, sir? What should I fear? Leave us, gentlemen.
Nau (*anxiously*) Your Grace, it is not ...
Mary Nay leave us, Claud.
Rizzio (*dubiously*) Maria ...

Nau, Rizzio and the Ladies go

Mary and Bothwell cross, slowly eyeing each other

Mary Well?
Bothwell Puir wee lass.
Mary (*amused and startled*) What?
Bothwell You're going to have a hard confinement. You're too thin for it, though.
Mary Indeed?
Bothwell I know what I'm talking about, too. You just bide quiet awhile. Don't ride so much; and don't ride so wild. And mind what you're eatin'. And altogether be a bit more sensible; and treat yourself more kind.
Mary Well, thanks; I will.

Bothwell Guid. When's it due?

Mary The time of our confinement is a thing we will announce when we are minded to, Lord Bothwell.

Bothwell July.

Mary Who told you that?

Bothwell You husband has been spending himself elsewhere since November, has he not?

Mary If you will speak of him, sir, you will study your respect.

Bothwell Let's speak of something else, then. You'd have to study hard to speak of Darnley with respect.

Mary I think this insolence is studied. Leave us.

Bothwell Look, I have matter which you ought to hear.

Mary I will not hear your matter.

Bothwell shrugs and is about to go

Unless you can attain a minimum of manner, too.

Bothwell (*mimicking her*) If my manner is offensive, so be it and good-night. I can no more.

Mary Oh, Jesus, are we there again?

Bothwell I like your manner fine.

She looks at him

It's very pretty.

Mary Good heavens, my lord, that is the second compliment within these same four years.

Bothwell Now fancy you rememberin' the first.

Mary Remember it? How not? A compliment in Scotland is a memorable thing. It stands out like a lily on a heap of dung.

Bothwell That's no' a bad description of yourself in Scotland.

She looks at him cautiously. They exchange a little mocking bow

Mary I'll hear your matter.

Bothwell It's men and means you want, I think?

Mary It is.

Bothwell You do not mean to meddle with the Kirk?

Mary The Kirk, sir? Are you pious?

Bothwell When the Kirk threw down the Catholic Church I got some fine broad meadow land; that used to belong to the Catholic Church. I'm awfu' pious about those meadows.

Mary If I got men and means from you I could not meddle with your meadows.

Bothwell That's true enough. What terms are you offerin'?

Mary No terms. I have taken out an option on the future, Bothwell; and you have wit enough to see it.

Bothwell (*smiling approval*) You're no fool, are you?

Mary No, sir; did you think I was?

Bothwell You married Darnley.

Mary ... What is it in me, Bothwell, that provokes you and your fellow lords at every turn and all the time to strip me of my dignity? Is it merely that I am a woman?

Bothwell A bonny woman.

Mary So?

Bothwell Worth strippin'.

Mary Is that another compliment?

Bothwell Yes.

Mary Your vein of courtesy's exhausted. Go.

Bothwell moves to go

It was a compliment for a courtesan.

Bothwell Am I to go or stay?

Mary You'll change your ways, sir, if you stay.

Bothwell I have no mind to change my ways. We're very much alike.

Mary You'll not tell me that's a compliment.

Bothwell Oh, I steal sheep and you steal revenues. Otherwise we're much alike.

Mary By God, there is another difference——

Bothwell There is.

Mary —I am a sovereign. And you, sir, are a subject.

Bothwell No. You are a woman. (*He approaches close*) Why don't you send me packin' now?

Mary Oh, sir, I am fascinated by your rough provincial masculinity.

Bothwell I think you are, a bit.

Mary Go!

Bothwell moves to go again

You are unfit for our purpose.

Bothwell Why, what was that?

Mary What, sir, do you smell promotion?

Bothwell Do I?

Mary A high promotion, Bothwell; you might come by further meadows.

Bothwell What is it?

Mary We had thought to make you Lord Protector to our child.

Bothwell Oh. (*He pulls at his beard, thoughtfully*)

Mary Ay. Now I think he'll change his ways.

Bothwell You'd want a Catholic for that.

Mary So change your church and be a Catholic. It would not cost you much.

Bothwell It would not cost me anything, to be a Catholic, for I am not a Christian. I
will not do it, though. For if our ways are different and you would like our ways to
match—you must change your ways! To mine!

Mary By Heaven, Lord Bothwell, I have heard about your ways. Even in Scotland
your name is morbid. You are a bloody villain, sir, a tyrant and a sodomist, an
enemy to innocence, a vampire and a demonist! It's only in your better moments,
Bothwell, that you are a thief.

Bothwell So *that's* what fascinates you.

Mary Go!

Bothwell starts to go

And go for ever—be banished to Dunbar—you will never see my face again!

Bothwell You're wrong, I think.

Mary *Go!*

Bothwell I was goin'—you keep stoppin' me.

Bothwell has gone. Unseen behind Mary, Nau and Rizzio enter

Mary glares after Bothwell

Mary Lout!

Rizzio Bothwell?

Mary Yes. (*She turns to him with a little laugh*) I do believe he thinks he's a lady's
man!

Rizzio Astonishing.

Mary No fooling, sir; I am not in the mood.

*The Light begins to concentrate into a small conspiratorial area at the table,
surrounded by shadow. Mary sits*

(*To Nau*) Did any other of the lords come forward, Claud?

Nau No, Your Grace.

Mary (*dipping her pen*) Well—(*she writes, rapidly*)—I will try my way now.

Nau sits and watches her unhappily. Rizzio, too, draws near

Nau You write, Your Grace?

Mary Yes, sir, I write.

Rizzio (*peeping*) In Latin, too.

Nau To whom does Your Grace write?

Rizzio He'll have difficulty reading it, whoever he may be.

Mary (*writing*) So you will make it fair. And you—(*looking up at Nau*)—will carry
it to Rome.

Nau (*sadly*) Oh, madam, Rome?
Mary And when you have got means, in Rome, I will send to Milan for mercenaries. Loyalty does not grow in Scotland, so I will import it.

Darnley enters, uncertainly, hanging off in the shadows. He carries a bottle

Rizzio My lord.
Darnley (*eagerly*) Good-evening, Claud—Signor Rizzio.
Rizzio My lord.

Nau and Rizzio withdraw respectfully as Darnley drifts towards Mary, who, after one glance round, one stare, returns to her writing. He sits and watches her

Darnley Good-evening, Mary.
Mary What do you want?
Darnley Might I not simply have come home, like any other man?
Mary You might. It seems improbable. (*She does not look up from her flying pen*)
Darnley (*after a pause*) Are you writing a letter?
Mary Yes.
Darnley Who to?

She thrusts it towards him at full stretch. He looks at it

It's in Latin.
Mary Yes.
Darnley I can't read Latin.
Mary No. (*She pulls it back and goes on writing*)
Darnley You're cruel, Mary.
Mary Oh, Harry, go away.
Darnley Mary, I'm sorry.

It is touching in its sincerity, pathetic in its infantile inadequacy. She shifts restlessly and stops writing, but does not look up, exhaustedly impatient

Mary Have you been drinking?
Darnley I'm not drunk.
Mary You're maudlin.
Darnley It isn't drink that's made me maudlin. Not this evening.

He waits. She struggles against it, but speaks at length, still without looking up

Mary What is it then?
Darnley (*pathetically*) Mary ...
Mary (*exasperated*) What?

Darnley Look at me.

She blows out an angry sigh, throws down her pen, and raises her glowering face. But seeing him, her expression alters. She rises, staring, and backs away. Rizzio and Nau come forward, alarmed. Darnley averts his face from them

Nau Your Grace.
Mary There are sores on his mouth ... Harry, look at me—what are those sores on your mouth?

Her reaction has appalled Darnley. He rises, stares wildly at Rizzio and Nau, then speaks defiantly

Darnley It's the frost!
Mary By God I know that frost.
Darnley Mary ... (*He approaches her*)
Mary Stand off!
Darnley Mary ...
Mary Sir, will you stand off? You are unclean ...!

Darnley almost runs to the exit, then turns

Darnley (*in a voice shaking with feeling*) God save me from a loving woman.

Darnley goes

Mary (*starting after him*) Harry ... (*She checks*) Oh, Jesus—the child ...!

Rizzio goes to her, alert and calm

Rizzio When was the child conceived, Maria?
Mary Four—four and a half months.
Rizzio And have you seen the sores before?
Mary No?
Rizzio The child is safe.
Mary Oh, Davie, do you really know?
Rizzio Cherto! In Padua this useful branch of knowledge was the most highly regarded of my many accomplishments. I was in great demand. But do you know I have never been so greatly in demand as I have since we came to this godly city of Edinburgh? I think it is the cold, you know, it brings people together. Ah good, you smile. And the child is safe.
Mary Thank God for Davie.
Rizzio I do, frequently.

She smiles again, but then her smile fades

Mary And him?

Rizzio Your husband. Hm. The English have a saying: You have made your bed and you must lie in it. Myself I have never seen the need for this; when there are other beds.

She drifts towards the exit, then turns and looks at him

Mary (*softly*) Davie, bring your lute.

Mary goes

Rizzio (*rising; delicately*) Aha!

Nau Signor Rizzio—don't go to her!

Rizzio Oh come, Claud, the Queen needs—(*he makes a deliberately ambiguous gesture*)—comfort.

Rizzio goes after Mary. Nau goes separately. The Lords enter and tramp across to the table. Morton picks up the letter

Morton Who here has lands from the old Church?

All I.

Morton Well, you're to lose them.

Ruthven Ach, she hasnae the men.

Morton Oh, she'll have taken thought for that. It'll be Frenchmen maybe, or maybe mercenaries, but no, no, she thought of that before she did this. (*He puts the letter down*) So what's to do?

Ruthven Fight.

Morton It's gey expensive fightin'. An' you can always lose.

Ruthven What then?

From behind the curtain at the head of the shallow pyramid of stairs, the sound of the lute is heard, playing Rizzio's tune. They turn and look. The Light begins to gather, ominous

Morton I'm getting to like that instrument. Verra seductive. Ay—a bagpipe's gey stirrin' on the moors but it's no help in a bedroom.

Ruthven What are you talking about?

Morton Her husband, you gowk.

Lindsey What, what can *he* do?

Morton Nothing while he's only that. But suppose he was the King. And suppose he was bound to us. Bound hard. Our man.

Lindsey He's no a man at all.

Morton Well, call him a man for courtesy. D'you see it?

Ruthven No.

Morton Well, I do, Ruthven. I see it clear. So either come with me or take yourself off and be damned.

Ruthven I'll come with you.

Morton Right, here he is.

Darnley enters, as before but without the bottle

(*Urgently, sotto voce*) Give him a bow, give him a bow.

The Lords bow. Darnley stops uncertainly

Darnley My lords ...?

Morton You look sick, sir. Are you?

Darnley Yes.

Morton And so are we, sir, of the same disease.

Darnley What?

Morton Domination! Domination by a woman. That we are sick of, and so is Scotland.

Darnley By God, you are right, Morton; that is my sickness.

Morton We know it, sir. We have watched you. And we think you are too patient. We think the husband of the Queen should be a King.

Darnley looks at them, breathing hard, pulling at his opened doublet, trying to sober up

Darnley Well?

Morton And you would be the King, sir, you must play the leader.

Darnley Leader?

Morton Ay. And if you'd be a husband, you must play the man!

The lute is heard again and a low laugh from Mary

Ha! They're vigorous enough, heh? They're diligent, heh?

Darnley Wha' ...?

Morton God's death, my lord, they're going *to* it—now!

Darnley Who ...?

Morton The monkey—and your wife!

Darnley *Whaaa-aa* ...! (*He reels towards the steps*)

Morton grips him by the arm and wheels him round and back

Morton (*with an admiring chuckle*) Did I not say there was a kingly spirit in this man? But see, Your Majesty, these things must be done majestically. I have here a wee paper. Which all of us will sign. (*He puts it on the table and gives a curt nod to his colleagues*) Sign.

The Lords sign

Darnley (*as they do so*) What is it?
Morton Our warrant.
Darnley Warrant?
Morton Ay—or say a promise which we make each to each other, ay and God Almighty too, that what we purpose here is a naething mair nor less than justice for yourself and David Rizzio; nae mair for you, nae less for him. The crown for the King, death for the adulterer. Now you sign. (*He thrusts the pen into Darnley's hand*)
Darnley Sign?
Morton Kneel, my lairds.

The Lords kneel

This is a solemn moment in the history of Scotland.

Still Darnley hesitates. Mary's low laugh comes again. He turns and looks up at the curtain

They're going to it now, my lord! Laughing! Making comparisons!

Darnley whirls back again and signs. The Lords rise. Morton takes the papers, grunts, satisfied, and puts it away. He pushes Darnley aside as done with. All draw daggers

Right, my lords. Quick and quiet.

In a swift padding rush they are up the steps and tear down the curtain, revealing Mary and Rizzio

Signor Rizzio!

He grabs Rizzio and throws him to the others. They fall on him like a pack of dogs

Mary (*in the uproar*) Ho there! Rescue! Treason! Bothwell! Bothwell!

The mangled corpse is let drop. Mary falls in shock. Darnley is hanging off, appalled and nerveless. Morton is angry

Morton Dagger him, man!

Darnley is paralysed. A lord leaps down to him, snatches his dagger and throws it to Morton, who plunges it into the corpse. Mary gives a cry of horror

Bothwell and Nau enter at the run. They check as the Lords present daggers, crouching. Bothwell spreads his empty hands, approaches and looks at the corpse

Bothwell God's death, my lords, you're very thorough. Lord Darnley, I think this is yours. (*He tosses the dagger to Darnley*)
Darnley (*piteously*) Mary, I ...

Darnley dashes from the stage

Morton Now, Lord Bothwell, are you here to hinder or to help?
Bothwell Neither, Lord Morton.
Morton Then you're in my road.
Bothwell Then may I get out of it?
Morton Right out of it, Bothwell, out of Edinburgh now.
Bothwell (*to Mary*) Your Grace.

Mary raises her head and looks at him

It seems that I must leave you to God's care. I'm for Dunbar.

Bothwell goes

Morton Now, madam, though this was rough yet it was justice.

Mary descends unsteadily, Nau hovering anxiously at her side. She crouches at the corpse and sees the wounds

Mary Oh, God ... (*She rises, bewildered*) He was my friend. (*She feels faintness coming over her, reaches for support, and swoons*)

Nau catches her and lowers her to the ground. Morton looks on gloomily

Nau Good God, my lord—what have you done?
Morton Our duty. Naething more.

Morton moves to go. The Lords follow. Morton snarls at them

Shift it!

Morton and the Lords go, dragging the corpse. Mary watches covertly

Mary (*when they have gone*) Morton, Ruthven, Lindsey, Douglas, Glencairn,
Falconside and Kerr ...
Nau (*startled*) Madam ...?
Mary Remember them! Remind me every day that they must die.
Nau Oh, madam, this is wild! The castle is full of their men!

She looks about, then rises from her knees

Mary So we must quit it.
Nau There is a guard on every door!
Mary There will be no guard on the kitchen door. Come. (*She moves to go*)

Nau follows her, shaken, bewildered

Nau But, madam, where?
Mary Where? To the Border—Dunbar!

They go

WARRIOR
by Shirley Gee

This powerful, exciting drama, based on a true story, is set in the mid-eighteenth century and tells the story of Hannah Snell who, having been deserted by her sailor husband, dresses as a boy and goes in search of him. For seven years she lives as a man in the Marines, boldly braving wounds, bloody battles and her own troubling visions. The story is told in flashback and these opening scenes are set in the madhouse, Bedlam, where finally she has been committed by the authorities.

Set: The madhouse, a house, a dockyard. Period: mid-1700s.

Cast: M4 F3.
Hannah, stubborn, passionate, fearful, brave, volatile. She makes a grand boy, but is entirely a woman. Her accent need not be strong, but should have a roughened edge. Sculley, madhouse keeper who gets a morose enjoyment from his distressing work. Mrs Sculley, his wife and attendant, coarse-grained, capable, tough and kindly. Susan, Hannah's sister-in-law, worn, impatient, sensible. Godbolt, Sergeant of Marines, hard, dark, haunted, moral, loyal, upright. Drubber, a marine, a swaggerer, a bully, strong; young. Cuttle, a marine, good, simple, but not a buffoon; older.

Playing time: 15 minutes.

The madhouse

Hannah in a harsh light, in a night-shift

Hannah I cannot ... I must ... they come into my mind. They say tell about me. Tell when the shadows lengthened on the grass, when the shadows—NO! The wind lifts the blossom, the wind blows, like it always blows, on all of us. (*She sings*)

> Now I went out to walk one day,
> The wind was rather strong that way,
> In fact it blew the lot away ...

(Speaking) Ten ... nine ... eight ... seven ... six ... five ... four ... *(She screams)*

The Lights come up on stage. Two attendants, Sculley and Mrs Sculley, are with her. Mrs Sculley holds Hannah, roughly but not unkindly. Sculley pauses in oiling the swing, a large, heavy contraption rather like a see-saw with a chair in which the patient is strapped at one end, a weight at the other

Sculley A penny a time to see the raving. *(He holds his cap out to the audience)* A penny to see them cured. *(He laughs, turns back to work)*

Mrs Sculley pulls off Hannah's shift, scrubs her down with a long-handled mop, as you might an elephant at the zoo

There's all sorts here. Cholerics. Melancholics. Hysterics. *(Turning to Hannah)* Which are you?
Mrs Sculley To be seen and enjoyed and lessons learned and a good day's outing.
Sculley Brutes, some of 'em. Brutes. And some is stones.
Mrs Sculley She's not, though. Are you, lovie? Not a brute and not a stone. Just her brain's gone topsy-turvy.
Sculley The brain's a noble organ.
Mrs Sculley It is, it is. Lords it over the rest of the body. But when it goes topsy-turvy—well.
Sculley What was it, now, as made her lunatic? Drink was it?
Mrs Sculley Or grief. *(She taps Hannah's foot)* Lift.

Hannah lifts her foot, Mrs Sculley turns to the audience

See? She's not unmanageable, like some. *(Scrubbing)* I'll put my penny on disappointment in love. *(She taps Hannah's other leg)* T'other.

Hannah lifts it

Sculley Whatever it is, bodily disorder, poverty, a sudden change in fortune, he'll seek out the cause. The doctor, he'll dig and he'll dig until he finds it.
Mrs Sculley He's wonderfully fond of causes. He's in high hopes of restoring her. *(Now drying Hannah, putting her shift back on)* But if he can't—this is your last chance.
Sculley If he can't——

Sculley has finished oiling the swing. He pats it. Hannah stiffens, stares at it. Sculley laughs

—she'll fly like a bird.

Hannah tries to run, but Mrs Sculley holds her

All the same when you face them with the swing.

Mrs Sculley You'll be all right. You can be cheerful for a long space of time, I've seen you. Be respectful. Answer him loud and clear. What's your name ... ?

Hannah Hannah. Hannah Snell.

Mrs Sculley How's that for an answer? How old are you, Hannah?

Hannah Thirty-one.

Mrs Sculley See. Lucid as any.

Hannah Hannah Snell.

Mrs Sculley Born in the year of our Lord ...

Hannah Seventeen hundred and twenty-three, in the city of Worcester. Moved to London, seventeen hundred and thirty-five. Married David Snell, sailor ... oh, Davey ...

Mrs Sculley Hold fast to your wits, dearie. Married David Snell, sailor ...

Hannah On a foggy day in January seventeen hundred and forty-four. A lovely lad, and a scoundrel. Oh, Davey ...

Susan's house

(A scream) DAVEY!

The Sculleys retire

Hannah, aged eighteen or so, stands alone, in her nightshift. She holds a letter

Oh, no. DAVEY!

Susan enters, startled out of sleep

Oh, Susan.

She holds out the letter. Susan takes it

Susan "Dear one. I'm not meant to be stuck ashore. I've signed back on the *Cloud*." The dog. "Sorry about the two pound. Never fear. I'll come back rich as a king, your loving Davey." The double dog. Gambling again?

Hannah He promised me. He swore.

Susan He'd eat a live cat for a wager. Two pound?

Hannah A bit above.

Susan How in God's earth will you find two pound?

Hannah I don't know, do I? I'd pledge the spoons, but there's no spoons left to pledge.

Susan You've nothing?

Hannah Less than nothing.

Susan Well, I'm sorry Hannah, but I have to say it. You've dug your own pit. Always a shilling behind, that's you. What'll you do? They'll come after you. They will. It'll be prison, Hannah.

Hannah (*looking round wildly*) There's the clock. That's ours. And ... and ... (*she can't see anything else*) and ... (*She takes off her locket*)

Susan Six shillings. Seven at most.

Hannah What'll I do? I don't know what to do.

Susan No use looking to me and Caleb, we can't help.

Hannah Course not. We're living on you as it is.

Susan Not that we grudge you, mind. After all, he is my brother. Even if he is the back end of a dog. And you're a good soul, Hannah.

Hannah Lord, I'm afraid of prison.

Susan Cassie Terson cut her throat because her husband ran off with her savings. Whatever will you do?

Hannah When he comes back I'll crack his head for him so hard.

Susan Comes back? He's forgotten you already.

Hannah Never.

Susan Did he tell you he was going?

Hannah No.

Susan Well then.

Hannah I think he tried. He cried in my arms last night.

Susan Well he might.

Hannah I can feel his tears on the back of my hand.

Susan Without your man you're nothing. Lost your place.

Hannah staggers suddenly, covers her eyes with her hands a moment, takes her hands away, stares

What is it? What——?

Hannah The sea. The sea. It's everywhere.

Susan Oh my Lord.

Hannah There's Davey standing in it, at the edge. He's staring at me. Oh, his eyes are sad. Now his shadow's left him ... and turned white ... and sank beneath the waves.

Susan I hate it when you're like this.

Hannah There's blood in the sea. Drops of blood, like ladybirds, on him. He's sinking now. He's gone.

Susan Oh, Hannah, you do frighten me.

Hannah dives suddenly for a clothes chest, starts to haul clothes out

What are you doing now?

Hannah Going after him. He'll drown. I have to stop him.
Susan You can't. Hannah, you can't.

Hannah is pulling on a shirt

It's only a dream.
Hannah I don't dream. I see.
Susan (*of the shirt*) That's Caleb's.
Hannah He'll get it back.
Susan It's his best.
Hannah It's not. It's the other one. (*Tugging on long johns*) You know it's a warning.
    Remember the bolting horse? And the fire? And the night your father died? I saw
    them all. He mustn't go to sea.

As Susan starts to speak

I know. They're Caleb's too. I'd have worn Davey's but he's took them all.
Susan Let him go. He's worthless.
Hannah He's good at heart.
Susan All because of some stupid, stupid dream——
Hannah Do you want the sea to have him? (*She puts on shoes and stockings*)
Susan You never stop to think. He's had the night's start. What if he's sailed already?
Hannah Then I'll go to sea as a sailor. Follow him.
Susan You don't know anything about the sea.
Hannah The sea is blue. And deep.
Susan And you've to watch it for it's after you to pull you down.
Hannah I've learnt to make a soup and light a fire and pledge a thing I haven't got.
    (*Cramming hair into a cap*) I'll soon get used to it.
Susan Sailors are demons.
Hannah Davey's a sailor.
Susan They live in sin and blood. And die in it. What if you get swept up in a war?
Hannah (*dressed now*) How'll I do?
Susan You wouldn't fool a rabbit.
Hannah Is it here? (*Her breasts*)
Susan It's all of you. Anyone could tell with half an eye.
Hannah I do swell, don't I. (*She rushes to the chest, pulls out a long piece of cloth,
    takes off her shirt, wraps it round*) Tie it. Oh, quick, Suke. Please.

Susan ties the cloth tight

I can't be a man, but I can be a boy.
Susan Man or boy, you'll have to breathe. How do you think you're going to manage
    among all those men?

Hannah I'll snarl and spit and march about a bit. (*Dressed again, she rolls a seaman's sock of Davey's, uses it for a codpiece*) How's that?
Susan Better. Much. How'll you do at night?
Hannah Snore. Belch. Fart. I shall fart all night if I want.
Susan Hannah, you can't.
Hannah I can do anything. Once you're a man you can kick the world like a king. (*She collects a few things—a mug, candles, matches, a knife, bundles them into a man's jacket*)
Susan You're determined, then?
Hannah Like iron. Don't worry, Suke. Soon as he sees me, he'll come back.
Susan You must be careful.
Hannah I will.
Susan (*crying*) You mustn't cry, no matter what.
Hannah (*not crying*) I won't.
Susan You must be gruff.
Hannah (*gruff*) I will.
Susan Better still, be silent.

Hannah nods

And grim.

Hannah nods grimly

You are the best ... the ... stupidest sister-in-law a body could ever ... If anyone finds you out ... oh, feel my heart. Leave it a week and see.
Hannah I can't. How can I? (*She sees Davey's kerchief sticking out of his trousers pocket, pulls it out, is sad. She recovers, and ties it round her neck*) I'll find him and I'll bring him back and there's my mind and there's the end of it. (*She marches upstage, turns*) The sea shan't have him. (*She salutes*) Everything strong and hearty.
Susan (*calling after her as she goes*) Hannah! You're off to the slaughter-house.
Hannah Not I. I'll sail like the moon in the sky.

Susan exits

As Hannah crosses and recrosses the stage she becomes more confident, more at home in her clothes. She kicks at stones, tries to whistle, fails, succeeds at last and is delighted with herself

She exits

The dockyard

A roll of drums. Godbolt and Drubber drum up recruits

Godbolt Roll up, roll up for the good life, lads. The good rich life. A gallon of beer
a day. A bountiful supply of clothing, the ladies flocking and the rest of your life in
peace and plenty.
Drubber Go the world over. See the Hanging Gardens of Babylon——

Cuttle bursts in, breathless. A man, not a boy

Cuttle I'm here.
Drubber The yellow men of China, the monsters of the deep blue sea——
Cuttle I'm game, sirs.
Drubber Chase the Frenchie fleet across the seas——
Cuttle By Christ I'll chase them off, whoever they are, the more the merrier——
Godbolt Welcome my fine sir. Name?
Cuttle Cuttle, sir. Billy Cuttle, sir.
Godbolt Mister Cuttle, sir.
Drubber (*aside*) Seems a bit of a dung barge.
Cuttle Here, sir, at His Majesty's service.
Godbolt (*to Cuttle*) A likely man indeed. (*Aside*) The Navy needs warm bodies.
Cuttle I'm game for anything, by hell I am.
Drubber (*to Godbolt*) He stinks of jail to me.

Hannah enters

Hannah Excuse me—
Drubber (*crossing to her, pulling her forward*) Now this looks a tall enough boy.
Hannah Excuse me. Can any man here tell me——
Drubber Holds himself smart enough.
Godbolt Good. Good. Come to the aid of your country like an Englishman.
Hannah No. Indeed no. I'm looking for a mate of mine. Shipmate. Name of Snell.

They shake their heads

Davey Snell.

They shake their heads

He signed aboard the *Cloud*.
Godbolt (*pointing to a board*) The listings are all there. I think you'll find you've
missed him.
Hannah Missed him!
Godbolt Here, I'll read it for you.
Hannah Thank you. Thank you.
Godbolt Never mention it. A man must help another. (*He blocks the board from
Hannah's sight, surreptitiously wipes out some of the names scrawled there in
chalk*) The *Cloud*. Sailed on the morning tide. Next port of call Lisbon.

Hannah Oh no. When's the next merchantman?

Godbolt The *Swallow*. Docked for repairs. The *Calico* ... sailed last week. The *Lady Mary* ... The *Drum* ... No luck, lad. there's none. No sailings for a week.

Hannah What'll I do?

Godbolt Looks like you're out of luck.

Hannah He's my ... my sweetheart's brother. I must find him. Bring him back.

Godbolt I can see it means a deal to you. What can we do to help this gentleman, Drubber? Tell you what, we're Lisbon bound, you could follow him with us.

Drubber That's it. Catch him up, and on the way see all the lands that's over the water.

Godbolt Hear the silver chink of a shilling a day.

Cuttle Oh sirs both, just let me at 'em.

Godbolt You still here?

Hannah I can't enlist. A merchantman, yes, but ...

Godbolt Give all you've got to get at the enemy of your country?

Hannah Yes, but ...

Drubber Come back with a Frenchie's ear?

Hannah nods

Not womanish are you?

She shakes her head

Godbolt If you want to find your Davey Snell, it's us or nothing. Name?

Hannah James. James Grey.

Drubber seizes her, forces her mouth open

Drubber All his own teeth. Must have your own teeth to bite your cartridge. (*He shakes her, tosses her to Godbolt*) See that, Sergeant? Free motion of every joint——

Godbolt (*flinging her back to Drubber*) Limbs nice and easy——

Drubber Seems like a proper specimen, Sergeant Godbolt.

Godbolt Very proper, Mister Drubber. (*He catches her, spinning her round the other way*)

Hannah staggers, dazed. Drubber holds up both hands

Drubber How many hands do I hold up?

Hannah (*gasping*) Two.

Drubber lets off a musket shot

Godbolt Can you hear that, lad?

Deafened, hands over ears, she nods

Drubber He's the proper use of his eyes and ears.
Godbolt In every respect fit for His Majesty's service. Sign, sir, sign for the *Rainbow.*

Hannah, still dazed, nods

Cuttle And me, sirs. I'll sign. I saw the two hands, clear. I heard the shot. My limbs
   is free.
Godbolt (*aside*) This one's a muckfly. (*To Cuttle*) Sign, then.

He pushes the book to Cuttle, who signs

Cuttle There's only been but one path before me, sir. At your side, sir.
Godbolt Depresses me to hear you say that.
Cuttle I'll fight so fair and I'll sail so sweet——
Drubber (*rolling his drum*) Billy Cuttle, James Grey, from henceforth in God's and
   the King's eyes you are a Christian and a Marine. (*He rolls the drums*)

Drubber and Godbolt start to go

Godbolt (*as they go*) Roll up, roll up for the good life, the good rich life. Sail the
   Black sea and the Red sea and the Yellow sea. Spend the rest of your life in peace
   and plenty ...

   Drubber and Godbolt exit

Hannah What do I know of soldiers?
Cuttle Their coats are red. They march over hills.
Hannah And guns are loud. And a ball can kill. Oh Lord, I've done it now.
Cuttle Ay, sir. That's done all right. You've done it and so have I and all the saints up
   in the sky cannot undo it.

Hannah on one side of the stage, Cuttle on the other, are kitted out. Shirt, shoes,
waistcoat, britches, coat, hat, bedding. They change into uniform. Cuttle is proud,
delighting in his new clothes, looking ramshackle as ever. Hannah is in panic

Hannah What have I done?

WUTHERING HEIGHTS
by Emily Brontë, adapted for the stage by Charles Vance

The once wild and temperamental Catherine Earnshaw is now happily married to her wealthy neighbour Edgar Linton and settled at Thrushcross Grange awaiting the birth of their first child. Heathcliff, the 'Gypsy boy' and close childhood friend of Cathy, fled Wuthering Heights where he worked for Cathy's hated, drunken brother Hindley. Having made his fortune in the intervening years, he appears, totally altered and immaculately dressed, at Thrushcross Grange to call on Catherine.

Set: Thrushcross Grange. Period: early Victorian.

Cast: M2 F3.
Catherine Linton, still spirited but much more controlled, pregnant; early 20s. Edgar Linton, master of Thrushcross Grange. Isabella Linton, Edgar's younger sister. Ellen Dean, housekeeper of Thrushcross Grange, formerly Catherine's childhood nurse. Heathcliff, the 'Gypsy boy' at Wuthering Heights, immaculately dressed.

Playing time: 11 minutes.

Thrushcross Grange

Catherine, Ellen and Isabella are sitting knitting or sewing baby garments which they show to each other at what is evidently the end of a session devoted to such work

There is a large window enclosure and a couch

Catherine There now! I think, Isabella, we have almost enough to clothe your first three nephews, provided Edgar and I are not blessed with twins!
Ellen (*as she collects the sewing gear and garments*)
     Pink is for a little girl
     Blue for a boy
     Cradle trimmings, Christening robe:
     White for parents' joy ...
Catherine And whichever it is, it will be welcome, although I hope one of the first three will be a boy to please Edgar!

Isabella (*a little coolly*) Yes, an heir will be splendid.
Catherine Even though it disinherits you, I am afraid I must wish it, Isabella.
Isabella The most natural thing in the world, my dear, and be sure I wish it too.
Ellen Such things are the will of heaven.
Catherine Bless your golden little heart, Isabella, I don't question your generosity;
I know you have Edgar's happiness very much in mind.
Isabella Yours too, Catherine dear. I think, though, the sewing has given me just a
touch of headache; you will excuse me if I retire?
Catherine Away with you and lie down, you shouldn't let the work tire you.
Ellen I had better think about tea; the master will be ready for his, I am sure.
Isabella (*as she goes*) I will come back for tea, and lie down afterwards.

Isabella exits

Catherine And I will go and entice Edgar from his books.

Ellen exits

Edgar comes in

Edgar Am I permitted to inspect the results of the afternoon's work?
Catherine Later, Edgar. Nelly has put it away. I was just coming to fetch you.
Edgar Then let us sit in the window; and wait for her. These late summer evenings
are delightful—the light is just fading—we shall soon have autumn upon us.
Catherine You can still see beyond the orchard and the park.
Edgar The whole valley is a sea of silvery mist.
Catherine And rising proudly above it—Wuthering Heights.
Edgar How are you feeling today, my love?
Catherine I am very well indeed, and quite content.

Ellen enters

*They pay no attention to her and she watches them for a moment sitting quietly in the
last of the afternoon sun. It is a very peaceful picture*

Edgar (*noticing her*) What is it, Nelly?
Ellen (*uneasy*) I wondered—should I bring the tea up here, sir.
Catherine Of course, Nelly.

Ellen turns to go, hesitates

Edgar Was there something else?
Ellen Oh and, a person from Gimmerton wishes to see you, ma'am.

Catherine (*without moving*) What does he want?

Ellen I didn't question him.

Catherine Well, close the curtains when the light goes, and bring the tea, Nelly. (*She rises, kisses Edgar lightly and goes to the door*) I'll be back again directly.

Catherine exits

The sun sets and it becomes progressively darker outside. In the room the firelight begins to take effect

There is a slight pause and then Edgar speaks

Edgar Who is it, Nelly?

Ellen (*busying herself about the room*) Someone the mistress doesn't expect! Oh, dear I wonder—oh! (*She clatters the fire-irons in annoyance*)

Edgar What's the matter?

Ellen It's that Heathcliff. You recollect him, sir? Heathcliff who used to live at Wuthering Heights.

Edgar What, Nelly! You mean the gypsy—the ploughboy?

Ellen Hush—please, sir ...

Edgar I don't understand. Is this a matter of consequence?

Ellen You must not call him by those names sir. The mistress would be sadly hurt.

Edgar Really? They were very close as children—I know that of course—but they are not children now—so—I really don't understand; you seem quite agitated.

Ellen He came upon me so suddenly—it was such a surprise. I didn't think—I see now, sir, I am to blame—I shouldn't have heeded him when he bade me give that message: "Just say 'a person from Gimmerton to see you.'" I should have told *you* sir.

Edgar If my wife had wanted to speak to him she would have gone in any case—there's no harm done.

Ellen They were more like brother and sister, and later on—she was heartbroken when he ran off; oh dear, I shouldn't have been so foolish and overawed by the man!

Edgar (*a little irritably*) Nelly, this is nothing; we'll dispose of it in a minute.

Ellen As you say, sir, and I hope you are right. And, as you say, sir, they are not children now—I hope you will remember those words, sir—(*quickly before he can silence her*)—and all I know is, sir, his return will make a jubilee for her!

Edgar goes to the window and, after watching for a moment, opens it

Edgar Don't stand out there, my love. Bring the person in, if it be anyone particular. (*He closes the window before there can be a reply and comes into the room with a slightly troubled expression*) You had better bring the tea, Nelly.

Before Ellen can move, the door flies open and Catherine bursts in, wild with excitement. She rushes to Edgar and flings her arms around his neck

Catherine Oh, Edgar, Edgar! Oh Edgar, darling! Heathcliff's come back—he is!
Edgar (*crossly*) Well, well, don't strangle me for that.
Catherine But he's back! Standing outside this very minute!
Edgar He never struck me as such a marvellous treasure. There is no need to be frantic.

Ellen exits

Catherine I know you didn't like him.
Edgar I wouldn't say that. I hardly noticed him.
Catherine Yet, for my sake, you must be friends now. You will?
Edgar Catherine, we are not children any longer, none of us. You are no longer——
Catherine Shall I tell him to come in?
Edgar Here? Into the parlour?
Catherine Where else?
Edgar (*snappishly*) In the kitchen I should think.

She stands away from him, regarding him with a droll expression, half anger, half amusement

Catherine No. I don't feel the kitchen.

Ellen enters with tea

Ah, Nelly! Set the tea at two separate tables! One for your master and Isabella, being gentry, *there*. The other, for Heathcliff and myself, being of the lower orders, *here*. (*Moving across the room away from the door, to Edgar*) Will that please you, dear?
Edgar Catherine, there is absolutely no need—
Catherine Or must I have a fire lighted elsewhere?
Edgar Catherine there is absolutely no need—
Catherine If so, give orders. (*She begins to move to the door*) I'll run down and secure my guest.

Edgar intercepts her

Edgar (*to Ellen*) Nelly! *You* bid him step up.

Ellen goes

And you, Catherine, try to be glad without being absurd.

She looks at him doubtfully then slowly goes to the window

Catherine I wonder if I am about to see an unsuspected side of your nature?
Edgar The whole household need not witness the sight of you welcoming a runaway
    servant as a brother.
Catherine (*working up to an outburst*) Oh dear, what a little ass you can be!
Edgar Once and for all, before there is any development——
Ellen Mr Heathcliff.

Heathcliff, immaculately dressed, is shown in by Ellen

*Catherine's ill-humour appears to vanish instantly in a smile. She goes to Heathcliff,
takes both his hands in hers and, crossing to Edgar, takes one hand of his and crushes
it into Heathcliff's. Edgar, amazed at the change in Heathcliff, is at a loss. Heathcliff
lets go the hand and coolly stands waiting for Edgar to speak*

Edgar Sit down, sir. Mrs Linton, recalling old times, would have me give you a
    cordial reception and of course I am gratified when anything occurs to please her.
Heathcliff I also. If it be anything in which I have part.
Edgar (*stiffly*) Then you are welcome, sir.
Heathcliff Good. Then I will stay a while with pleasure. (*He goes to sit*)

*Catherine almost dances about; she catches hold of Heathcliff's hands again and
sits him beside her on a sofa. She seems oblivious of her husband's presence*

Catherine I shall think this a dream tomorrow! I shall not be able to believe I have
    seen and touched and spoken to you once more. Yet you don't deserve this
    welcome—three years of silence—and you never thought of me.
Heathcliff A little more than you thought of me! I came back with a plan. Then I
    heard you were married. So I must modify the plan. I thought about this very hard,
    just now, while I waited below in the yard.

*The power of his personality holds them in silence while he looks from one to the
other*

Your welcome has put these things from my mind!
Catherine Oh Heathcliff!
Heathcliff You'll not drive me off again. I have fought through a bitter life since last
    I heard your voice and you must forgive me, because I struggled only for you.
Edgar Catherine, unless we are to have cold tea—
Catherine Yes, now, let us have tea. Tea, Heathcliff?
Edgar (*striving to preserve an ordinary tone and a measure of politeness*) Mr
    Heathcliff will have a long walk wherever he may lodge tonight—and I'm thirsty!
Catherine You haven't rung for Isabella.

He does so

Catherine pours out tea. She never touches hers. Edgar hardly touches his; only Heathcliff, completely at ease, finishes his

Ellen comes in

Ellen Miss Isabella is not feeling well, sir and asks to be excused.
Edgar Tell her I will come to her presently.
Catherine Does she know Mr Heathcliff is here?
Ellen No ma'am. Unless she saw him approach through the park.
Edgar You must tell her the great news, Nelly.

Ellen goes out

Are you going to tell us your adventures, sir?
Heathcliff No.
Edgar I am sorry I cannot offer you ...
Heathcliff (*without looking at him*) I expect nothing from you, sir, I shall stay at Wuthering Heights.
Catherine The Heights?
Heathcliff Hindley invited me when I called this morning.
Catherine Hindley!
Heathcliff Invited me. And indeed, now you know of my—availability—I must go. (*He rises*) It has been a short stay, but a pleasant one.
Catherine Going so soon? This is ridiculous. Edgar, make him stay!
Heathcliff Well, Mr Linton, are you inclined to make me stay?
Catherine You mustn't tease Edgar.
Edgar I am inclined to respect my guest's wishes and speed him on his way.
Heathcliff I thank you, sir. I shall come again—always being careful of course not to outwear my welcome!

Without any further formality Heathcliff goes

Catherine is about to follow him but Edgar prevents her

Edgar Ellen will see him out.

Catherine runs to the window and then comes back to Edgar

Catherine Yes—he'll have a fine old talk to Nelly! She will know far more of his past doings and his future intentions than us! Oh, Edgar, you can be tiresome. Why didn't you encourage him to stay and tell us about himself?
Edgar You must give me credit for making the attempt.

Catherine You are sulking because I'm glad of something that does not interest you.

Edgar That is most unkind. You cannot expect me to respond to your Heathcliff in any other way. I have always had an aversion to him.

Catherine Of course, and why? Because he was always dirty and rough—can't you understand, he was purposely reduced to that state by Hindley? That was not his real nature. And look at him now! Isn't he quite the gentleman? Isn't he worth anyone's regard?

Edgar I cannot continue with this—you are cruel and selfish.

Catherine And you are silly and pettish.

Edgar I am going to my study and I would appreciate not being disturbed for the remainder of the evening.

Catherine Oh, go to your study! Go and snivel and think yourself badly done to! There are times when I could shake you!

Edgar goes without replying

Catherine goes to the window, which she opens, and calls

Goodbye, Heathcliff, come again soon!

Index of Authors